# THE SUCCESSFUL SELF

Born in Australia in 1930, Dorothy Rowe worked as a teacher and as a child psychologist before coming to England where she obtained her PhD at Sheffield University. From 1972 until 1986 she was head of the North Lincolnshire Department of Clinical Psychology. She is now engaged in writing, lecturing and private practice. Her research and therapy are concerned with the questions of how we create meaning and how we communicate.

Her other books are *The Experience of Depression* (1978) reissued as *Choosing Not Losing* (1988), *The Construction of Life and Death* (1982), *Depression: the Way Out of Your Prison* (1983), *Living with the Bomb: Can We Live without Enemies?* (1985), and *Beyond Fear* (1987).

D0281809

# DOROTHY ROWE

# THE SUCCESSFUL SELF

**FONTANA/Collins**

First published in 1988 by Fontana Paperbacks
8 Grafton Street, London W1X 3LA
Third impression October 1989

Copyright © Dorothy Rowe 1988

Set in Linotron Sabon

Printed and bound in Great Britain by
William Collins Sons & Co. Ltd, Glasgow

CONDITIONS OF SALE
This book is sold subject to the condition
that it shall not, by way of trade or otherwise,
be lent, re-sold, hired out or otherwise circulated
without the publisher's prior consent in any form of
binding or cover other than that in which it is
published and without a similar condition
including this condition being imposed
on the subsequent purchaser

To Jo and Jeremy

# Contents

## THE SUCCESSFUL SELF

# Preface

*The Successful Self* is my sixth book, and is another stage in the journey of exploration and understanding which began for me as a small child when I puzzled about why my beautiful mother (I have a clear memory of her when I was tiny and she a young woman) behaved in such a way that she caused herself and her family such pain. Now I know why, and this is what I write about.

After the manuscript of my last book, *Beyond Fear*, had been delivered to my publishers, my editor, Michael Fishwick, and I started talking about ideas for the next book. Michael was intrigued with my notions about extraverts and introverts, especially when he discovered after I 'laddered' him that, having spent his life thinking he was an introvert, he was really a shy extravert. At first we talked about doing a snappy little book on extraverts and introverts, the 'people persons' and the 'what-have-I-achieved-today persons', but decided that the subject matter was too complex and too important for that. Moreover, I wanted to look more closely at the way people cope, or fail to cope, with their lives.

I have spent years observing and talking with copers and non-copers, and can describe the difference simply. People who cope with their lives value themselves and are optimistic, while people who do not cope with their lives do not value themselves and are pessimistic.

However, dividing people into copers and non-copers, or the sane and the mad, overlooks the fact that among the copers or the sane are some very dangerous people, a great many dangerous people.

Our society is made up of people engaged in doing one of three kinds of things, namely:

(1) Believing that they are intrinsically bad and unacceptable, they feel so threatened that they have to defend
themselves with depression and any of the other defences
which psychiatrists call the symptoms of mental illness.
They do not cope very well with their lives.

OR

(2) Accepting and valuing themselves, they feel secure in
themselves, neither burdened nor driven, being freely
themselves. They are the Successful Selves.

OR

(3) Working hard at being good and overcoming, to some
extent, their sense of intrinsic badness, they assume a
multitude of obligations with their attendant guilts and
shames. They are driven and burdened, and worry about
how well they are coping. When they take great pride in
their goodness and obligations they become dangerous
to other people, because, while they claim to be sensitive
and caring, they in their blindness and ignorance inflict
pain on others, and because they believe they know what
is best for others they do what they can to prevent other
people becoming independent adults, that is, Successful
Selves.

People engaged in this third category of activity are sometimes
totally unaware both of the damage they are doing and of their
own misery. There are many men who pride themselves on their
achievements and on the strong, manly person that they are, and
who feel that it is most unjust that they should be burdened with
a wife who is depressed and children whose behaviour leaves
much to be desired. There are many women who are so enthralled
with themselves as good wives and mothers that they fail to see
any connection between the criticism they lavish on their husband
and children and the fact that their husband has withdrawn from
them, and their children are disturbed or delinquent.

I meet these men and women regularly as the husband, wife, or
parents of my clients. They take no responsibility for my client's
predicament, and if they are paying my client's fees, it is on the
understanding that I convert my client into the kind of person

they want their relative to be. They have better things to do with their time than read my books.

However, there are many people engaged in this third category of activity who are, dimly or quite clearly, aware that there is something not quite right with their lives, that they are not as happy and fulfilled as they could be, that they are lonely, and that they may be hurting the people they love. This book is for them, and for the people who are not coping. The Successful Selves might like to read it to tell me where I have gone wrong.

The words and lives of many people are recorded in this book. Some of them were pleased to appear as themselves, and so their names and occupations are given in full. Others preferred to appear anonymously and so chose a first name for themselves when they read what I had written. They chose anonymity not so much to protect themselves as to protect their families. To all these people I give my grateful thanks.

Dorothy Rowe
Sheffield
January, 1988

# Introduction

# I

# Constructing the Self:
# the Hope and the Threat

One day, when I was seventeen, I stood outside the glass doors that led into Manning House, the Women's Union at Sydney University, and could not bring myself to enter. I had every right to do so. I had been admitted to the university as an undergraduate. I had even won an Exhibition, a scholarship, to go there. I should have been able to enter that door proudly and confidently.

But I could not do so. I hovered there in the garden and finally turned away.

It would be easy to explain my behaviour in terms of my being young and shy. I had grown up in a country town in a family descended from Irish convicts and goldseekers and Scottish miners. There was a tradition of respect for education but no understanding of what education was beyond the basics needed to get a steady job. My father and I, loving and close when I was a child, had drifted apart, while my mother and sister were, as ever, long on criticism and short – non-existent – on praise. I was torn between knowing myself to have the capacity to achieve much and feeling myself to be fat, clumsy, incompetent and stupid.

It would indeed be easy to explain my hovering outside that door in terms of my youth and inexperience. But I knew, even as I hovered there, that something more was there, holding me back.

It was that going up to that door, opening it, and going through it meant acting upon the *world outside me*, and the problem was that I had no trust in the world outside me, that world which, years later, as a clinical psychologist, I learned to call my *external reality*.

Years later I came to realize that not only were there many people who were like me, doubting their external reality, but there were many people who doubted their *internal reality*. Their external reality, the world they lived in, was solid and true. But that reality inside them could become vague, shifting, strange and empty. They would say to me, 'I don't know who I am,' and while one part of me would be thinking, 'How stupid. You must know who you are. I know who I am,' another part of me would be recognizing the panic and desolation that comes when the less real of our two realities falls away into distance and strangeness.

Now I am fifty-six I know why some of us stand hesitant to act upon the world and remain inside the only security they know, and why others of us scurry around in the hard brightness of the world, fearing and denying the darkness within. I also know why some of us go forth confidently. These are the people who have confronted their unreal reality. If the world outside them seemed unreal, they acted *as if* it was real, and, lo, it became real. If the reality within themselves was dense and dark, they journeyed into it and made it light. They took their little, frightened self, standing hesitant upon the threshold of an unreal reality and made the unreal real. Thus they created for themselves The Successful Self.

Such people lead successful lives. This does not necessarily mean that they are successful in terms of fame, wealth and power, though many are, but that they are successful in terms of their own values and aims. Given that life is a chancy business, they are secure, and given that relationships are always complicated, they live comfortably with themselves and others.

Real success, that success which does not turn eventually into emptiness and lonely bitterness, is based upon the creation of the Successful Self. Such a creation is possible for all of us.

## OUR TWO REALITIES

All of us, all the time, are aware of two realities, external reality and internal reality.

*External reality* is around us, outside us. We act in and upon our external reality. We share external reality with other people, but other people do not necessarily see our external reality in the way that we do.

*Internal reality* is inside us. Here we think, feel, imagine, and keep our secrets. In our internal reality we are always alone. No one else can enter, no one else can know, though some may try to guess, the nature of our internal reality. Our internal reality is both a refuge and a prison.

# HOW REAL IS REAL?

Because we know both realities we might expect that the two realities would appear to be equally real. But in fact they do not.

*For some of us external reality is more real than internal reality.* 'Reality' means for these people external reality, the world and what goes on in it. This is what is, and even though external reality may, at times, be confusing, it is always real. It is internal reality which seems less real, an unknown and unknowable territory. Such people think and feel and imagine passionately, but all their thoughts, feelings and fantasies are directed outwards, to what they see as the real world. They do not entirely trust their internal reality, and under stress they rush into external reality to act and to talk to others. Internal reality can become for them a dangerous, unknown emptiness.

*For some of us internal reality is more real than external reality.* Such people know that the word 'reality' is often used to mean the world and what goes on in it, but they do not entirely trust external reality. As they experience it, external reality is not as it appears to be, it is not solid and definitely defined, and it can change at any time. (If you are one of these people you know exactly what I mean here. If you aren't, you won't.) What for them is real and eternally existing is their internal reality, and it is into this reality that they withdraw when stressed and confused.

Many of the people who find their external reality less than totally real spend much of their lives trying to ascertain just how real external reality is. Prince Hans-Adam, Crown Prince of Liechtenstein, told me, 'Until I was about 19 or 20 I was not so optimistic. I was brought up Catholic and I didn't much believe in the church and all this kind of thing, the meaning of life, etcetera, etcetera. So then I tried to think things out. I tried to do it all logically, and then I saw that everywhere I had to accept belief in something. So I tried to cut down the beliefs. I came to the point where I said there is only one thing I can say with logic and that is, "I think, therefore I am – *cogito, ergo sum*." That is the only thing we can have with logic. All the rest we have to assume a certain probability. That means that I look at everything only with a certain probability that it might be like this. I don't have beliefs really. I just think that there's only a fifty-fifty chance that it is like this. I think I don't take things so seriously. You can die tomorrow, or there's a chance that the world will explode tomorrow. Probably there's a universe and that we go on, perhaps it will not explode. Perhaps it's only in my head that it will explode. That's the way I thought. I think out everything with logic, but also knowing that it's something where there's only a fifty-fifty chance that it exists. I have thought if I can think, I exist. I still can think, even if I perhaps don't exist in my body here. It's an interesting experience going on. I think that life is an interesting experience whatever happens.'

By contrast, when I was talking to Jean Hale, an extremely successful lawyer, writer and artist in Boston, Massachusetts, I described how, for some people, external reality seems, as it does for Prince Hans-Adam, not entirely real. She said, 'I don't know quite what you're talking about there, about external reality. Does that make sense, that I don't? So what should be my deficit?'

As we went on talking I explained how for her it was internal reality which seemed less than real.

She said, 'That's what I said to you, I'm very pragmatic. If something's wrong it's much less interesting to me as to why it's wrong or how it might not have gone wrong. It's much more likely that I'll look at how I can fix it. I like problem solving. Finding causes is somewhat less interesting to me. Is that because – internal reality – it's scary?'

'Yes.'

She turned her question into a statement. 'Because it's scary. That makes sense. But if you look inside you might not like what you see and you don't want to get into that. Messy. That's interesting. That makes sense. I think I'm that way.'

All of us belong in one of these two groups. However, some of us have the wisdom to recognize that *to cope with living we need to strive to make our two realities equally real*.

To do this we have to feel good about ourselves, for if we don't each of our realities will contain dangers, internally the sense of our own badness and externally criticism and rejection by others, from which we have to protect ourselves by staying within the one reality we can trust. Feeling good about yourself means having confidence in yourself, valuing yourself, accepting yourself, being yourself.

# FEELING GOOD ABOUT YOURSELF

Babies are born feeling good about themselves. They come into the world *being themselves*. They don't have to work hard at valuing themselves and accepting themselves, for they have not yet encountered the people who will not value and accept them as they are. They know how to be themselves because no one has yet taught them that it is wrong to be yourself.

This is how we all came into the world. We all know how to be ourselves because this is how we began. But even though we know, we may not dare to let ourselves know that we know. We were taught, sometimes within weeks of our birth, that we could not be ourselves because we were not good enough. The messages from others came through loud and clear.

Who did we think we were, assuming that just because we had been born we had the right to exist?

Who did we think we were, expecting to be fed when we were hungry?

Who did we think we were, expecting to be cuddled when we were lonely?

Who did we think we were, complaining when we were cold and wet?

Didn't we realize that we were dirty and disgusting and that we had to learn how to be clean?

Didn't we realize that we had no right to get angry?

Didn't we realize that we weren't as important as adults?

Didn't we realize that we had to obey adults?

Didn't we realize that we ought to be grateful to adults, especially our parents?

No, as babies we didn't realize these things, but by the time we were two or three we did realize all these things, even though we weren't always successful in showing to our parents' satisfaction that we did. We couldn't put our realizations into words, but we knew all this because we had lost our innocent self-acceptance. We had been taught the concepts *good* and *bad*, and we knew that we were bad, or certainly not good enough, and had to spend the rest of our lives working hard at being good.

And so the sense that we were imperfect, unsatisfactory became the part of that structure which later in our lives we called our *self*.[1]

# STRUCTURING OURSELVES AND OUR WORLD

Over the centuries many of those people who found their external reality less real than their internal reality turned their private obsession to public use and became scientists and philosophers who studied questions like 'What is reality?' and 'How do we know what we know?'

Out of all of this has come the understanding that whatever exists, what we usually call 'reality', or what Douglas Adams calls 'Life, the Universe, and Everything,'[2] is not something we can ever know directly. We can only catch distorted glimpses of it through the *structures* we create. For instance, the world to most of us looks to be full of colour. But it looks like that only if you have the right kinds of physical apparatus inside your retina. Colour isn't out there. It is in the structure of our eyes.

The language that we speak structures the reality that we know. Arabic speakers have a keen eye for a camel – some four thousand words are needed to make the discriminations they find necessary – but to us English speakers a camel is a camel. At present I am but to us English speakers a camel is a camel. At present I am engaged in creating a garden and am trying to learn how to distinguish hundreds of kinds of plants, shrubs and trees, each with its own special name. If I were a gaucho in Argentina I would find that four names would be adequate to cover the entire plant world. Just as they make a fuss about gardening, the English have always made a fuss about privacy – 'an Englishman's home is his castle,' as they say – but the Russians are so little concerned about privacy they don't even have a word for it. Could this explain why Communism took root in Russia but not in England?

Even where we share the same language, the way we use our language creates a different structure to reflect 'reality'. Sometimes when I am in America I feel that I delude myself when I think I understand American English.

It is not just different words for things – 'apartment' for 'flat', 'sidewalk' for 'pavement' and so on. It is the values that are placed on things. Something which came out again and again in the interviews I did and about which I have written further on in this book is the different way that Americans and Europeans talk about self-confidence and success.

The differences in the way we use our language are not merely national. They are individual. We each speak what the linguists call an 'idiolect', an individual language which is made not just of words but of attitudes, values, opinions and beliefs. All these attitudes, values, opinions and beliefs form the structure which is our self and our individual world.[3]

# THE STRUCTURE OF THE SELF

The innocent self-acceptance with which we arrived at birth was a self-acceptance without an awareness of a self. Our self was something which we had to construct.

The first of the structures that made up our self are images without words, for when we created them we were too young to have language. There are images of being held close and warm, and images of being cold, struggling and unsupported. There are images of being fed and comfortably satiated, and images of screaming with the pain of hunger. There are images of friendly, loving, welcoming faces, and images of terrifying emptiness. The images we acquire create our expectancy of what life will be, and for the rest of our lives they haunt our fantasies and our dreams.

As soon as we are born we look around eagerly to engage people in conversation, and if we are lucky they respond. When people talk to babies they usually tell the babies about themselves. 'Aren't you a big boy?' they say, or, 'What a dear little girl you are!' This information becomes for the infant the second kind of structure of the self, the definitions and values which other people impose on us.

Thus, we learn not just that we are a boy or a girl but how the people around us value boys and girls. 'Not another boy in the family!' greets one baby boy. 'What a pity you're not a boy', a little baby girl is told, while in other families boys are welcomed as boys and girls as girls.

In our hearing our supposed similarities to past and present members of the family are discussed. We may find ourselves being praised for being as pretty as our mummy, or deplored for having Uncle George's ears. Some of us are told that we are as intelligent as our clever father, and some of us are seen as having a distressing resemblance to the grandfather who was the mad one, the odd one out in the family.

We gradually become aware of other definitions and values being imposed on us. 'You're an American and America is the greatest country in the world.' 'You're lucky you're an Australian.' 'You're English and you must be kind to that little West Indian boy because he hasn't the advantages you have.' We learn, too, that we have been born into the One True Faith, whichever it may be, and that we are different from those who do not share our beliefs. Again, we learn of our ancestors and what race, or races, defines our appearance and place in society. We learn whether we belong to the upper, middle or working class, whether we are rich or poor, and whether such characteristics make us feel good or make us despise and denigrate ourselves.

When we are small we usually accept without question the definitions and values which adults impose on us because we believe that adults know what reality and truth is. As we get older we discover that adults make mistakes and do not always tell the truth. Then, if we wish, we can, with relative ease, discard or modify those structures of our self which derived from such definitions and values. We can learn that we don't have to accept the labels that other people put on us.

It is the third kind of structure which is less easy to change. This is the structure which came from the *conclusions* we drew from our experience.

When I was four years old I went into hospital with suspected diphtheria. In those days children died of diphtheria, and so my parents were very worried when they handed me over to the nurse. I remember looking back at their anxious faces as the nurse carried me up the stairs, and I cried. She put me in bed in a strange ward and said, 'The sooner you stop crying, the sooner you'll go home.'

I was a logical child. I stopped crying immediately, but I did not go home, not for a long while. I drew a conclusion from this. I had already discovered that my mother, often depressed and with an unpredictable and violent temper, and my sister, six years older and much disposed to teasing, were not to be trusted. From this experience with the nurse who lied I drew the conclusion that all women were untrustworthy. I knew I could trust my father, and I generalized this belief, foolishly as it turned out, to all men. I was in my late thirties before I modified my belief in the untrustworthiness of women, and then only because I had known the consistent loyalty of one woman friend and I had encountered the enlightenment of the Women's Movement.

Each of us has stories like mine, some far worse and some much happier. From these events, some of which we remember and some we don't, we drew the conclusions which became the rules by which we organize our life and make our decisions, that is, important parts of the structure of our self.

All these parts, trivial preferences and vanities and the major moral principles by which we live, all interrelate, and all depend upon one basic and essential structure, how we experience our existence.

# EXPERIENCING OUR EXISTENCE

Everything we know comes to us in the form of a contrast. If there isn't a contrast, we can't know. We know hot because there is cold, happy because there is sad, perfection because there is imperfection, life because there is death. Some of these contrasts simply provide an interesting variety. Others pose constant dilemmas in our lives.

One such contrast and dilemma is being a member of a group as against being an individual. We all want to belong in a group with our family, or our friends, or our colleagues, while at the same time each of us wants to be an individual. Meeting these contrasting and competing needs is a constant problem in living.

However, for each of us the need to be an individual and the need to be a member of a group are not evenly balanced. Each of us has a preference, and this preference relates to how we experience our existence.

Later in this book I shall explain how to discover, or, at least, to put into words, how you experience your existence. You have known this since your moment of birth. You just may not have ever put this knowledge into words. Here, to explain what this book is about, I shall simply describe the two ways in which we experience our existence. Each of us experiences our existence in one of these two ways.

> We experience our existence as being a member of a group, as the relationship, the connection, between our self and others.

OR

> We experience our existence as the progressive development of our individuality in terms of clarity, achievement and authenticity.

Each of these ways of experiencing our existence has a contrast. If we know *self* we know *not-self*, and the threat of *not-self* is the greatest danger we can ever know.[4]

# THE THREAT OF THE ANNIHILATION OF THE SELF

I always use the word 'annihilation' to refer to the destruction of the self, rather than 'death', for the destruction of the self is to us far worse than bodily death. We can come to terms with bodily death by imagining how some part of our self will continue on in our soul or spirit, or in our children, or in our work, or in the loving memories held by friends. But if our self is destroyed, we have vanished, like a wisp of smoke in the wind or chalk off a blackboard. We become an emptiness or crumble into dust.

We feel the fear of this threat whenever someone treats us like an object of no value, or we are rejected or criticized by someone whose love or approval we need, or whenever we fail at something important to us, or lose control of something crucial which we thought we could control, or whenever we cringe in shame or guilt.

Just as we know how we experience our existence so we know how we see the threat to the annihilation of the self.

**Those of us who experience our self as being a member of a group, as the relationship, the connection between our self and others, see the threat of the annihilation of the self as complete isolation, being left totally, utterly and forever alone, thus withering, fading away, disappearing into nothingness.**

**Those of us who experience our self as the progressive development of our individuality in terms of clarity, achievement and authenticity see the threat of the annihilation of the self as losing control of your self and your life and falling apart, falling into chaos, fragmenting, crumbling to dust.**

Two friends, each talking to me at a low point in their lives, illustrate these different ways of experiencing the sense of existence and the threat of annihilation.

Stephanie Alexander, a writer in South Africa, whose letters to me I cherish, wrote, 'I still have the feeling, though not as strongly as I used to, that I disappear. I knew – was certain despite all evidence of their care and forethought – that when I was not in the room, or, at least, in the house with my parents I had vanished from their world altogether. Now, though I have a stronger sense of being me, I often feel in low moments that the only time I am really real is when my little black cat comes to me. She is the only one of my cats who chooses to be with me (and prefers it to being with anyone else, or even going and playing in the sun) and for whom I have to do nothing but be me. I am not at all confident that there has ever been a human being in my life of whom I could say the same. All required something: pleasing, entertaining, supporting or giving support, or so it seems to me, and unless I worked (or work) at these various requirements I tended to vanish away.'

Jeremy Halstead, a clinical psychologist with whom I worked for many years, bought an old farmhouse on a wild and lonely Yorkshire hillside, only to be told of some important facts about its location which he had not anticipated. He said to me, 'I knew that buying this wonderful old house was an idiosyncratic choice. I could have been sensible and conforming and bought something in town, but conforming always seems to me like throwing away my existence. By conforming I achieve nothing, and might as well not exist. Someone else might as well do it. It needn't be me. I trusted my own judgement in buying this house, and when it went wrong I thought I'd been an awful fool. My father and teacher were right all along. I'm irresponsible. I wasn't angry. I just felt like breaking down and crying. I felt that if I'd got that wrong, if I hadn't foreseen what could go wrong, then perhaps I'd got everything, absolutely everything, wrong. I couldn't be certain about anything. Nothing was the way I thought it was. I felt that I wasn't holding everything – myself – together any more.'

We spend our lives maintaining and elaborating how we experience our self and in avoiding and defending our self against the threat, as we perceive it, to our self. Just how we do this relates to how we perceive our two realities.

# EXISTENCE AND REALITY

If you experience your existence as the connection between your self and others then your attention is directed to your external reality. External reality appears to be more real than internal reality.

If you experience your existence as the progressive development of your individuality in terms of clarity, achievement and authenticity, then your attention is directed to your internal reality. Internal reality appears to be more real than external reality.

How we experience our existence and the threat of the annihilation of our self underlies every decision we make and appears often in our conversation. Of course we do not say, 'I experience my existence as . . .' but such statements are there, nevertheless. We might create our own individual metaphors or we might select from the range of banalities and clichés which relate to existence, annihilation and the purpose of life those which best sum up our own experience.

When I interviewed Andrew Wallace, the racing car driver, in 1987 he had just moved up to driving Formula 3000, a necessary step on the way to fulfilling his ambition to become a Formula 1 champion. In 1988 he won Le Mans for Jaguar. Andrew told me, 'Racing was something I really wanted to do. Everything in my life I used to push to one side, my job, everything, and concentrated on what I was going to do. I just figured that if you're going to do it you've got to give it your best shot. When you win you've proved yourself. You've started out to do a job and you've done it. That's achievement.'

Andrew recognized that winning depended on a good team. 'The driver's contribution I wouldn't put higher than thirty per cent,' he said. But he set himself goals which were beyond what the team set.

This year, in a new car, 'The team goal is to be scoring points. My goal is to be winning races.' He had explained to me that no one had ever won a Formula 3000 race in the first year of driving in that class. Now he said, 'I feel I need to be winning races this year. Since I started seven years ago I haven't had one year where I didn't win a race.'

What was coming through in what he was saying was the sense of experiencing his existence in the need for individual achievement. He measured his success not in terms of public acclaim but in terms of achieving the goals or standards which he had set for himself. The recognition he wanted was 'from the Formula 1 managers, not from the people watching'.

The sense of experiencing his existence in the need for greater clarity was apparent in his description of how he developed his driving skills and what he called 'the excitement of winning'.

He defined developing his driving skills as 'You come up against a problem and you learn how to get over that problem. There's always a better way you can do it.' He spent a great deal of time thinking about a problem, analysing and clarifying it, and testing out his analysis in discussions with his team manager and in driving.

'Excitement' was the word Andrew used for the sense of

enormous pleasure which came from meeting a challenge, learning something by seeing something more clearly, meshing what he had learnt with what he already knew and achieving the goal he had set himself.

For Andrew the opposite of 'excitement' was 'boring'. A boring life would be one without challenges. That would be the life of 'somebody who works on an assembly line in a factory. You're not able to think for yourself. You'd just be a machine.' That is, if you cease to make your own decisions, and thus control the circumstances of your existence so that you can develop and achieve, your self ceases to be.

Andrew said, 'If I can't get into Formula 1, or if I can't earn my living doing racing I'd have to go back to a proper job, a boring, ordinary job, and I couldn't cope with that.'

Formula car racing is a very dangerous business. I asked him, 'If you had a choice between a short life as a very successful driver or a long life in a proper job, which would you choose?'

He said, 'I think it's probably best to have a short life as a successful driver.'

For Andrew 'a proper job' would be a fate worse than death.

If Andrew's sense of ambition was put beside Jean Hale's there would be no difference in size. Both want to be top in what they do. But where Andrew puts all his ambition into one highly skilled and dangerous field, Jean has put hers into many different fields. The friend who had written to me to suggest that I interview Jean said, 'Jean is an extremely distinguished lawyer, a successful writer and artist who has raised three children on her own. Just a terrific person who is wickedly funny and refreshing and perhaps one of the most beloved people in the publishing business.'

When we met I showed Jean her friend's description and asked if that was a fair summary of her achievements. She said that it did list the facts and commented, 'The thing that I like the most is "one of the most beloved people in the publishing business".' She went on, 'I do have a reputation for being extremely nice. And I am very nice. I can also be mean and vicious and nasty and extremely catty and tear people to shreds. But I'm very careful who I do that with.'

As we talked what came through clearly was that she experienced her self as needing to be in a relationship with other people. I often refer to such a person as a 'people person'.

'Yes,' she said. 'I'm a people person. I like people a lot, although, of course, I like some people better than others. I can generally handle people. I can generally figure out people better than most people can. I am happiest doing things that involve people. Before I came to this law firm, I was in a firm where I mostly did research. I had very little to do with people. I hated that job for a lot of different reasons, but one was that the best of my skills were unused. Now I'm in a firm where all my skills are brought into use. They say in law that there are four kinds of lawyers – the finders, the binders, the minders and the grinders, which I think is self-explanatory. I'm a finder, what they call a rain maker. The skill I have, which isn't that common, is that I get clients, and that's in large part because I'm good with people. Most lawyers, to use your construct, would be introverts, isolated people. I can do research, but there are people who do that much better than I. There aren't many people who do what I do as well as I do. Yes, I'm a person who defines herself in terms of other people.'

When she spoke of all the things she did and did so well she said, 'I've almost reached the point where I can accept that I can't be brilliant at everything. Not quite, but I'm getting there. I'll be there by the time I'm fifty. I know I should concentrate on and value the things I do the best. That's hard, because you want to be able to say – you want to be the complete lawyer, the successful writer and so on. I do a lot of things. I can't seem to slough off any of them, get rid of any of the things in my life that give me reason for self-esteem, a pat on the head. I am always looking for approval, for someone to say, "That was very good, dear. Aren't you terrific, dear," and I get a lot of that. And I probably do as much as I do because I need a lot.'

At the beginning of our conversation I asked Jean which of all her achievements was the most important to her. She said, 'Most important to me is that I have three splendid children. Failure to bring up my children well would have been the most extreme failure. Everything else can be dismissed, changed, dealt with. But to have failed in bringing up one's children is irretrievable.'

Bringing up her children was most important to her 'because I think that's where you have the most chance to make a difference. It's the one thing that only you can do. I have a friend, a writer, who says you should do things that only you could do. For instance, if a magazine asks you to write an article, if you feel that thirty-eight other people, or three or two, can do it, you shouldn't do it. If you're the only one who can do it, that is the thing you should do. That's a good way of cutting down on the things you are asked to do in life. Only you can be a mother to your children. It's the most profound and focused thing you can ever do in your life. You get to the end of the road and you have this degree and that honour and this much money, and that many people who think you're terrific, and if you've got three less-than-what-they-could-have-been human beings, how does it compute? How could you possibly put your so-called achievements against that? Does fifteen million dollars and forty-three degrees make up for three human beings that I didn't go the route with, or didn't do as much for as I could have? I don't mean to imply that I've done everything for my children that I could have done. In many ways I did a far from perfect job. So far they look very good, but you can't say your children really are in good shape until they have grandchildren and still look good.'

Jean thought in terms of grandchildren, of extending her family group. But she also thought of the greatest threat to her group and what that would do to her. She said, 'I have often thought that if my children, perish the thought, were to die I would be gone in twenty-four hours.'

Andrew and Jean, like everyone else, know how they experience their existence and how they see the threat of the annihilation of their self. However, describing this is not very easy. It is often hard to find the words. Even more, describing to another person how you perceive the threat to yourself means showing your greatest weakness. As Jean said in discussing trust, 'What is it you trust people with nowadays? You can tell almost anybody about the affairs you've had, your abortions, whatever. The thing you don't show is *you never show need*. That's what you show to the people you trust. It's not your sex life you have to keep secret. It's that you're needy, or that you're not on top of things, or that you have lost some kind of power.'

There is another reason for not making explicit and conscious how we experience our self and its annihilation, and that is that we do not like to admit to ourselves that this structure of our self is just a structure. We want to forget that the structures we have created which we call our self and our world are just structures. We want to see them as solid reality. 'This is the person I am and this is the world I live in.'

Here we come up against another one of these contrasts which are a life-long dilemma, the contrast between freedom and security. Both are desirable, but in life the more freedom we have, the less security, and the more security, the less freedom. This applies at both the political and personal levels. A State which gives its people great security in terms of income, housing, welfare, education and health takes away a great deal of their freedom: a State which allows great freedom for its people offers little security. As individuals, the more we insist that the structures we have created are absolute and solid reality, the less freedom we have to change them. The more we see that the structures we have created are structures, the greater insecurity we shall feel, but with that we have the knowledge that if they are just structures then we are free to change them.

The need to see our structures as solid reality can blind us to the fact that other people see things differently from us. This can lead us to think that anyone who sees things differently from us is either mad or bad, or perhaps both. Because how we experience our existence and the threat of the annihilation is so basic to our structure we can assume that everyone else perceives their existence and annihilation in the same way. This assumption lies at the root of most of the discord between people, especially the discord between couples, typically made up of one 'people person' and one busy developing his or her individuality.

Whatever degree of absolute and universal truth we choose to perceive in our structures, there is one structure which we are constantly developing, and that is our story.

# THE PATTERN OF OUR STORY

All we ever actually experience is the present, a lifetime of moments in the here and now. What we do with our experience in the present is to organize it into structures which we call the past and future.

Our creation of the structures of the past and future enables us to create our favourite structure, the story. All our understanding of people and things comes to us in the form of a story. Nothing fascinates us more than to be told a story, be it the story of how to build a motor car or solve an equation, or a story about the latest comic disaster to befall our friends or the latest mega-catastrophe involving our favourite soap-opera characters.

The story which fascinates and engages us the most is our own story. Even if there is no one to listen to us tell our story we constantly tell our story to ourselves. We remember our past: we plan our future.

The structure of a story is that of linear progression. First this, then this, then this and so on to the end. All our stories have this structure. However, within each story is a recurring pattern which makes every story an individual story. This pattern is created very early in our life story and relates to how we experience our existence. Once created, the pattern recurs again and again in our story. To some extent we are aware of this pattern. We may see it as something we constantly choose to do, or we may see it as a recurring fate or an unsolved problem. Later in this book I shall tell the stories of some people who saw the pattern as fate or an unsolved problem. Here I shall tell the stories of two people who saw very clearly the recurring pattern in their lives and who saw it as something they chose to do.

Often in our stories the recurring pattern is loss and the defences against future loss. Children are very much affected by the loss of a parent, but just how each child is affected depends on how the child experiences his or her existence.

Milta McLean Dennis is a remarkable woman. At thirty she is Public Affairs Director for WRKS, the very popular KISS Radio Station in New York. As a university student she had worked at

WRKS to gain experience, and the management there were so impressed with her then that, apart from eighteen months travelling in Europe, she has worked there ever since and now heads a department which under her leadership has won many awards.

She told me, 'I have set goals for myself as young as I can remember. I have always been the kind of person who is very cautious. I'm a strategic planner. I try to plan everything like so. I had to plan so that I could reach this point. But even in my personal life it's the same way. I look maybe ten years down the road and I say to myself I'd like to have this and that in that amount of time. Often people say to me, "You're very successful in what you've done. You should be happy with those things you have." Sometimes I feel guilty about wanting more, because if I look around me I see other people who are far less fortunate than me. Sometimes I do feel guilty, and then the real me surfaces and supersedes and I'm back to where I was again. I could not understand for the life of me why I was that way. It wasn't until about two years ago when I started what I considered to be a self-evaluation. Why am I the person that I am? What made me the way I am?'

The answer she came to was, 'Why I am the way I am is because when I was five years old my father passed away.'

As head of a young black family in North Carolina, Milta's mother, a school teacher, had little money for all the things a bright and imaginative child like Milta would desire. 'I guess at some point I said when I become of age I am going to have all those things that I've always wanted, and I'm going to work for it. But why am I such a strategic planner, why do I look ahead and say I'm going to do this now because I want to be ready for the next step? I realize it's because when my father passed away it was something totally out of my control. I had no control over that, and it had such a devastating effect on me. His death had such an impact on our lives. My parents were in the process of building a home. I kept saying to myself, "If he had lived we'd have lived in that house. I would have had all those things if my father had lived." I decided that from now on I needed to have total control. If I can control my destiny I'm going to see to it that I'm never caught off guard again. So I planned my life very strategically based on what happened to me when I was five years old. Even in little things I do, I say, "What happens if this happens?" For instance, if my husband and I take a trip some place I will plan to take something small and simple which would make a difference if we found ourselves in a situation which was an emergency. I would be able to pull us through because I'd thought of this before becoming engaged in whatever it was. It's worked well. So far, I haven't been caught off guard. I don't know how long it's going to last. I realize that I'm afraid of being caught off guard.'

'What do you think might happen?' I asked.

'I don't know. There have been times when there've been catastrophes in the family, and somehow I've been able to spring back. I ask why I am able to spring back, because it's the kind of situation which would normally take someone a long time to overcome. It's because people, friends, people I work with look at me in a way which says, "Milta will always succeed, Milta will always overcome this." This has helped a great deal. People have faith in me, and because of the faith they have in me I can carry on. I often think what could happen, what would be the biggest catastrophe where I was caught off guard. I don't know what could happen. I guess that's why I'm afraid of it. I don't know that if it was a big catastrophe whether I'd be able to cope with it. I was five when my father passed away, it took so long for me to become accustomed to that, because I missed him for years and years. I felt as though there was a part of me that was missing. I guess that was why I was always an over-achiever, because I was always trying to compensate for something I didn't have. I tried to be the best that I could be. I was never competing with the other person, I was always competing with myself.'

When she was describing to me her attempts to learn to cook she said, 'I want to know why. I have to be told why so that it will help me to remember later on. Knowing why will help me to better understand.'

'Why is it important to understand?' I asked.

'That's a good question. So that I relate to whatever the situation is. It helps me to relate better to what it is I'm trying to do at that particular time.'

'Why is it important to relate better?'

'I guess it reverts back to my childhood, so I'm not caught off guard. It's to prepare myself for whatever my destiny is, whatever my goal is. It's important to me to understand these things and to be able to relate. I guess it's about life. What is life all about? It's about relating to one another, relating to what you're doing, it's being meaningful, taking whatever you do seriously. We have a purpose here, and I think my purpose is trying to help those who are less fortunate than I am and that's one of the reasons I like what I do because I'm able to help someone with the information that I disseminate over the airwaves. I'm giving them pertinent information, and hopefully they're taking that information and turning it around, using it. And that's why it's important to me.' (That is, 'The clarity and organization I have developed for myself I wish to pass on to others to assist them in their search for clarity and organization.')

Jean's father didn't die. He simply abandoned his wife and child. Jean said, 'I didn't see him for a great many years and then I got back in touch with him. My children sometimes take me to task because I'm not very considerate to my father. They say, "How can you do that?" and I say, rather archly, but I mean it, "He abandoned me when I was a child, so I'm allowed to do anything to him. If I abandon you, you can do anything to me. But I didn't so you can't." I'm sure if I were in analysis the psychiatrist would make a great deal of this, but I use it primarily as an excuse for not being punctilious, not, say, writing him a thank you note. My father doesn't make a whole lot of difference in my life. I don't expect to be much affected by his death. My mother died when I was twenty-four, when I wasn't very close to her, so I wasn't particularly affected by her death. I've often thought that, if my life goes in a normal course, God willing, I will not outlive my children, and I will never be greatly affected by death.'

Milta had experienced the loss of her father as loss of control with the danger of being destroyed in total chaos, and so she created the recurring pattern of organizing, planning, achieving in order to prevent such devastation ever again. Jean felt the loss of her father as being rejected and abandoned, with the danger of the complete isolation which would cause her to disappear, and so she created the recurring pattern of forming relationships where abandonment should not occur. As a child she protected herself by gathering other people around her. An only child with little opportunity to make many friends, she discovered a multitude of friends in books. She peopled her world with a vast array of characters who became her true friends who shared her daydreams and her play acting. Books and their contents have always been her friends. She said to me, 'When you talk of isolation, one thing that would make me check out when I was ninety-eight years old would be if I couldn't read.'

Jean did not simply create imaginary friends to give her a sense of existence. She developed her talent to be a good friend, and, as the opportunities presented themselves, she made many friends.

Friendship depends on faithfulness. A good friend does not abandon you. When her father abandoned her, Jean, in justified anger, drew up the rule that 'If someone abandons you, you have the right to abandon that person. If you abandon someone, that person has the right to abandon you.' Her father had abandoned her, so she had the right to abandon him. She had never abandoned her children, so they did not have the right to abandon her.

An important feature of such recurring patterns in our life story is that the pattern can be both inhibitingly defensive and expansively creative. Milta and Jean structured their pattern when they were weak and vulnerable children. This weakness and vulnerability they still felt in adulthood, so they maintained the pattern as a defence. They also used the pattern with great success as a way of going forward in life purposefully and creatively.

However, there is a flaw in the reasoning of both Milta and Jean. No strategic planner, no matter how intelligent, perceptive and powerful, can guard against every contingency. We cannot control the constantly changing world which is influenced by a universe which is beyond even our understanding. Neither can we control or even predict the behaviour of all other people. Similarly, just because we are loyal and faithful does not mean that the objects of our loyalty and faithfulness will always be loyal and faithful to us.

We all employ in the structures of our self rules which are basic to its structure and which are neither logical nor reasonable. These rules have to do with how we see relationships and the degree and kind of risks we are prepared to run, and were developed from the conclusions we drew from our early experiences. Like a faulty foundation of a house, they may not cause us any difficulty until we come under stress. Then, if we refuse to see that these rules are illogical and unreasonable and instead insist against all the evidence that our rules are the Absolute Truth, we find ourselves behaving in those ways which psychiatrists call the symptoms of mental illness.

Thus Milta in her determination to prove that she could control everything, could become increasingly obsessional, and Jean, to ward off the panic of the threat of her self disappearing after she had been abandoned could become unable to venture from her own four walls, and both could deny the discrepancy between reality and what they wished it to be by retreating into the safety of the prison of depression.

However, neither Milta nor Jean would be so foolish as to do these things. They each see very clearly where they are vulnerable, and they are wise in the ways of the world. Milta knows that she cannot guard against all possible catastrophes, and she also knows that with the support and reassurance of her friends she will be able to survive the unexpected. Jean knows that adult children cannot be protected by their mother from all disasters and that, in the ordinary course of life, adult children do tend to get wrapped up in their own affairs and neglect their mother. As she said, 'If they do neglect me, I expect I'll be annoyed and upset, but I won't be destroyed.'

Milta and Jean are well aware that to survive in this world we need to be flexible. We can try to impose our structures on the world, but when the world persists in refusing to conform to our structures we should acknowledge this and try to find the right point where we should abandon our structures and create something new.

The reason that Milta and Jean can do this is because each woman values and accepts herself. When we feel like this about ourselves we have an inner security which allows us to see our structures as structures, as statements of possibility and not as Absolute Truths. When we do not value ourselves we want to see our structures as solid and unchangeable, for if they shift and change we fear that we shall fall apart or disappear.

Valuing and accepting yourself is an essential part of creating a meaningful story for yourself.

# A MEANINGFUL STORY

For a story to be meaningful it must have a beginning, a middle and an end, and one part must connect in a meaningful way to the next.

Over my years as a therapist many people have told me stories which do not have these criteria of meaningfulness. They have said things like, 'I have no future', or 'My future is a blank wall', thus robbing their story of a hopeful ending, something which we must give our story if we are to live our lives in confidence and courage. They have said, 'I can't remember my childhood', thus creating a story without a beginning, something which we must have if we are to feel rooted in time and place and connected to those who went before us. They have talked only of an unhappy past and an even more unhappy future, while the present, the middle of their story, is somewhere they cannot be. Yet if we cannot live in the present we cannot live anywhere, for the present is all that we really have.

Their stories have all contained mysterious gaps. They have said things like, 'I have a good husband, a wonderful home and lovely children. There's no reason why I should be depressed', or 'I couldn't have had better parents. No, I can't talk to them', or 'Dorothy, I'm amazed that you think there's a connection between me being sexually abused as a child and my panic attacks'.

These gaps and inconsistencies in our story which rob it of its meaning appear when there are events in our lives which create for us the greatest threat, that of the annihilation of our self. As small children, helpless and in the power of adults, we have few ways of dealing with such events other than by denial. We can 'forget' that the event occurred, or we can remember the event but not the powerful emotions that accompanied it (what Freud called the defence mechanisms of repression and isolation). For the child these are essential and effective survival techniques, but when they are carried forward into adult life they cease to be appropriate and become instead structures which inhibit and cripple. They force the person to retreat into the preferred reality and to use the preferred reality as a hiding place and refuge, and not as a starting place and a resource for creativity. Such a way of existence is a meagre survival, not a full and creative life.

# LIVING A FULL AND CREATIVE LIFE

It seems that whether we find our internal reality more or less real than our external reality is laid down in the kind of neurological system with which we are born. The research which shows this can be interpreted in two ways. Some people believe that our genes determine our fate, and thus the holders of this belief make themselves the helpless victims of their supposed genetic inherit-ance. They can be no more than what their genes allow them to be. Other people, myself among them, see our genetic inheritance as our *potential* which we can develop in an infinite number of ways.

We do not have to live within the reality which we find the more real. If we are wise we venture into our less real reality and make it real.

Prince Hans-Adam, whom I had met first at a conference and second when I interviewed him in his office at Schloss Vaduz is charming and courteous, not just interested in people and events, but as actively involved as his royal position will allow. It is difficult to see in him the introspective teenager who concluded that all he could feel sure of was his own thoughts. He has taught himself the social skills necessary for success in our external reality, just as Andrew Wallace, a man given to deeds, not words, has taught himself the art of social conversation, in particular the art of giving interviews, something he recognized as a skill needed by a racing driver seeking sponsorship. I first met Milta McLean Dennis in 1986 when she interviewed me about my book *Living with the Bomb.*[5] So skilled was she in making me feel comfortable and getting me to talk at length that I did not realize until I interviewed her a year later that she had not been born a 'people person'. Jean Hale, a 'people person', revealed in the depth and clarity with which she talked about herself that she had recog-nized the necessity of journeying inward and acquainting herself with her internal reality. Moreover, she had discovered quite early in her life something which many 'people people' fail to discover, that being alone is not a danger but a pleasure and a renewal. All these people, while being well aware of their weaknesses and vulnerabilities, value and accept themselves.

# BECOMING A SUCCESSFUL SELF

Becoming a Successful Self begins with awareness and understanding.

It is possible to live our lives without awareness and understanding, and indeed many people do. We can respond to events and act without wondering why we do so: we can live in accordance with a set of instructions handed down to us by our parents and leaders, and never question the rules that rule our life. We can explain other people's behaviour solely in terms of whether they are like us, and if they are not we say they are mad or bad. If we live like this, our lives are narrow and meagre, limited in time and place, and barren of curiosity and wonder. We can choose to live such lives as a way of avoiding pain and uncertainty, but then when we encounter, as we must, loss and the unexpected, we have few resources to deal with the pain and uncertainty that follows.

*Awareness* means using our ability to act, feel and think while observing our actions, feelings and thoughts. It means responding to other people's actions while wondering what thoughts and feelings lie behind such actions.

*Understanding* means becoming aware of how we explain why people behave as they do, checking our theory about people against what we observe, and then modifying or changing our theory. We might be using the theory that all people think and feel as we do, but discover that all people do not, and so we have to enlarge our theory, and then check it again against our observations.

An important part of that awareness and understanding is making conscious our knowledge of how we experience our own sense of existence and the threat of annihilation, and how our two realities differ in their degree of reality. Along with that awareness comes the understanding that while some people experience their existence, the threat of annihilation, and their two realities in ways similar to us, others do not. Moreover, we need to understand that even when such similarities do exist, no two people elaborate and express these similarities in the same way. We are all individuals, and as such we each have to find our own awareness and understanding.

Thus no two Successful Selves are the same. A Successful Self can be defined only in the most general way, as follows:

> **The Successful Self is not engaged in a constant battle to avoid the threat of the annihilation of the self.**

> **The Successful Self feels valuable, self-accepting and self-confident.**

> **The Successful Self has developed flexible and creative ways of elaborating the sense of existence.**

> **The Successful Self has made the less real reality real by developing the skills necessary to live within that reality.**

> **The Successful Self uses the preferred reality not so much as a refuge but as a resource for creativity.**

> **The Successful Self has created a life story without the gaps and inconsistencies which inhibit and cripple and which goes forward in courage and hope.**

A Successful Self is not a state of being which once achieved is ours forever. It is always a mode of being and becoming, a journey of continual discovery.

# Extraverts
# and Introverts

# 2

# Our Two Realities

While you have been reading the first chapter you might have wondered whether the two ways of experiencing our existence relate to being an introvert or an extravert. Indeed they do. I am just not very happy about using the words 'extravert' and 'introvert'. They each have so many meanings that conversations where they are used can be very confusing. So in this chapter I shall talk about some of the ways the words are used, and I shall try to define very clearly what I mean when I call someone an introvert or an extravert.

There are three main ways that the words 'extravert' and 'introvert' are used:

(1) as descriptions of the ways people behave,

(2) as labels for that kind of group which psychologists call a Type,

(3) as the preference each of us has for internal or external reality.

## 'INTROVERT' AND 'EXTRAVERT' AS
## DESCRIPTIONS
## OF THE WAY PEOPLE BEHAVE

When someone is rather withdrawn, quiet, not very talkative we can describe that person as 'introverted'. If that person behaves like this persistently we can describe that person as 'an introvert'.

When someone is very happy, talkative, sociable and active we can describe that person as 'extraverted'. If that person behaves like this persistently we can describe that person as 'an extravert'.

Most of us can behave in both introverted and extraverted ways.

When we feel tired, or sad, or worried, or shy we can become withdrawn and silent. If the conditions that make us tired, or sad, or worried, or shy persist over a long period of time we can be so silent and withdrawn that people might describe us as 'an introvert'. We might think of ourselves as being 'an introvert'.

Similarly, when we feel very happy, or excited by news of good fortune, or with friends who stimulate us, we can become excited, sociable and talkative. Some of us are very good at being excited, sociable and talkative so that the people we are with won't see how sad and worried or shy we really are. If the conditions which make us excited, sociable and talkative persist people might describe us as 'an extravert'. We might think of ourselves as being 'an extravert'.

## 'INTROVERT' AND 'EXTRAVERT' AS TYPES OF PEOPLE

One form of structure we all use all the time is that where we see some feature which a number of people possess we use that feature as a way of grouping those people together and labelling that group. This is how we bring order into the chaos of a multitude of individuals where no two people are the same.

The first of the structures we call a group which we create is 'mother and me', which later we extend to the group 'family' with the contrast 'not family'. At the same time we are creating groups we call 'male' and 'female', 'adults' and 'children'. Then we go on creating groups wherever we see some aspect of people which we think is important – friends and enemies, blacks and whites, golfers and non-golfers, and so on.

Useful though this technique is in reducing confusion, it is dangerous because it can lead us to forget that in creating the structure of the group we have ignored certain important characteristics of each individual in the group. Thus, we can come to believe that if a person is in such and such a group the characteristics of that group explain everything about that person. Then we say things like, 'You behave like that because you're a man', or 'You must be good at sport because you're an Australian and all Australians are good at sport', or 'You and I will get on well together because you're a Sagittarian and I'm a Virgo, and Sagittarians and Virgos always get on well together'.

Dangers like these have never stopped doctors and psychologists from putting people in groups, slapping labels on the groups, and then explaining everything about each person in terms of these labels. Woe betide you if you find yourself put in a group and labelled 'schizophrenic' or 'hypochondriac' or 'neurotic extravert' or 'Type A personality'. It's no use jumping up and down and waving your hands and saying, 'I'm not like that. I'm me, an individual, like nobody else'. The doctor or the psychologist has put you in a group and labelled you and that's that.

Down the centuries, when doctors and psychologists have wanted to explain why people behave as they do, they have said that there were various groups or *types* of people, and everyone was one of these Types. These Types were based on things like 'bodily humours', or 'temperaments', or constellations of stars, or the bumps on a person's cranium, or the yet unidentified set of genes a person is born with, or the answers a person gave to a set of questions.

Thus, you might think that you feel frustrated, angry and disappointed because from your earliest childhood your family have prevented you from being yourself and doing what you want to do, but according to the Typologists you are wrong. You feel like that because you have a 'choleric temperament', or were born when the sun was in the ascendant, or you have a big bump on your cranium, or you have a 'manic-depressive' gene, or because you got a high score for Extraversion and Neuroticism on the Eysenck Personality Inventory.

Thus do Typologies take power from us and give it to 'the experts', and prevent us from changing.

Whenever we become very interested in a typology it is very easy to see it operating everywhere. You can pick a Sagittarian by the way she walks down the street or a Neurotic Introvert by the way he behaves at a party. But if we are interested in finding the truth and not just in proving ourselves to be right we have to ask, 'Does this aspect of people really exist or is it just something I have imagined and then projected on to the rest of the world around me?'

I used to think that that aspect of people which is usually called 'introversion-extraversion' was just a figment of some psychologists' imagination and bore no relationship to real, lived experience. Early in my career as a psychologist it was the fashion to use a statistical technique called 'factor analysis'. Psychologists were always claiming to have found such and such a 'factor' after having given their subjects a 'battery of tests' (a 'battering by tests' is a better description of what actually went on). There were great arguments over the existence of these 'factors'. Some psychologists said we all had one big Factor G of General Intelligence and lots of little S Factors of special abilities, while other psychologists said there was no Big G, only lots of little S factors. What neither side would admit was that whether a psychologist ended up with a Big G or not depended on the way he did his sums and grouped all the correlations he had done together. Meanwhile, other psychologists were discovering all these different Personality Factors. (Which Personality Factors were found depended which professor the psychologist worked for. Psychologists working for Professor Cattell in America found factors different from those psychologists working for Professor Eysenck in England.) We were all supposed to have these Intelligence and Personality Factors, large and small, inside us. If you believed all this you could think of yourself as being like a sweets jar, jammed full of different sized lumps of candy. What you were supposed to do with these 'factors' was never explained, although everything you did do was explained in terms of one or other of these 'factors'.

However, as time went by, evidence that the distinction between extraversion and introversion did exist kept appearing in my own research, first in my work using the Rorschach Inkblot Test, and then in my studies in Personal Construct Psychology. I had to go back to re-reading psychologists as opposed as Carl Jung and Hans Eysenck, both of whom group people into extraverts and introverts. I could see in their work links with mine.

Jung, in his book *Psychological Types*,[1] wrote that, 'Introversion and extraversion, as a typical attitude, means an essential bias which conditions the whole psychic process, establishes the habitual mode of reaction, and thus determines not only the style of behaviour but also the quality of the subjective experience.

Not only that, it determines the kind of compensation the unconscious will produce.' In Jung's view, an harmonious life for the individual comes from a balancing of the attitudes of introversion and extraversion.

My research has led me to agree with Jung thus far, but after that we part company. Jung felt that grouping people into extraverts and introverts was not enough. In his obsessional way he went on subdividing his groups. He created Thinking as against Feeling, Sensing as against Intuiting, and Perceiving as against Judging Types which could be combined in one person in different ways.

Sixteen different ways in fact. The Myers-Briggs Type Indicator[2] identifies sixteen combinations of Jung's Types and describes each combination in positive terms. The MBTI is becoming increasingly popular, especially in business and health care institutions where people working together amicably and actually talking to one another is actually much rarer than it should be. Seminars where a group of colleagues fill in the questionnaire and discuss their answers can be an extremely useful exercise in discovering that each of us has an individual and unique way of perceiving ourselves and our world. Also, knowing that you are an ISTJ, or an ENFP or whatever, can be very useful in providing you with an excuse for your bad behaviour. Then you can say things like, 'Of course I'm outspoken. I am an ESTJ, and all ESTJs say what they think.'

However, when a senior executive decides that all his management team should be the same psychological type, as measured by the MBTI, he shows that he has not understood why every organization, be it a family or a multinational business, needs to be made up of individuals with contrasting and opposing perceptions. That way we can complement each other, make up for one another's deficiencies, and, by comparing and contrasting our different perceptions, have a better chance of discovering what is actually happening as distinct from what we imagine is happening. Thus we can act more effectively.

If you read through the descriptions of the sixteen Myers-Briggs Types you can feel that you wouldn't mind being any one of these types. Each of them seems really nice and tremendously sane. You won't feel like that if you fill in the Eysenck Personality

Inventory. It is full of traps – a Lie score to show if you cheated, and a Neuroticism score to show how crazy you are, even though you might never have set foot in a psychiatrist's office. You do have a chance of ending up being labelled a Stable Introvert or a Stable Extravert, but equally you run the risk of being labelled a Neurotic Introvert or a Neurotic Extravert.

Hans Eysenck would lay no claim to being 'nice'. He is honest, truthful and plain-speaking, qualities which can prevent a person from being thought to be 'nice'. He is, in William James's terms, 'tough-minded', and he has no time for 'tender-minded' psychologists, nor for 'unscientific' thinkers like Freud and Jung. He has stirred up enormous controversies. He has also had an enormous influence on research in psychology, both in the way psychologists do research and in what research they do.

Initially, the Eysenck research method was to take large groups of people, give them a number of different tests and look at the correlations of test scores that emerged. Such correlations, Eysenck said, could be considered to be 'dimensions of personality',[3] which became the title of his first book in 1948. One dimension which appeared consistently in his research results was what Eysenck called 'extraversion-introversion', and as a quick and reliable way of measuring where a person stood on this dimension Eysenck devised the Eysenck Personality Inventory (EPI), a short questionnaire which is regularly used in a wide variety of research. What this research shows is that those people labelled 'extravert' and those labelled 'introvert' differ in many important ways, such as in the pattern of changes in body temperature, which affects how efficiently we can work at different times of the day and night, and the quickness of recovery from jet lag. Introverts have a slower recovery rate from jet lag than do extraverts. Andrew Wallace, who would score high on Introversion on the EPI, had his only 'large shunt' (large accident) in a racing car when he got off a plane from Australia at Heathrow and went straight to Silverstone to practise. He discovered that his reflexes were not as quick as they usually were.

Eysenck and his colleagues were not satisfied with just describing these differences. They wanted to know why, and to answer this question they looked at the neurological functioning of extraverts and introverts. This research, carried out with large groups of a wide variety of people and with a variety of methods has led Eysenck and his colleagues to conclude that a person is born and remains either an extravert or an introvert. The bases of extraversion and introversion are brain states which are innate and genetically determined. Eysenck wrote,

'Introversion is produced essentially by high arousal levels in the cortex; this high arousal level, in turn, is produced by an over-active ascending reticular formation . . . People have a preferred level of arousal – if this is too low, they are bored, while if it is too high they are upset. Extraverts tend to have a level which is too low most of the time, unless the environment can provide excitement and stimulation; hence they are stimulus hungry and sensation seeking.'[4]

Thus to the extravert external reality is immensely important, for only it will provide the necessary level of stimulation. For the introvert external reality can be dangerous, for it can become painfully overstimulating. Withdrawal into the physical stillness of internal reality means a dangerously low level of stimulation for the extravert, while the quietness of internal reality allows the introvert to reduce stimulation to its optimum level. Anything we see as dangerous we also see as strange. Thus the reality which is dangerous is less real. The reality which is safe is the real reality.

All living organisms, of which we are one species, are very competent in seeking not just the conditions which will allow them to survive but the conditions which will enable them to function at their optimum level. To do this organisms have to have some inner representation or structure which relates to what the organism needs and the conditions which will meet that need. In some organisms this structure is at a level we call 'instinct', and in other organisms the structure involves a system of mental representations which we call thinking.

Up to recent years human beings, in their vanity, claimed that as they were the only animals who thought, talked and used tools they were the highest form of all the species, the pinnacle of creation. Now the claim to such superiority has to be made for other reasons, for what has become increasingly clear is that many species use a structure of internal representations which allow them to create a system of communications and, in some cases, tools. (To form the idea of a tool you have to have some notion of past and future and some mental picture of how one object relates spatially to another.) All we can claim now is that human beings use the most complex structure of internal representations which we reveal in the way we talk and act.

To survive physically we need a properly functioning neurological system, and to live well we need the conditions which allow our neurological system to function at its best. When we are born we have the potential to create structures which are internal representations of our needs and the conditions which will fulfil these needs. We immediately proceed to do this. We think and we engage others in conversation. As babies we know how to turn our heads away when the stimulation around us is too much and how to fuss and cry when the stimulation is too little. As adults we adjust the level of stimulation with statements like, 'Turn the radio down. I can't stand all that noise', or 'It's dead boring here. I'm going down to the pub'.

Thus the words 'introvert' and 'extravert' can be used to label two groups of people according to the levels of stimulation their neurological system requires. They can also be used to label these two groups of people according to which reality, internal or external, the members of each group prefers.

However, once we start talking about *preferences* we are talking about *meaning*, and when we talk about meaning we are talking about individuals, because, while we share certain structures of meaning with other people, the set of structures which we each create and call 'myself and my world' is different from all other such sets of structures. Each of us is an individual. We each can be classified as belonging to a multitude of groups, but no one group describes us completely. We are each in a group of one.

## 'INTROVERT' AND 'EXTRAVERT' AS THE PREFERENCE EACH OF US HAS FOR INTERNAL OR EXTERNAL REALITY

We may come into the world possessing one of two kinds of neurological system, but this is simply *potential*. We can use this potential in an infinite number of ways.

The neurological system we are born with determines which reality, internal or external, we find the more real, and it is in the more real reality that we have our sense of existence.

External reality contains other people, so when our sense of existence resides in our external reality our structure of self from its very beginning involves other people. We experience our sense of self in relationship to other people.

Internal reality is aloneness, oneness, so when our sense of existence resides in our internal reality our structure of self from its very beginning concerns just ourselves alone. We experience our sense of self in our own individuality.

From the moment of birth we begin elaborating our sense of existence. As babies we devise ways of getting the world around us to respond to us in the way we want. Thus the extravert infant has to develop ways of engaging the world (something like, 'If I smile at Granny and bounce up and down she'll pick me up and play games with me') and the introvert infant has to develop ways of quietening the world down while still making it interesting (something like, 'If Granny shakes a rattle at me I'll cry, but if she sings to me I'll smile at her'). Amongst developmental psychologists there is no doubt that babies from birth are very adept at carrying on an interchange with an adult and rewarding the adult for a response which the baby wants and punishing or ignoring the adult who fails to give the desired response. Just how each baby does this depends on the individual baby and what the environment has to offer. Parenting adults differ in just how well they can understand their baby's communications and respond to them.

We are all aware of how we experience our existence long before we can put it into words. The words I use to describe the two ways of experiencing our sense of existence are a distillation of the many descriptions I have been given over the last twenty years. So, when in the rest of this book I use the word *extravert* I mean experiencing your existence as being a member of a group, as the relationship, the connection, between yourself and others.

When I use the word *introvert* I mean experiencing your existence as the progressive development of your individuality in terms of clarity, achievement and authenticity.

Extraverts can make themselves a member of a group in a

tremendous variety of ways. They can, for instance, gather a large family around them, or have hundreds of friends, or play team sports, or run a business with colleagues, or enter one of the helping professions and enjoy being needed, or become an actor or a musician or a singer and feel close and loved by the audience.

Many extraverts as children have bad experiences with other people and grow up feeling very nervous about being with people. They become loners, or people with very few friends, and may think of themselves as being introverts, but are in fact shy extraverts. They can survive very successfully by creating their own group, perhaps of fantasy figures from books or television with whom, in daydreams, they share adventures, or by worshipping from afar certain heroes and heroines (as a fan you can imagine that the singer whom you worship has a special relationship with you and you can find in a fan club a few people you can trust), or by joining a group of people who are as fanatically devoted to bird watching, or train spotting, or collecting picture postcards as you are, but where you don't have to give your fellow fanatics the same high degree of trust that you give to your real friends, the birds, or the trains, or the postcards.

If you have always found people to be completely untrustworthy, you can find a loyal group of people in your pets, or in the objects which to you have taken on the characteristics of people. An extravert friend of mine, showing me the garage he had converted into a totally book-lined study, gestured towards the books and said, 'These are my friends. I rarely lend them and I always know where each one is.' Some years later, when his wife phoned to tell me that they had separated, I asked, 'Has he taken his books?' and when she said, 'Yes' I knew that the separation was not a temporary one. She is an introvert, a magnificent artist who, as wife and mother, has painted far too little. She was devastated by his leaving, so, to offer some hope, I said, 'You could use the garage as a studio.' She said, 'I've already put up some track lights.' I knew then that she would survive and prosper.

Introverts can develop their individual sense of clarity, achievement and authenticity in a tremendous variety of ways. They become thinkers, and thinkers are everywhere, designing a space probe, sorting out the world's economy, formulating a new theory in pure mathematics, or philosophy, or religion, or art, or education, or feminism or football. Some of the thinkers think simply so that they can understand and see things clearly, and others use their thinking to advance their own individual achievement. One such achieving thinker might win the Nobel Prize and another might run a successful fish and chip shop. Some thinkers, having gained greater clarity, want to share this new understanding with others in order to help them see things more clearly, and so they enter one of the communication professions, be it in the media, or writing, or education, or in the helping professions. Some thinkers seek greater clarity because they want to be themselves, and you have to find and know yourself so that you can be yourself. A seeker after authenticity places great emphasis on honesty and truth, and as such can become a person whom others find to be marvellously real and strong. But such a person can also become an eccentric.

The continuing problem for introverts is that it is very easy to lose touch with external reality. This is why other people are of vital importance to introverts. They keep the introvert in contact with external reality. Many introverts recognize this, and so they work hard at learning the social skills that come easily to extraverts. These introverts are often taken to be extraverts, though they rarely consider themselves to be extraverts. Many introverts become creative in one of the arts where their mode of working is by observing external reality, taking some aspect of that inside themselves, reworking this in an idiosyncratic way, and then putting their creation back into external reality.

Other introverts, having had in their childhood bad experiences with other people, are very cautious in their relationships with others. They may solve the problem of needing other people by marrying an extravert who has to socialize for both of them, or they join one of the helping professions (medicine particularly) where they have contact with others but are always in control behind the barrier of the professional relationship, or they develop relationships with animals or objects as their means of relating to external reality.

If introverts fail to maintain their contact with external reality and stay inside their own internal reality they can develop individual worlds of tremendous variety but which have no connection with anyone else's world. Such introverts if rich are tolerated as eccentrics, but most usually find that other people do not like this way of living and seek to restrain it with tranquillizing drugs, electroconvulsive therapy, lobotomies and locked doors.

Just as we can elaborate our sense of existence in a multitude of ways, so we can defend against our fear of the annihilation of our self in a multitude of ways.

The words I use to describe the two ways of experiencing the fear of the annihilation of the self are a distillation of many people's words.

*Extraverts* see the threat of the annihilation of the self as **complete isolation, being left totally, utterly and forever alone, and thus withering, fading away, totally disappearing into nothingness.**

*Introverts* see the threat of the annihilation of the self as **losing control of your self and your life and falling apart, falling into chaos, fragmenting, crumbling to dust.**

The defences that extraverts create against this fear always have to do with maintaining membership of a group. If you are an extravert and you value and accept yourself you will expect that other people will value and accept you. You can feel sure that wherever you go you will be valued and accepted, and that even if some disaster takes away all the people in your group you will soon find another group who, valuing and accepting you, will gather around you.

But if you are an extravert and you do not accept and value yourself, then you will always be afraid that you will be rejected and be left totally alone. So to avoid this you spend all your time in trying not to be rejected.

You may decide that, if no one will ever love you for yourself alone but only for what you can do for them, you must always be doing things for other people. If people won't love you, you can at least make them need you, and then they won't turn you out. So you become a self-sacrificing parent, a health worker who is always a tower of strength, an executive who is indispensable. You try not to think about what will happen to you when your children are grown up and independent, or when you are too old to work. There is the daily danger that if you demand anything, even the smallest thing, for yourself, people will reject you, just as they will if you dare to get angry. So you go through your life not seeing that your needs are met, never getting angry or even annoyed, or trying never to get angry and then sometimes shamefully, frighteningly, bursting out in uncontrollable anger. You live in fear of anger. Being anxious becomes part of you, like breathing, and if you can think of something to worry about, however trivial, it takes your mind off the most terrible fear that, because you are unlovable, one day people will cease pretending that they love you and will reject you and you will be no more.

These kinds of thoughts, and events which remind you of other times when you have been abandoned can culminate in some place where you feel exposed and vulnerable and are suddenly overwhelmed by heart-stopping terror. The dread of this experience is not dissipated by your doctor calling it 'a panic attack' and explaining it in physical terms as the body's response to something perceived as dangerous. You guard against it happening again by avoiding those circumstances where it first occurred and circumstances where, if it did occur again, you know you would be embarrassed, shamed, rejected and alone.

If as an extravert you believe that you are basically bad, of little value, unacceptable to yourself and to other people, you see this badness and unacceptability as residing in the darkness of your inner reality, and as that in itself is dangerous, you must flee from it into external reality. You can make yourself very busy there, rushing around, even achieving great things, but if the sense of badness and danger increases, you have to become increasingly busy until your level of activity ceases to be ordinary activity and becomes the frantic activity which is called mania.

The defences which introverts create against the fear of the annihilation of the self always have to do with control and keeping things in order. If you are an introvert and you value and accept yourself you believe that you have the capacity to be in control and keep things in order. Because you have such faith in yourself you can tolerate a high degree of disorder and lack of control. You can easily identify those parts of your life which need to be orderly and leave those less important parts in some degree of doubt or disorder or in the care of other people.

When, as children, we have bad experiences involving adults we usually draw two conclusions. One is that we are bad and unacceptable ('If I was really good my parents wouldn't treat me like this'). The other is that people cannot be trusted. At any moment they might reject you and abandon you, or create chaos around you.

If you are an introvert and you do not value and accept yourself you see everything inside you and around you likely to go out of control at any minute, and, as you don't trust anyone else to keep order, you have to be constantly on guard, controlling and organizing. You set standards which have to be reached and maintained, and you draw up rules about how these standards should be reached and maintained. To counteract your sense of badness you set very high standards ('If it's not perfect it's no good'). You believe it is wise to look for trouble before it starts, and so you become very adept at predicting trouble. You become very good at worrying about possible future events. Once the actions you have organized have been carried out you can start to worry about whether they have been carried out properly. Because as an introvert your external reality isn't all that real to you, you can always worry about whether something really did happen, or is really like it appears to be, or only seems like that to you and it is actually different. Introverts are expert worriers and doubters.

If you can keep your need to organize and control and your doubting and worrying within the limits our society regards as sensible and virtuous you can be very effective at what you do, but once you go over these limits trouble begins. You can arouse great anger and resentment among your family and colleagues who get tired of your obsessive cleaning and organizing, and find yourself increasingly isolated. This isolation and/or a further loss of self-confidence can make external reality seem even less real, and in the effort to maintain contact with it you can become increasingly obsessional and compulsive, needing, say, to wash your hands so often that the skin cracks and bleeds, or to check the electrical equipment in your house in such a complex ritual that you can't complete it to go to work or to bed. When such obsessions and compulsions fail to maintain contact with external reality, you can retreat into an inner reality from where your communications appear to those outside as no more than hallucinations and delusions.

## CONSTRUCTING THE SELF

What we experience as our self is a construction which we begin creating from birth. The foundation of our self is how we experience our sense of existence and how we perceive the threat of the annihilation of the self. All the conclusions we draw from what happens to us, all our opinions, attitudes and beliefs, and all our decisions, big and small, relate together and depend upon this foundation.

Psychologists like me call the parts which make up our structure of self 'constructs', and we show how they relate to one another and lead ultimately to the most abstract and most important construct of all, how we experience our self and the threat of the annihilation of the self, by a series of questions we call *laddering*.

# 3

# Which Reality Do You Prefer?

I had gone to New York for the wedding of two friends. They arranged for me to stay with one of their friends, someone I had not met. This was Margot Ely, Professor of Education at New York University. My friends described Margot as being greatly valued by her students because she regards the subjects of her research as real people with value and dignity, and not as mere cases to be analysed objectively or as numbers to be manipulated.

Margot welcomed me with tremendous warmth and friendliness. She apologized for what she saw as the inadequacies of the room I was to use, but I found it and the whole of her apartment splendid. She had many beautiful paintings and sculptures, gathered on her world-wide travels. Just about all of them were of children and mothers.

We talked and found that we shared many interests. After dinner one night I showed her what I meant by *laddering*, the method of questioning which reveals how we construct our sense of existence and our fear of the annihilation of our self.

I began by asking her to give me the names of three kinds of food.

She replied, 'Vegetable, meat, grains.'

I asked, 'Can you tell me one way in which two are the same and the other different?'

Teasingly she replied, 'If grain and vegetable are linked – animals that move around and grains that stay waving in the wind.'

I refused to be teased. 'Which do you prefer?'

'I'll go with the animals that move around.'

'Why is that important?'

'Because what I saw in my mind were people, and I go with people, because, with all my sorrow and sometimes desperation with people, I still would put in my lot with people.'

'In that way are you saying you feel related to people?'

'On my off days I also feel related to grains waving around,' she laughed.

'Yes,' I said and went on to ask a cruel question, 'What would happen to you if there were some change in your life and you were unable to relate to people?'

She said, 'I could give you a romanticized answer, and hope to overcome and be creative, but even Robinson Crusoe had someone. I would be desolate, I'd be lonely. I would try to do something with myself as a person. Would my personage disappear also? Would I still be allowed my person?'

'What do you think would happen to your person?'

'Oh, well, what I'm saying is that my person would change. I know that. Because people respond, among other things, to other people and relate to them and if that were taken from me, well, I would have to find ways to relate to myself. I know I would change. I would be the poorer, I suspect.'

'You wouldn't say what would happen to you ultimately?'

Margot spoke very quietly, 'Ultimately I would die.'

On that visit to New York I met for the first time Molly Friedrich who later became my literary agent in America. She greeted me with great warmth and friendliness, and proceeded to explain to me with absolute clarity and organization the complexities of getting a book accepted by an American publisher. Some weeks later, one hot summer night, I sat with Molly on her back porch and, over wine and coffee, I 'laddered' her.

I began by asking, 'Could you give me the names of three books that you represent?'

Molly named three books written by two authors whom she represented.

I asked, 'Can you tell me one way in which two of them are the same and the other different?'

'The first two have been written by the same author. The third book is by another person.'

'Which do you prefer, the books by the same author or the one by the other person?'

'The books by the same author.'

'Why is that important?'

'It's important because he's a better writer and a clearer thinker, and because I also have more material from him. I have the full manuscripts as opposed to a detailed proposal, so the third book is speculative. He promises a lot. I don't know that he'll deliver it at all.'

'So there you've given me a whole lot of different things, so what if I just chose one – what about – the clear thinker. Why is being a clear thinker important to you?'

'Because I think it enables you to sort out the world and your responses to it realistically.'

'And why is it important to sort out the world and your responses to it realistically?'

'Why is it important to me? Because I think it is important to approach life honestly and clearheadedly. It's something I value.'

'And why is it important to approach life honestly and clearheadedly?'

'Because I think that that's the only way to go through life. Sometimes you realize things in your life that aren't good. It's better to be honest about them. Because I value honesty.'

'What would happen to you if you found yourself in a situation where you couldn't sort things out in that way?'

'I would seek help. I would seek advice. I would seek suggestions from those whose opinions I respected.'

'What if none of that was available? What would happen to you?'

'If I was absolutely unable to – I would feel utterly alone and probably in shambles.'

'That's a good word, "shambles". I must remember it. I usually use the word "chaos".'

'Where things are collapsing,' said Molly.

Thus Margot and Molly, both very bright, sociable, successful women, each experiences herself and perceives the greatest danger in very different ways. Margot is the extravert and Molly the introvert.

# HOW TO LADDER

When I teach a psychology class about the structure of meaning I often, as a demonstration, call for some volunteers to go through a process of questioning which demonstrates how the most trivial of decisions which we make is based upon a series of judgements, each more abstract than the one preceding it, and all ultimately dependent upon a judgement about the nature of the individual's sense of existence.

I begin by asking the person to name three kinds of some particular class of object. The object could be food, or flowers, or musicians or anything about which the person has some experience. One object frequently chosen is motor cars. So I begin by asking, 'Would you give me the names of three kinds of motor car?'

The person can reply in many different ways, but for the sake of this example, I shall say that the person says, 'Chevrolet Corvette, Ford Escort and Cadillac.'

I then ask, 'Can you tell me one way in which two of these are the same and the other different?'.

Here the person can answer in many different ways, but, whatever is said, the person is giving a construct which he or she uses to evaluate these objects.

Suppose the person replies with, 'One of the cars is cheap and the other two are expensive.'

I then ask, 'Which do you prefer, an expensive car or a cheap car?'

The person can choose either 'expensive' or 'cheap', and for whichever is chosen I ask the same question. Suppose here the person chose 'expensive'. I ask, 'Why is an expensive car important to you?'

To answer this question the person has to give another construct which is connected with his/her construct of 'expensive' and which is important to him/her.

Suppose the person says, 'I prefer an expensive car because expensive cars are more reliable than cheap cars.'

I ask, 'Why is reliability important to you?'

The person may give an elaborate answer to this, but one which says, in effect, 'Because people depend on me.'

I ask, 'Why is it important that people depend on you?'

The person may answer this in many different ways, but the essence of what the person says is that the whole point and purpose of his/her existence is to be needed by others, to relate to others, to be part of a group.

I then ask, 'Suppose that things changed in your life so that no one in the entire world needed you, or depended on you or wanted to relate to you in any way. What would happen to you?'

This is an extremely cruel question, for I am asking the person to contemplate and to put into words the very conditions which would bring about the annihilation of that person's self as he/she experienced it. In answering this question people use words like 'I'd disappear', 'I'd wither away', 'That would be the end of me', or like Margot, 'Ultimately I would die'.

> Here the person is saying that he/she experiences his/her existence as being a member of a group, as the relationship, the connection, between his/her self and others, and his/her annihilation as complete isolation, being left totally, utterly and forever alone and thus withering, fading away, totally disappearing into nothingness.

Suppose that another person has chosen the same three cars, given the same construct 'expensive – cheap', with the preference for 'expensive'.

I ask, 'Why is an expensive car important to you?'

The person says, 'An expensive car is always an individual car. It's different.'

'Why is being individual and different important to you?'

Here the person can answer in terms of being an individual, being distinct from all other people, or the person may talk in terms of individual achievement, not simply in the sense of having expensive and individual possessions, but in the sense of developing, becoming an individual. Such answers contain at their core a sense of the ongoing development of individual clarity, authenticity and achievement.

Again the cruel question. 'Suppose that the conditions of your life changed so that you could not, in any way, develop your individual clarity, authenticity and achievement. What would happen to you?'

The answer is always in terms of loss of control, falling apart, falling into total chaos, or in Molly's terms, 'a shambles where things were collapsing.'

> **Here the person is saying that he/she experiences his/her existence as the progressive development of his/her individuality in terms of clarity, achievement and authenticity, and his/her annihilation as losing control of his/her self and life and falling apart, falling into chaos, fragmenting, crumbling to dust.**

# LADDERING IN THERAPY

I would not ask these questions in such a direct and persistent way of someone who was greatly troubled. These questions can often seem threatening and disturbing.

However, quite early in therapy, usually in the first meeting, I like to establish whether my client is an extravert or an introvert. At that point in therapy this distinction probably won't mean much to my client, but it allows me to understand what my client is afraid of and what are real possibilities for change. For instance, if the client is in an unhappy marriage, the possibility of leaving the marriage will, at some time or other, be discussed by us. If my client is an introvert, the prospect of leaving the family group will be much less threatening, particularly if leaving the group means a better chance of achieving, than if my client is an extravert.

So, in this first conversation, when the client's use of a construct suggests that it is of great importance to him or her, I might ask why.

For instance, a client might say, 'I just can't stand my home to be untidy.'

I might then ask, 'Why is it important to you to keep your home tidy?'

The client might say, 'I worry about what people think of me,' and thus reveal a fear of being rejected by the group.

Or the client might say, 'I like to have everything organized and under control', and thus reveal a fear of chaos and loss of control.

Sometimes, 'Why is that important?' is too important a question to ask.

A young woman, Ester, came to see me recently at the request of her stepfather. Over the past two years she had largely given up eating and had become life-threateningly thin. She had been in and out of hospital, and she, her mother and stepfather had been questioned, advised, counselled and therapized by consultant psychiatrists, junior doctors, 'key workers', psychiatric nurses, social workers and community nurses until the three of them didn't know what was happening and what they should do. Ester's stepfather hoped that I might be able to bring some order into the chaos.

Ester began by telling me that it was very important to her that she should not get fat. I knew that if I asked her, 'Why is it important to you that you don't get fat?' she would hear that question as coming from yet another person who wanted to prove that she was stupid, immature and neurotic, and that she should do as she was told, eat properly, and grow up. So I hastened to show her that my interest in why she didn't want to get fat had a different intent and meaning.

I said, 'There are two kinds of reasons why people don't want to get fat. Some people feel that if they get fat other people will reject them. Nobody'll have anything to do with them and they'll be left completely alone. That's the very worst thing that could happen to them. Then there are other people who don't want to get fat because they feel that if they get fat they'll have lost control of themselves and their life, and losing control is the very worst thing that could happen to them.'[1]

Ester looked at me steadily while I spoke of being rejected and alone. When I mentioned the word 'control' her head nodded in assent, and she went on nodding in agreement all the way through my explanation of why an introvert would choose to become anorexic.

I first noticed this head-nodding distinguishing extraverts from introverts when I began talking about how we experience our sense of existence and perceive the threat of annihilation in my lectures on depression. I would be describing how extraverts experience their existence and perceive the threat of annihilation, and about half the heads in the audience would be nodding in agreement. Then I would talk about introverts, and the first lot of heads would become still and the rest of the heads would begin nodding in agreement. Remembering who nodded when often makes answering questions at the end of the lecture much easier.

Since Ester was an introvert she assessed her situation in terms of control, achievement, clarity and authenticity, and she measured her success in terms of the standards set by the people whose approval she desired. She saw it as very necessary to control her weight and diet, for these were the only areas of her life where she saw herself as having any control. All other areas were controlled by other people. It was in weight and diet that she could achieve. She denigrated everything else that might be an achievement – her eight 'O' Levels ('My sister and cousins got more'), her writing ('It's no good, no one would publish it'). An ultraslim figure was her achievement, a personal statement of clarity and authenticity. It showed, she said, that she was not greedy and uncontrolled.

The people whose approval she desired and whose standards she wished to meet were her mother and stepfather. Both of them wanted her to eat in the way that they did, and this Ester could not agree to do. To comply would mean giving up the last vestige of autonomy. Moreover, in urging her to eat they were, Ester felt, giving her two contradictory messages. 'Eat more,' they seemed to be saying, 'and do not be greedy and out of control. We do not approve of people who are greedy and out of control.' I guessed that from the way she spoke about not being greedy that in her childhood Ester had been harshly punished for possessing this vice.

No doubt if I had questioned Ester's mother and stepfather about this they would have said that what they were advising was moderation. But Ester cannot be moderate. She despises moderation. She feels pushed to the extreme and so she takes things to the extreme. To experience, to justify and to elaborate her sense of existence and to fend off the threat of annihilation of her self, she will hone her body to its finest, even if it means that she might die.

How very similar Ester is to her contemporary and fellow introvert, Andrew Wallace. Andrew hones his body to the finest strength and responsiveness, so as to hurl it at enormous speeds in a tiny car around a dangerous race track and so risk death. The people whose approval he so strongly desires expect him to do this, and if he fails to meet their standards they will reject and ignore him.

The difference between Ester and Andrew lies in how they value themselves.

Andrew has a good opinion of himself. He accepts and values himself. He believes that he has the power and ability to achieve what he wants to achieve and to stay alive. Ester does not value herself. Starving herself is both an achievement and a deserved punishment. Her death, she feels, would be a sacrifice to expiate her badness.

In her childhood Ester had many experiences from which she drew the conclusion that she was bad and worthless. What Ester needs now is not people who fuss about what she eats and who punish her when she doesn't, but people who convey in their every word and act that they accept and value her as the person she is. In therapy she needs someone who will help her examine her feelings of being bad and unacceptable and the experiences which gave rise to those feelings, so that she can see that that feeling of intrinsic badness is nothing but the weight of rubbish that other people have loaded on her. We don't have to accept other people's rubbish.

Many of the experiences which led Ester to conclude that she was bad and worthless had to do with wanting something for herself and being told by powerful adults that she was wicked to be so greedy. She must consider other people before herself. Many of us are taught in childhood, often quite harshly, that to be virtuous, respected and accepted we must always put other people's needs before our own. We must not be greedy and selfish, but always altruistic. This is one of the reasons why the process of laddering is so dangerous.

# LADDERING IS NOT A GAME

Whenever in teaching I do a laddering exercise I find that some people go to the top of their ladder without hesitation or difficulty, while others go up a rung or two and then begin to prevaricate. They go round and round in circles, showing all kinds of resistance.

The reason that we resist being taken to the top of our ladder in public is because we know, usually with the first 'Why is that important?' question where the series of questions will lead, and we don't want our answers to be publicly revealed.

If we reveal how we perceive the threat of the annihilation of our self we are revealing our greatest weakness, and many of us believe that it is dangerous to reveal weakness. If anyone wants to torture and destroy us they now have the means. Extraverts are most effectively tortured and destroyed by being put in complete isolation. Introverts can cope with isolation by retreating into their internal reality which for them is full of interest. The most effective way of torturing and destroying introverts is to deny them the means of organizing their sense of time and space and by telling them that they have misconstrued external reality. Don't let them have a clock, or see daylight, and bring them their breakfast when they had calculated it was time for supper. To make an introvert prisoner doubt his perception of external reality an interrogator might have a long conversation with the prisoner, and on his next session insist that he has never met the prisoner before. The Secret Service Departments of most countries have manuals of instruction on all these techniques.

Some of us resist being laddered not so much because we don't wish to appear vulnerable as because we don't wish to be seen as wicked. We have been taught that selfishness is wickedness, and at the top of our ladder is total selfishness. There it is revealed that we are in the business of looking after ourselves. We use other people to maintain our own existence: we are concerned only with the development of our own individuality.

We need to remind ourselves that to be of any use to other people we have to be alive and whole, both physically and in ourselves. Dead we are of no use to anyone. Feeling empty or fragmented leaves us with nothing of ourselves to give to anyone. To live with other people in sharing, giving, loving relationships we need to feel whole. We need to feel that the structure of the self we have created is safe from threat and that we can elaborate our sense of existence.

To do this effectively it is important to know clearly and consciously how you experience your sense of existence and see the threat of your annihilation. If you are going to find this out by laddering, perhaps it is best to do so in the privacy of your own head.

# 4

# Different Ways of
# Seeing and Doing Things

The way we experience our sense of existence and see the threat of the annihilation of our self underlies our every act and decision, be it eating breakfast or getting married, be it choosing eggs and bacon or this particular person.

Because there are two different ways in which we can experience our sense of existence and the threat of annihilation every aspect of life is dealt with differently by 'people persons' and 'what have I achieved today?' persons. Extraverts and introverts have their own particular style of doing things and reasons for doing things.

It is possible to draw up lists of 'Extraverts Do This' and 'Introverts Do That', but such lists are simply general descriptions and not Real, Absolute and Immutable Truths. Each of us, introvert or extravert, is an individual and we each have our own individual way of elaborating our sense of existence and of defending ourselves against the threat of annihilation and thus our own individual styles of making decisions and of acting. Also, we are always capable of choosing to learn another way of making decisions and of acting.

When I say that 'Introverts do X' I do not mean that extraverts *never* do X, and when I say that 'Extraverts do Y' I do not mean that introverts *never* do Y. We are all capable of doing a great many things. But there are certain things which introverts do easily, naturally, unthinkingly and persistently, even chronically, and which extraverts would, if ever they chose to do them, do with some difficulty, with forethought and preparation, and then only occasionally. Similarly, there are certain things which extraverts do easily, naturally, unthinkingly and persistently, even chronically, and which introverts would, if ever they chose to do them, do with some difficulty, with forethought and preparation, and then only occasionally.

However, while as persons we are each an individual, as simply *bodies* there are some characteristics which we share as extraverts or as introverts.

# PHYSICAL CHARACTERISTICS

Neurological psychologists explain differences between introverts and extraverts in terms of the state of *arousal of the cortex* of the brain. That part of the brain which is called the ascending reticular activating system sends a stream of signals to the cortex to keep it awake and thus able to deal with what is happening in external reality. According to this research some of us have an ascending reticular activating system which is very busy keeping our cortex in a highly aroused state, and others of us have a lazy ascending reticular activating system which makes our cortex sluggish and underaroused. To function reasonably efficiently the first group of people must reduce stimulation from external reality and the second group must seek extra stimulation from external reality.

Thus it is not surprising that introverts, having a highly aroused cortex, see the annihilation of their self as falling apart, which would be, in neurological terms, the experience of an overloaded and overstimulated cortex, and extraverts, having an underaroused cortex, see the annihilation of their self as a disappearance, which would be, in neurological terms, the experience of a cortex coming to complete stillness.

But neurological psychologists are never concerned with concepts like 'the sense of self'. They like concepts they can see and measure, and so all their research is directed at human and animal activities which they can see and measure.

Psychologists engaged in this kind of research have found that they do not need to measure the functioning of their subjects' ascending reticular activating system to divide them into extraverts and introverts. Getting their research subjects to answer the Eysenck Personality Inventory will do that satisfactorily, and then they can be set the tasks which the experimenter wants to examine.

Psychologists have always been interested in how people learn, and so thousands of college students and white rats have been expected to learn all sorts of things under all sorts of conditions. One of the simplest forms of learning is called *classical conditioning*, where, in the case of Pavlov's dogs, food which makes the hungry dog salivate and the sound of a bell are presented together on a number of occasions, and soon the dog learns to salivate at the sound of a bell.

Measuring how much people salivate at the sight or thought of food is somewhat undignified, so experimenters often prefer to send a puff of air towards the subject's eyes. The subject blinks, and, if a bell is sounded at the same time, sooner or later the subject will learn to blink when the bell is sounded, whether or not there is a puff of air. Learning this is for some subjects much sooner than later, and these tend to be introverts. Hence it is often said that introverts condition more quickly than extraverts.

It is hardly surprising that this is so. A couple of disparate things happening together means for the introvert something that needs to be understood, sorted out and dealt with quickly so as to maintain order and control in a busy cortex. A couple of disparate events happening together means for the extravert the variety and excitement necessary for adequate stimulation.

Eysenck, ever ready to point out our faults and failings, says that this explains why introverts become *neurotic* and extraverts *psychopathic*, so that psychiatric hospitals are filled with introverts and prisons with extraverts.[1]

Here is an example of how, according to learning theory or *behaviourism*, this could come about.

An introvert child, as children are wont to do, steals some sweets, and his father, as fathers are wont to do, beats him. The introvert child quickly associates the pain of the beating with stealing and decides to steal no more. He also associates the fear inspired by his father beating him with his father, and so spends the rest of his life being frightened of his father and of all the people who remind him of his father. Such a fear could be regarded as irrational, and the person holding such a fear as neurotic.

An extravert child committing the same misdemeanour and punished by his father makes no such strong associations. He makes no connections between stealing and punishment, and so goes on to steal again, unreminded by the presence of his father or other father-like figures that such behaviour is unwise. He could come to regard the pain of punishments as a form of exciting stimulation.

Freud and his disciples had, before Eysenck, noted the preponderance of extraverts as psychopathic characters, but had explained this in terms of the development of the superego. The psychoanalytic explanation is much more complex than the behaviourist explanation. However, whichever explanation we prefer, we need to remember that if you're an introvert you don't have to be neurotic, and if you're an extravert you don't have to end up in gaol.

Some researchers, by no means all, have found a relationship between body temperature, the time of greatest mental alertness (that is, being a *morning person* or an *evening person*) and extraversion-introversion. Thus extraverts are supposed to be 'owls' and introverts 'larks'. According to Jim Horne, Director of the Sleep Laboratory at Loughborough University, the best way to discriminate an 'owl' from a 'lark' is to ask whether the person would prefer to do a mentally demanding task at 7 a.m. or 10 p.m. He says that this preference shows no relation to extraversion-introversion.[2]

Perhaps one reason why different researchers in this field get different results is that they use the Eysenck Personality Inventory (the EPI) to measure extraversion-introversion. On this questionnaire introverts who have learned to enjoy being sociable will score as extraverts, while extraverts who are frightened of other people and are therefore shy will score as introverts.

Now the EPI doesn't just claim to measure extraversion and introversion. It claims to measure 'neuroticism' too, and so when you read the research papers where these differences in body temperature have been applied to the serious questions of how people adapt to long aeroplane flights or shift work, you'll see the words 'neurotic' or 'stable' preceding the words 'introvert' or 'extravert'. If you're an introvert *never* say that you suffer with jet lag or can't cope with shift work, for according to this research the people who find jet lag and shift work hardest to cope with are *neurotic* introverts.[3]

Something else you need to be wary of is agreeing to do the Weschler Adult Intelligence Scale (the WAIS), not unless you are absolutely sure that your scores on it won't fall into the hands of the CIA. There could still be someone in the CIA using a system for interpreting these scores to select people to spy for America or to wreak vengeance on foreign spies.

Back in the 1940s a psychologist, John Gittinger,[4] was director of psychological services in Norman, Oklahoma. He became interested in those itinerant men who, in summer, worked as short order cooks and dishwashers and, in winter, got themselves admitted to the psychiatric hospital. In the 1940s the main occupation for psychologists was giving intelligence tests, and so Gittinger applied his skill in administering the WAIS to these itinerant cooks and dishwashers. He found that they fell into two distinct groups. The cooks were good at the sub-test in the WAIS called Digit Span. The dishwashers were not.

In the first part of the Digit Span test the psychologist reads out in a measured pace a set of digits, say, '4-9-7-8-1.' The person being tested has to repeat the set correctly, and with each successful repetition the set gets longer. In the second part of the test the psychologist reads out the sets of digits and the person has to repeat them backwards. Thus, '6-5-2-9.' '9-2-5-6.'

To do this test you have to be able to pay close attention to what the psychologist is saying and to ignore anything that might distract you from your task. This, indeed, is what you need to be able to do if you want to work as a short order cook. Ignoring all that is going on around you, you listen to the customer's order and repeat it correctly. If you can't manage to do this, you'll have to be a dishwasher.

Gittinger called the men who worked as cooks and could do well on Digit Span 'Internalizers' and the dishwashers bad on Digit Span 'Externalizers'.

He saw this grouping as two distinct, inherited personalities which were at the bottom of other layers of personality which had developed from the person's experiences. These further layers could be identified by other tests in the WAIS, and the whole pattern of test scores could be interpreted in particular ways so as to describe some 1,024 personality types.

It took some while for Gittinger to develop his Personality Assessment System (PAS) and he never regarded it as complete, but from 1950 the CIA used his system, so much so that during the Cuban missile crisis Gittinger was asked to advise President Kennedy as to how Khrushchev was likely to react.

Gittinger taught the PAS to CIA officials concerned with selecting the right type of spy for certain missions. Gittinger wrote,

> 'In an intelligence context, two people were asked to go next door to describe something there. It happened a fire broke out. Each returned independently to report. I had test scores on these two people; one was an Externalizer, the other an Internalizer. The E came in and said, "I couldn't see a damn thing because there was a fire next door." The I, in contrast, came with complete details of what he was supposed to report. Then he was asked about the fire. His reply: "What fire?"'

Thus, if you want a spy who will pick up lots of general information about everything that might be happening, choose an Externalizer, and if you want to find out all about one specific thing, choose an Internalizer.

Similarly, just as the PAS identified the strengths of the Externalizer and Internalizer, it also identified their weaknesses, and thus just how that person could be made to feel confused and frightened and in danger of losing his sanity.

Some of the CIA-funded research was directed at how Internalizers and Externalizers responded to alcohol and LSD. This research showed that alcohol made Internalizers more withdrawn and the Externalizer type called 'uncompensated' more talkative. With LSD Externalizers were more likely to have bad trips than Internalizers. Sheldon Kopp, whose books should be read by everyone on the journey of self-discovery, wrote, 'It is sometimes said that a bad trip is not so much a matter of actually running into something terrible within oneself, as it is a terror-stricken flight from whatever it is that one *might* encounter in the unplumbed depth's of one's mind.'[5] That is, if our inner reality is unknown and therefore perceived as dangerous, we must flee from it.

The history of psychology is filled with psychologists busy fleeing from their inner reality. Not all have been extraverts. Many have been introverts who can cope with their inner reality only so long as it is organized and controlled, but any emotion, theirs or other people's, terrifies them. Just about all these psychologists were men, and so, whether extravert or introvert, together they could strive to uphold the traditional male view that being Rational and Objective is Good (and Masculine) and being Irrational and Subjective is Bad (and Feminine). Thus they demonstrated that admirable skill which we all try to emulate of taking our fear and our defences against it and defining them not as a weakness but as a virtue.

The result of all this was that for most of their science's history psychologists studied what they called Behaviour and Cognition, and all those disorderly aspects of humanity were lumped together under Emotion or Personality and reduced to chemical changes or inherited traits.

Psychologists like Gittinger could see that what kind of person we are affects how we use our intelligence, but such an understanding did not fit with the way psychologists wanted to work. They wanted to ignore the fact that when research subjects come into the laboratory they do not leave their life history, their hopes and fears, their attitudes and beliefs at the door.

Over the same years psychiatrists were holding firmly to the belief that the life history, the hopes and the fears, the attitudes and beliefs of their patients were of no importance at all. Their patients, the psychiatrists believed, were suffering from mental illnesses caused by some bodily malfunction – a defective gene or an aberrant biochemical change.

Then along came a sociologist called George Brown. He and his colleagues showed that if we have a great many losses and disappointments in our lives we are likely to become depressed.[6]

Of course many people before George Brown had observed this. He was the first to put this observation to the test using the methods of social research. He introduced the term 'life events' and showed how a person's life history could be assessed in terms of not just how many life events had occurred but the magnitude of stress each of these events produced.

Soon the term 'life events' began appearing in the research reports of psychiatrists and psychologists, along with a new way of using the old words 'stress' and 'attitude'. There was another new term, the 'auto-immune system', referring to our body's capacity to ward off noxious influences. It seems that 'stress', that is, the particular attitudes and feelings we have about what has happened to us, affects how our auto-immune system functions. Defining an event as bad and thus feeling hurt, confused, frightened, angry, guilty, shamed, resentful, envious, helpless, all or even just some of these, is very stressful. Too much stress and our auto-immune system develops faults and we become vulnerable to a host of diseases. Once ill, we can affect the course of our illness by holding those attitudes which reduce stress.

Some of this research involves the use of questionnaires which give scores on extraversion-introversion. Thus at the Common Cold Research Unit in Wiltshire it has been shown that introverts infected with a cold virus developed much worse symptoms than extraverts, but a complicating factor was the number of stressful events in the person's life. A follow-up study showed that not just whether the person is an extravert or an introvert but, as either, what obsessional habits a person has affect both the course of the cold and the possible beneficial effects of the drug interferon.[7]

It would seem, then, that the better we know ourselves the better chance we have of avoiding becoming physically ill and of looking after ourselves if we do become ill.

Like needing to know ourselves, something else we all share, whether extravert or introvert, is our need for other people.

## NEEDING OTHER PEOPLE

'People who need people are the luckiest people in the world.'

Whenever I hear Barbra Streisand singing this I wonder whether she means just 'people persons' or all of us. For good or ill, we need one another.

Extraverts define their sense of existence in a very direct relational way to others. Their answers to the question, 'Why is that important?' always include or imply other people. When I asked a dear friend why, in the midst of her busy life as wife, mother, psychotherapist and friend to thousands, she maintains a large allotment where she grows organic vegetables, she replied not just in terms of maintaining the health of her family but in terms of her relationship to the earth. Nature, to her, is a person with whom she has an intimate relationship.

Introverts, even in a whole series of 'Why is that important?' questions, usually do not mention other people at all. But that does not mean that other people have no primary role in the introvert's sense of existence. People do play a vital part in the introvert's sense of existence, but such people are inside the introvert's head and not necessarily existing in external reality.

The introvert is concerned with some kind of individual achievement, but how do you know whether you have achieved anything if you haven't got a standard to measure it against? Introverts always do have such a standard. It is the achievements and opinions of a small group of people whom the introvert has selected as being sufficiently admirable for their achievements and opinions to matter (to the introvert, not necessarily to the rest of the world).

The first of these figures inside the introvert's head are the parent figures, a reworking of childhood experiences of parenting adults. The actual parenting adults may be long dead, but the figures in the introvert's head have a degree of reality and importance which real, live people rarely (for the introvert) assume. Sometimes these figures hold impossible standards of perfection and achievement, so that the introvert may think, 'I'll never be as good a person as my mother', or, 'No matter what I achieve my father will never see it as enough.' Sometimes these figures may be hated and despised with the same implacable certitude with which other figures are admired, and thus they provide absolute standards of achievement. 'I shall never give way to anger. I shall never be violent like my father.' 'I must always be strong. I shall never be weak and vacillating like my mother.'

The other figures in the introvert's head may be images of people who have achieved what the introvert wishes to achieve, and thus possibly people whom the introvert has never met. Or they may be images of those people, like Andrew Wallace's Formula 1 managers, who can admit the introvert into a select group of high achievers.

Once the introvert has achieved something of note, the figures in the head include those other achievers who meet the high standards which the introvert has set. Speaking as an introvert, I could list, in order of priority, those psychologists whose praise of my work affords me the greatest pleasure and to whose comments and criticism I pay the greatest heed, while criticism by those people not on my list I dismiss with, 'The person's a fool.' Remember, when an introvert says to you, truthfully, 'I value your opinion', you are being paid the highest compliment an introvert can bestow.

In this way introverts are awfully snobbish, though most of them have good enough manners to try to hide it, especially when they recognize how, in another way, they desperately need other people, not just the figures in their head, but real people in their external reality.

It is all too easy for introverts to withdraw into their inner reality and drift away like an untethered balloon into an idiosyncratic and lonely life. To prevent this, wise introverts create and maintain connections of love and concern with other people, sometimes just a few people, but enough to keep the introvert's attention turned to external reality. Introverts fear loneliness just as much as extraverts, not because they fear that if they are alone they will disappear, but because they fear an eternity of solitude in an empty universe.

Because we have such fears we all, from time to time, make fools of ourselves over other people. We select certain people as the recipients of our hopes and fears, the fulfilment of our desires, and when these people fail to respond in the way we wish we may retire hurt but, more frequently, we behave outrageously in the attempt to force the person to meet our hopes and desires and to dispel our fears. The people we usually select as the recipients of our hopes, desires and fears are our lovers, spouses, children and friends. We reserve our best behaviour for strangers.

The people we need most are those who we think will best assist us to elaborate our sense of existence and to defend ourselves against the fear of annihilation. The more fiercely we feel this need, the more we see these important people only in relation to us and less as people in their own right.

As babies and toddlers we regarded our mother as a person who existed solely to meet our needs. We kissed her when we felt love and bit her when we felt anger. We climbed into her arms to get warm and on to her lap to reach a toy. We had no idea that she had needs of her own unrelated to us, and so when she went into the bathroom and closed the door on us we screamed with rage. How dare she abandon us!

As babies and toddlers we behaved outrageously because we knew that we were weak and could not take care of ourselves. If, as we got older, we gained confidence in ourselves, we did not feel threatened as we discovered that other people have lives of their own. We could accept that the only universe of which we are the centre is our own. In other people's universes we play a minor part.

But if we have that kind of childhood which teaches us to regard ourselves as bad and unacceptable, we, as adults, live in fear that the people we see as necessary for the maintenance of our existence will reject and abandon us. If we allow ourselves to see that other people have lives of their own and interests which do not include us we shall feel even more frightened. Thus, though we may love the people we need passionately and would sacrifice ourselves and everything we own to maintain their existence and welfare, we cannot let them be themselves.

Extraverts and introverts who do not value themselves differ in how they refuse to let people be themselves, but they each devise roles for people in the story which they have created of their life.

Such extraverts see their life as a great romantic drama in which they are the hero or heroine and all other people as characters in this drama whose every thought and action relates in some way to the central character. Such thoughts and actions need not be loving and benevolent. For the hero of such a drama it is better to believe, 'My brother passed me in the street today without speaking because he hates me,' than, 'My brother didn't notice me in the street today because he is so worried about his job.' The great romantic drama will not end in happily ever after but in the tears for what might have been. Any possibility that it could have a happy ending must be nipped in the bud.

One such extravert was Richard. He had been the last of a large family, an unwanted child to parents whose anger with one another prevented them from giving love to their children. As a child Richard felt closest to Moira, the eldest child, who mothered him. She was ten years older than Richard, and when she left to get married Richard, then ten, felt confirmed in his belief that his role in life was to be rejected and abandoned. He made friends at school but only, he felt, because he gave them presents and helped them. As an adult he was a charming, generous, attractive man who, to an outside observer, was blessed with a host of friends.

But Richard lived a life of anxiety and jealousy. He kept a score of how often Moira, now a busy mother, visited their sisters and compared it jealously with the number of her visits to him. That she might think that sisters coping with small or ill children might need her more than her bachelor brother did not occur to him. He kept score, too, of how frequently friends visited or phoned him, all without recognition that they might have problems or obligations in which he played no part. He had no notion that we can have friends whom we love dearly but whom our busy lives prevent us from visiting. If, for whatever reason, a friend failed to contact him as he expected the friend should, Richard would assume that the friend had rejected him and so, when they did meet, Richard would behave coldly towards his friend. Some friends saw this as Richard's peculiarity and persisted in their friendship, but others returned his rejection with rejection, and so Richard felt confirmed in his expectation. A longtime girlfriend, who would love to marry him and live happily ever after, told me, 'Richard sees rejection where none exists. I tell him I love him but he doesn't believe me.'

Romance is fantasy which is based in external reality, whereas tragedy can have its roots not so much in events as in principles, the substance of internal reality.

Introverts who do not value themselves reject the notion of life as a sentimental romance. They choose the drama of tragedy with themselves in the role of the heroic individual, virtuous but flawed, the object of the gods' envy and spite, alone and doomed. Any possibility that the tragedy might be averted and the hero saved must be fiercely resisted. The theme of this tragic drama is that the hero recognizes that he must maintain the Absolute

Principles and Standards of Life which the other characters in the drama often fail to uphold. That these other characters do not make these Absolute Principles and Standards the centre of their life is seen by the hero as evidence of the character's perversity and not as the person's right to see things differently.

Kate had been born into a family where people said one thing and meant another. The result of this was that often in her childhood she had been faced with so much confusion and uncertainty that she had felt very strongly the threat of annihilation. To defend against this she decided that the most important Absolute Principle and Standard of Life was Truth. Never would she tell a lie. To tell the truth, no matter what the consequences, was the greatest virtue, and she was determined to be good. When, in adult life, she was in the grip of depression and longed for death, she would accept no compromise, and where she was asked to compromise most was over her husband Gavin and the less than virtuous life he led.

She had met Gavin at church and fallen in love with his warm brown eyes and what she thought was his God-fearing soul. When she discovered that his interest in the church's choir and debating society included drinking in pubs and less than platonic cuddles with women choir members and debaters she was devastated, not merely by the discovery that he was a drinker and a philanderer, but that, to carry out these activities, he had lied to her. If only he would tell her the truth everything would be all right. What she could not see was that truth telling was not very high on Gavin's list of priorities. Under his veneer of charm and gaiety he was an insecure extravert, desperate to have everyone liking him. He believed that the one sure way to get everyone to like you was to tell them what they wanted to hear. This was not necessarily the truth. No matter what Kate said, he had no intention of relinquishing the belief which gave him some measure of security.

Long before she had met Gavin, Kate had been engrossed in the tragic drama of the girl who suffered for Truth. Marrying Gavin was one sure way of continuing and intensifying the drama, and becoming depressed was both an increase in suffering and a way of refusing to see that Gavin existed as a person in his own right, trying as best he could to maintain his sense of existence and to ward off the threat of annihilation. He was acting out his own romantic drama while she was engaged in her own tragedy, and both plays could not be performed together on the one stage of their home life. Fortunately for Kate, after years of suffering, she came to see this, and left to find her own stage where she could act out what she now sees as an ironic comedy.

Life as ironic comedy is that lived by introverts who value themselves, while extraverts who value themselves see life as romantic comedy with many happy endings. That way they all laugh a lot. Valuing yourself means that you don't have to take yourself and your life totally seriously.

But even where introverts and extraverts share perceptions and opinions, they differ in the style with which they present them.

# DIFFERENT STYLES IN DOING THINGS

Many of us, introverts and extraverts, love clothes. We want to make a statement about who we are and what our life is by the way we dress. We want people to notice us. So clothes are very important to us. Just how we express that importance depends on whether we are extraverts or introverts.

There are two main differences. The first concerns what kind of notice we want. Introverts are concerned with being admired by others, especially by the people whose opinion they value. Extraverts are concerned with being thought to be attractive by everyone.

The ideas of admiration and attraction have within them concepts of separation and closeness. Introverts prefer admiration whose distance reduces clutter and confusion, that is, the dangers of over-stimulation, while extraverts prefer attraction with its intensification of relationships and the possibility of greater stimulation.

These notions of reducing or increasing stimulation underlie the actual choice of clothes. For some extraverts and introverts the choice is between 'dramatic' as against 'sophisticated'. For other extraverts and introverts it is between 'bright and colourful' as against 'cool and simple', or 'lots of jewellery, frills and scarves' as against 'plain and uncluttered'. Even amongst extrav-

erts and introverts who don't care what they wear, this last
distinction is important.

This difference in the way extraverts and introverts feel about
clothes is one of the reasons mothers and children argue about
clothes. An extravert mother might enjoy dressing her introvert
children in bright, attractive clothes, while the introvert child feels
overloaded and embarrassed at attracting attention. Similarly, an
introvert mother might dress her extravert children in plain,
sensible clothes, while they desperately desire T-shirts with bla-
tant messages and clothes in a kaleidoscope of patterns and
colours.

The traditional picture of extraverts and introverts is that
extraverts talk non-stop while introverts are mostly silent, but I
know many extraverts who are taciturn through shyness and
many introverts, myself included, who are great talkers. One
reason we introverts talk so much is that we have a head packed
full of ideas, and talking about them is a great relief. Talking is
an escape from that inner reality and a chance to maintain contact
with external reality and the friends that make external reality
worthwhile. Non-stop introvert talkers, as I sometimes find in
therapy, are often trying to prevent their listeners from uttering
the kind of criticism which devastated them in childhood and
which wounds them still. Extraverts who do talk a great deal
have found that talking usually ensures other people's attention
and with that their sense of existence. Non-stop extravert talkers,
unsure of their existence, believe, 'I talk, therefore I am.'

However, the main difference between extraverts and introverts
is not how much they talk but the way they talk.

When I was young I used to envy the friends who always
seemed to have such a good time. They might be doing much the
same things I did, going to the beach, visiting relatives, having the
occasional party, but where I found the things I did always
ordinary and mainly dull, these friends were always involved in
events which were interesting and exciting. It took me years to
realize that the difference between these friends and me was not
in what we did or what we felt about what we did, but how we
talked about what we did.

I didn't realize this until I had for a few years been head of a
department of clinical psychology and involved in interviewing

and appointing staff. Introverts, I found, give an account of their experience which minimizes it, while extraverts maximize it. Asked, say, if they had had experience in marital therapy, an introvert will make ten cases of marital therapy sound like an inadequate introduction to this type of therapy, while an extravert will make ten cases sound like a lifetime's experience as a marital therapist, and all done without actually boasting. In the actual practice of their profession, which I could see once I had made the appointments, the introvert and the extravert might be equally skilled. They simply differed in the way they talked about their experience.

These contrasting ways of talking about experience arise from the different ways that extraverts and introverts observe what goes on around them. Extraverts take in a multitude of surface details. Their accounts of their observations can be wonderfully descriptive and witty, conveying their sense of excitement and amazement. Introverts' observations are more focused. They select certain items and comment on them, not simply to describe them but to remark upon their underlying significance and the pattern that they make.

An illustration of this is in the contrast between the story-telling styles of Robert Ruark (an extravert) and Quentin Crisp (an introvert). Robert Ruark died before I had a chance to meet him, but he loomed large in my youth, when he was one of a band of adventurous reporters whose lives of travel and writing I longed to emulate. Robert Ruark said of himself, 'There was a time when I could go anywhere, eat airline food, use gin as a substitute for sleep, fight against the Mau Mau, chase elephants on horseback, slug athletes, enjoy being jailed, and wrestle with leopards, all for the love of the newspaper business.'[8] His writing conveyed a wonderful sense of what he was experiencing, and nowhere better than in his book about his childhood, *The Old Man and the Boy*. Here he described how his grandfather taught him all the lore of hunting and fishing on the North Carolina coast, and the beauty of those woods and sea and the excitement of acquiring hunting skills fairly leap off the page to make the reader as excited and happy as he was. He wrote of his new rowing boat, 'When I was out alone in that boat, I never had to worry about amusement. I was Captain Blood looking for pirates, or I was actually on Treasure Island, running from Long John Silver. I was Zane Grey catching marlin off New Zealand – wherever that was – or I was Hawkins or Drake . . . But mostly I learned about how much fun a man can have amusing himself, and about how exciting solitude can be if you play it right. I would get up early in the morning, row her out to one of the sand bars, jab an oar deep in the sand, and make her fast. Then I would kick around in the ooze, feeling for clams with my feet and looking for soft-shell crabs. When I had a mass of clams, I would take the cast net and prowl in the shallows for mullet and shrimp for bait, casting the net in a great circular spread that drove upward sharp slivers of water as she settled with the shrimp and the mullet bucking and arching inside the cords . . . I found out that you don't actually need companionship to amuse yourself; that there are actually times when you can have more fun without people.'[9] This was an important discovery, but nowhere in the book does he explore what it meant. He had found that there was nothing to be afraid of in being alone – provided that he was amused and busy. He led a life of frenetic activity, and never did discover that it is possible to be alone and quiet and not disappear.

Quentin Crisp has raised being alone and quiet to an art form, but it would have been an unknown art form had not his autobiography, *The Naked Civil Sertant*[10] been made into a television film – overnight he became famous. After the publication of his second volume of autobiography, *How to Become a Virgin*,[11] he left England for New York, and it was there he very kindly agreed to talk to me and my tape recorder. But then, as he explained, he would not dream of refusing.

He said, 'Someone I know said that my humility is ironic. And that worried me, because I think that my humility is real. I remind myself almost every day that I am nothing and I have nothing. Otherwise you think you have rights, and once you start to think you have rights, you are a terrible nuisance . . . When I was asked to explain the difference between the notions of the pursuit of happiness in England and America, I dwelt on this at great length and then the people who asked me wouldn't touch it. But I'm sure I'm absolutely right. In England, the English don't want to be admired, they want to be obeyed. Americans want to be loved, failing that, to be admired, failing that, noticed. If you took a huge hall and you filled it with the great psychologists and the great scientists and the great economists and the great generals and the great admirals and the great statesmen, and Mrs Burton, everything would stand still when she arrived because she lived in the Big Time. It's quite extraordinary. And now I live in what I call the Peanut Circuit. If you lived in America, if you lived here for more than six months, you would start to receive in your mail invitations. They would invite you to various occasions – the opening of an art gallery which will turn out to be in a dim cellar further along the street, somebody's birthday party who you've never heard of, the refurbishing of a discotheque. And, if you can keep going, you can live on funny things on sticks, the peanuts. If you can live on peanuts and champagne, you need never buy food again. Your half of the bargain is that you are willing to be interviewed and photographed. If you are shown some kind of privilege, favouring, then you owe it, and I never refuse to be interviewed and photographed.' All of the stories Quentin told me over a two hour conversation were witty and precise in their descriptions of people and place, and every story contained a reference to his meditation on his experience to find its underlying meaning and the moral issues contained within it.

This difference in the way of observing makes extraverts, on the whole, better at remembering details about the people they meet – details like the person's name, whether he or she is married, has children, is working and so on. At further meetings the extravert can draw on this knowledge to engage the person in easy conversation. This is one of the skills which an introvert, trying to develop the balance of a Successful Self, has to recognize as important and work at acquiring. An introvert who has not recognized how important this skill is will continue a lifetime's habit of not remembering details like the person's name but instead remembering something of interest only to the introvert, like some facet of the person which fitted in with one of the introvert's theories, such as something as idiosyncratic as, 'Never trust anyone who drinks herbal tea'.

These two modes of observation are very much affected by a lack of self-confidence and paranoia. The more we feel inadequate, weak, helpless and anxious the more wrapped up in ourselves we become and the less able to observe and remember other people as they actually are. Much of life passes us by, and what we do observe of other people concerns simply whether they make us feel more, or less, frightened. If, on top of that, we have constructed ourselves a life drama where we are the victim of malignly powerful people then we become adept at picking out those aspects of our experience which confirm our beliefs about our life. Thus we can observe and remember all those people whose slightest word or gesture identifies them to us as our enemy.

When we despise ourselves and with that feel weak, helpless and in danger from others, we become locked into our own individual world of meaning, unable and unwilling to make the effort of checking whether our perceptions of other people are correct. In this state we retreat to the particular way of constructing our world of meaning which unenlightened extraverts and introverts use. For such extraverts all meaning resides in external reality, and for such introverts all meaning resides in inner reality.

I came across an example of this when I was talking to a friend, Tony, about the break-up of his marriage to Eleanor. I had been acquainted with them for some years and so knew that Eleanor was an extravert and Tony an introvert. Tony said of Eleanor, 'She inhabits a space and she explains everything which she sees as impinging on that space in terms of things outside that space, never inside it.'

The reason that Tony was talking to me about such personal matters was that he was trying very hard to resist the temptation to retreat into his own inner world and explain the whole painful business in terms of his own elaborate and idiosyncratic theories about how people and the universe function. Such theories give him a sense of order and control which the real world containing a wife determined to confound and confuse him could never give him. But he had the wisdom to know that such a retreat was dangerous and that he had to continue to deal with external reality and to tolerate the uncertainty and confusion it engendered.

These different ways of observing have a deeper significance than just different styles of doing things. They relate to the reasons that we have for doing things.

# DIFFERENT REASONS FOR DOING THE SAME THINGS

When I was staying with friends in Columbus, Ohio, I was impressed with the acres of immaculately mown lawns which surround each house. In England there are many gardens where all the flowers stand to attention, not a leaf is out of place, and no weed dare appear, but, equally, there are many houses surrounded by an untamed wilderness. One day, as we drove home from the university, I asked my friend Robert what would happen if a citizen of Columbus decided not to mow his lawn. Robert threw up his hands in horror. 'You have uttered the unthinkable. Here everybody keeps his lawn cut.'

If I had taken the time to question the citizens of Columbus as to why they mowed their lawns, no doubt they would have said that if they did not mow their lawns they would be prosecuted. There is a local law that says a householder must keep the lawn mowed. If I then asked why it was important to avoid prosecution, the answers would have diverged. Some people, the extraverts, would talk in terms of public shame and of not spending money on a fine which could be better spent for the benefit of the family. Others, the introverts, would talk in terms of the loss of self-respect and the disorganization of their life. Many of the citizens would say that even without the threat of prosecution they would mow their lawn. The extraverts would want their garden to be attractive and to fit in with the other gardens in their suburb; the introverts would want their garden to be well organized and to give them a sense of achievement.

Most of us have some area of our life which we keep well organized, clean and tidy. It might be our garden, our house, our car and garage, our body, or simply the top of our desk. We might think that the virtue of such organization, cleanliness and tidiness is self-evident, but, if we force ourselves to question the importance of such virtues, we find our answers concerned with avoiding the dangers of rejection or of chaos and with promoting the satisfactions of relationships with others or of personal achievements.

Such an examination of the reasons for our virtues can lead to a statement of what we see as the purpose of life.

**Life**, say the introverts, **is about personal achievement**.

**Life**, say the extraverts, **is about people**.

Thus the reasons why we do the things that we do come to the two different ways we experience our sense of existence.

Here follows an account of just some of the things we all do, but for different reasons.

For instance, we all like to succeed.

## SUCCESS

Whether it is in making a million or getting the children to school on time, we all like to succeed. Success makes our self-confidence expand. Failure makes self-confidence shrivel. Whether we are extraverts or introverts success is very important.

Some of us see success in terms of achieving the goals we have set – getting a good job, buying a home, having children. Some of us see success in terms of winning, of beating the competition. Whether it is success in terms of achieving goals or success in terms of winning the differences between extraverts and introverts still apply. Extraverts see achieving goals and winning in terms of relating to other people, both by caring for other people and by gaining or maintaining their acceptance and affection. Introverts see achieving goals and winning as ways of achieving their personal development, maintaining their high standards and gaining the approval of those whose opinion they respect.

Extraverts can be as competitive as introverts. Harry Gration, the kindly, caring and much-loved extravert television presenter on BBC North, becomes a killer once he steps on to a squash court. He told me, 'I am very ambitious. I would like to think that one day I could work in sport in London. I've always liked the competitive element in games. You like to get one over on people occasionally – I'm talking about sport. I don't like to lose. I have a battle with one of the guys here. We play squash twice a week and it's always close and absolutely no quarter is given on the court at all. We hammer each other and swear at each other

– in the nicest way. I like to win, and if I lose I get upset about it for a while. I need to feel occasionally that I'm doing something better than someone else – or as well as. You don't want to be a loser all your life.'

David Sutton, of David Sutton Motorsport, so renowned in the motor rallying world and an introvert often taken to be an extravert, told me, 'In my business I'm surrounded by a competitive world. I don't accept that when I build a car for a competitive rally it's going to be second or third. Quite often they are, and sometimes they don't finish at all, but I never go to the start of a rally thinking that they're going to be anything less than first. I think if you start saying to yourself second is good enough, or third is good enough then after a while you'll start to say that fifth or sixth is good enough. I think if you are in competition you've got to lead with the only result that is acceptable.'

When I questioned Harry and David about why winning was important they each at first wondered why I was questioning the self-evident, and then they answered in terms of how they experienced their sense of existence. To Harry the sporting world is the one he wishes to belong to, and being a good sportsman ensures this. David sees his life in terms of improvement, achievement and doing things properly, and this he applies to everything whether winning an international rally or mending the fences on his farm.

If success were simply a matter of us maintaining our self-confidence and elaborating our sense of existence we could, relatively easily, develop a way of life which did just this. But for most of us success is more complex than this. Our sense of what is success is very much affected by the pressures we feel emanating from our past and from the society in which we live.

Leo Braudy concluded the preface to his book on fame, *The Frenzy of Renown*, with, 'Although I began the work when both my parents were alive and vigorous, neither has lived to see its completion. But their loss impresses on me still more the feeling that writing this book has nurtured. In the heart of aspiration is the desire for recognition by those whose approval is unconditional and therefore need never be sought, but also can never be assumed.'[12]

This is the pressure from our past, our parents, whose attitudes and actions so impressed themselves on us as children that we spend the rest of our lives trying in some way to satisfy, not just our real parents, but the parents we carry around inside us. 'Satisfying our parents' means winning their total acceptance, approval and affection, showing them that they were wrong in expecting so little of us, and making up for the deficiencies of the past. Unfortunately, our internal parents can seem unchanging and insatiable, and so we go on and on trying to achieve the unachievable.

Our internal parents remain unchanging so long as we cling to our childhood belief that we were the cause of what happened to us. If only we had been *really* good, or *more* competent, we would never have been rejected, betrayed, punished, left bereft. We like to believe that we were the author of our own disasters because the other option, that we were the helpless victim of powers beyond our control and understanding, is too painful to contemplate.

Thus Harry cannot feel confident that the rejections he experienced in his childhood will not occur again, and so he goes on trying to prove his acceptability, not just by being a successful sportsman, but also by being exceptionally kind and caring, even though all of us who know him would tell him, and do, that such proof is totally unnecessary. David, as he told me of how his father lost his business and plunged the family into poverty, said, 'I was about fifteen at the time. I always felt that had I been that couple of years older I might have been able to contribute more to the business and perhaps keep it going.' He has proved a million times over that he is a better businessman than his father, but he is unreassured, just as he continues to chide himself for not doing more for his mother who did so much for him.

In talking to Harry and David I was impressed, as I am when I talk to my clients, with their sheer *goodness*. It is one of the ironies of human life that those childhood experiences which cause us in adult life to be anxious and driven can also be the experiences which create in us the kind of goodness about which we are truly humble.

Like the pressure from our internal parents, the pressure from society very much affects how we think and talk about success.

In my conversations with Americans who are successful in their chosen field I was often struck by the confident way they spoke of achieving further goals. By contrast, when English and Australian people talk about achieving their goals, whether small or large, there is a hesitancy, a sense that simply speaking of such aims could in itself frustrate them. These hesitant statements are often prefaced or followed with one particular phrase, 'Touch wood', and usually accompanied by a gesture towards any available wood-like surface.

'Touch wood' is an acknowledgement of the sin of hubris, when vaunting human ambition challenges the gods and provokes their envy and spite.

Perhaps what the English and Australian people are warding off with 'Touch wood' is not just the envy and spite of the gods but the envy and spite of their fellow citizens. In Australia we speak of 'tall poppies'. Anyone who stands out above the crowd is likely to be cut down, and so many incipient 'tall poppies' leave Australia, never to return.

Quentin Crisp, comparing his life in England with his life in America, said to me, 'The real difference between England and America is that in America they want you to succeed because they feel you may drag them forward with you, and in England they want you to fail because they fear you may leave them behind.'

I met only one American who was aware in her own life of the sin of hubris. This was Jean Hale. She said, 'I'm bad at correcting mistakes. The single, most self-destructive quality that I have is I devote an enormous amount of time to not making mistakes because, when I make a mistake, I find it almost impossible to correct it. I will let it get worse and worse and I will not take care of it. I have to make trouble for myself. I'm Jewish, and there's a tendency among Jews to feel that if you have it too good it's all going to be taken away from you. You can't have a perfect life, because if you're perfect or your life is perfect it's tempting the gods. They will strike you down.'

Jean here illustrates one of the forms of magical thinking that we all use to delude ourselves into thinking that we have everything under control and that we are safe. We see that in this imperfect world our lives can never be perfect, but we think that if we *choose* a particular bit of our life to be imperfect, then we have our fair share of imperfection with a proportion of pain and anxiety which we can predict and survive, and so we can never be struck by the unjust, random forces of the universe. We have made a bargain with the gods. Using this kind of magical thinking we fail to see that the gods do not enter into bargains with mere mortals, and neither do viruses, earthquakes and the many forms of death. All we achieve with such magical thinking is to rob ourselves of some possibilities of happiness.

Thus magical thinking prevents many people from attaining the success they desire and, even worse, of exploring and fulfilling their potential, what we could be if only we knew it.

The success that many of us desire is fame. Famous, we are significant, noticed, approved of and desired. Famous, we become more real than real. 'I saw you on television' has a far greater reality value than 'I saw you in the street'. Fame, for both extraverts and introverts, is a way of proving that you exist.

However, the way in which fame is defined today by society creates for us some insoluble conflicts. A famous person can no longer be simply different from the rest of the populace, in the way that Alexander the Great and Henry VIII were, as semidivine rulers, different from their subjects. Nowadays, wrote Leo Braudy, 'A famous person has to be a socially acceptable individualist, different enough to be interesting, yet similar enough not to be threatening or destructive. Thus the urge to fame intensifies the basic conflict between society and individualism, and the paradoxes of fame come from the effort to balance thinking about oneself with the obligations of belonging to a society. That these paradoxes are becoming more obvious is due to the effort of both American and European culture to maintain a public rhetoric of individualism that offsets an increasingly pervasive web of institutional and corporate relations ... In Europe individualism has generally been considered antisocial, while in America it seems encouraged by society, although subject to society's often hidden terms. Every American therefore draws with each breath simultaneous urges to conformity and distinction. No other country in the midst of creating a modern state, has so defiantly evolved so many institutionalized differences, so many ways of being outside. No other country so enforces the character-wrenching need to be assertive but polite, prideful but humble, unique but familiar, the great star and the kid next door.'[13]

English society has a tradition of relishing, or at least tolerating, the 'English eccentrics' who built follies and led peculiar lives. This tradition is withering away in the face of society's pressures on the individual to conform. A popular press ridicules the heir to the throne who chooses to spend some time in the quiet contemplation of nature, while ordinary people who in earlier times might have added interest and enjoyment to their lives by undertaking unusual feats and competitions, have now to protect themselves from public ridicule and rejection by undertaking such feats and competitions only 'in a good cause'. If you make a fool of yourself for charity you will be applauded, but make a fool of yourself to find out something more about yourself and to add to the enjoyment of your life and you will be punished.

But if we cannot risk making fools of ourselves how can we elaborate our sense of existence? Elaborating our sense of existence means venturing into the unknown, attempting things never tried before, and risking failure. Undertaking enterprises where success is certain is not elaborating one's sense of existence but defending oneself against the threats of rejection and chaos.

This is why, as I listened to so many Americans talk of the confidence they had in their future success, I ceased to feel nervous for them in their hubris and I began to suspect that what I was hearing was another age-old, magical way of dealing with the terrors of this world, whistling in the dark.

I checked this out with my friend Scott Budge, Assistant Director of Counselling at Pace University, New York, and astute observer of the American and European scene. He agreed that this was very much so in the two groups of people he knew in his work, the university students and the members of the Forty Plus Club, that is, managers and executives who had been 'let go' by their firm.

Scott said, 'The students assess one another according to how self-confident they are. People who are self-confident know exactly where they are going. They are goal directed. They know what they want. Anyone who doesn't or who hesitates publicly risks tremendous humiliation. You must look like you're confident. There's a real fear that someone can see through the veneer to an essential lack of confidence. To not have confidence is a sin here. There's a very strong moral dimension to it. Another dimension of whistling in the dark is there for managers and executives. When you get fired you get a glimpse of the fact that you are nothing without an organization. You are not an accountant except in so far as someone has hired you. Ask an American who he is and he'll tell you what he does. Who are you? I'm a psychologist. One's identity is vocational. But then, if I am not employed by somebody, there must be something wrong with me. It's either I'm successful, I'm a self-made man, or I'm a failure and it's my fault.'

So it is that if a nation creates a philosophy that individuals can achieve anything they set their minds to, then failure must be the individual's fault.

This takes no account of the fact that there are forces outside our control, such as a hurricane which destroys the people on whom our sense of existence depends or the stock market crash which destroys everything which we have achieved.

How can we not be afraid? And do we not try to hide our fears, so that other people will not see that we are afraid and despise us? So whether we speak of our successes with brash self-confidence or disarming modesty, we are all playing the same game of defending ourselves against the threat of annihilation of our self.

In the long run success and fame may not protect us from this threat, for they can create more rather than less issues in our relationships with other people, issues which have to be dealt with by extraverts and introverts in their own individual ways. One such issue is that of leadership.

# LEADERSHIP

When we begin our working career, joining an organization, entering a profession or apprenticeship, being 'the junior' in a factory or shop, we are expected to conform to the rules of the system we have joined and to the demands of the more experienced people in our team.

Introverts, unless they have grown up in families which required total conformity and obedience, usually find this stage of their career very difficult. They prefer to pursue their own goals and to act in their own idiosyncratic ways. Extraverts, usually quicker than introverts in picking up the conventions of behaviour in a particular system and wanting to be accepted into the team, do not find the first stages of a career as threatening as do introverts, that is, provided the extraverts think reasonably well of themselves. If you, as an extravert, despise yourself, you will expect that everyone, from the managing director to the tea lady, will reject you.

'A good team member' is an accolade the extraverts find easier to earn than introverts. Introverts have to work hard at it, learning and remembering to use the language of the team – 'we' rather than 'I'. Their high standards and their need for clarity and order often conflict with their extravert colleagues' way of doing things which, to the introvert, often seems slapdash and incomplete. The introvert, doubting and looking beneath the surface of things, will question what the team is doing, while the extravert, who is often prepared to complain to colleagues, will be less inclined to challenge the status quo.

It is often with a sense of relief as well as achievement that an introvert becomes a team leader. 'Now I can be myself and do things my way.' This is not to say that all introverts make good leaders. They are often so taken up with their own ideas that they do not perceive the needs and wishes of the people they are leading. It is simply that, to the introvert, becoming a leader is not a threat to the sense of self.

However, for the extravert, becoming a leader is a threat to the sense of self and wise extraverts have to work at developing the necessary understanding and skills as the wise introvert has to work in order to become a good team member. This is why many competent and experienced extraverts become depressed and anxious when they are promoted to a position of authority. The loneliness of command can seem to be the isolation which threatens to annihilate the self.

Many of the anxious and depressed men I have had as clients were in this predicament. One such, Chalky, about whom I wrote in *Depression: the Way Out of Your Prison*, had been promoted from teacher to deputy headmaster and subsequently crashed into a deep depression. He had all the skills necessary for his new job, but decision-making and especially taking the daily school assembly with the critical eyes of his colleagues upon him created in him an unendurable fear against which he protected himself by becoming depressed.[14] I wrote of Chalky, 'If you take as your rules for living trying "to please everybody all of the time" and trying never "to offend people or show annoyance" but always wanting "to be the peacemaker", then you must never take a position of authority and decision-making. In a position of authority, whatever it is, you cannot avoid offending some people and you cannot avoid being criticized.'[15]

I had thought that the solution to Chalky's problem could be for him to modify the rules by which he lived his life and to accept the truth of the old saying, 'Try to please all and you shall please none'. But doing this is never easy and usually requires some reflection upon oneself and one's life. If, as a child, you have been punished and humiliated for being angry, anger itself, yours and other people's, carries the threat of annihilation. Many extraverts find the thought of looking into one's inner reality very scary. 'It's not good to go too deeply into these things,' they will say of psychotherapy, preferring as a patient or doctor to take or to offer drugs to blot out awareness of the threat to the self. Chalky ended our meetings ('She expects me to talk about my childhood', he said scathingly to his doctor who reported this to me) and solved his problem by relinquishing his post and the extra salary that went with it and returned happily to the security of his classroom and the pupils who liked him.

Being liked is the key issue here. For extraverts being liked is as necessary as air. Introverts like to be liked, but for them it is similar to ice cream, very pleasant but not necessary. Successful extraverts in positions of authority develop ways of ensuring that people like them, no matter what they do. Thus President Reagan, an extravert, no matter what blunders he committed and how many people he disappointed, appeared before the cameras and, with his boyish charm, wooed and won his audience's affection. Whereas Mrs Thatcher, an introvert and supremely indifferent to whether people like her, forcefully states and repeats that she is Right and her critics Wrong. President Reagan was liked and Mrs Thatcher is admired, and thus, in their own terms, they are successful.

Mrs Thatcher has revealed in interviews attitudes to leadership and being liked similar to those expressed to me by David Sutton. He said, 'One of the sad facts of life is that the world is full of

losers, and if I can set an example to the people around me that
by determination you can succeed then this is what I'll do.
Leadership is very important. If a company or a team has strong
leadership people will react positively to it. I don't have people
around me to like me. I have people around to respect me. When
I go into a meeting to negotiate a major contract, I'd be lying if I
said I was not going for myself, but I'm also going for the people
that work for me and their families. I believe that I'm going as
the leader of a team. I'm going for all of us. I'm setting an
example. I like to be popular. I don't think in motor sport there's
a person who hates me. There are quite a few who are envious. I
like to be popular, but it's not the number one priority. Most
important is leadership. My mechanics know that they can count
on me a hundred percent.'

David's mechanics also know that if they get anything wrong
David will tell them about it most forcibly. As an extravert Jean
Hale uses other methods to get people to do what she wants. She
said, 'It's always been my view that you can mostly get people to
do what you want without them being angry with you. There are
ways to do it. In a lot of cases by being polite, or pleasant, or
things like that. I worked in one firm where people treated
secretaries like dirt, or machines, and I always said please and
thank you, and that was a great job that you did, or I know that
this is an enormous imposition but do you think you could
possibly . . . , and everybody liked me and worked harder for me
than they did for anyone else. Now I'm a very successful
negotiator. I feel that I have elevated my particular style of
niceness and reasonableness to its highest potential level.'

Over the years, in therapy sessions and in workshops, I have
often posed the participants a question which summarizes the
issue of leadership and being liked. It is,

> 'Suppose you were faced with a situation where you could
> act in only one of two ways. If you act in one way people
> will like you but you won't respect yourself, and if you act in
> the other way people won't like you but you will respect
> yourself. Which will you choose, being liked or respecting
> yourself?'

Introverts find this question quite straightforward. Without
hesitation they choose maintaining self-respect, irrespective of

whether people like them. Extraverts hesitate. They know that choosing self-respect is the socially acceptable answer, but they know that the answer is not natural and easy for them.

When I was talking to Prince Hans-Adam he told me how early in his adult life he had to deal with the problem of being liked and respecting himself. On leaving university he was given the task of re-organizing the family business and this involved making a number of decisions which many people did not like. This worried him at first, but his experience had proved him right. He said, 'I prefer to be unpopular and have a clear conscience. I'm being honest to myself. I've seen myself that if I made a decision so as to be liked by the people, that might turn out good for the moment, but I soon found myself in difficulties. So I think it's better to go straight away for what you know is right, even if it's not popular at the moment. I try not to tell people in an undiplomatic way, to stamp on everybody's feet. I try to say it as nicely as possible.'

When I put this question to Margot Ely there was a long, long pause before she answered. Life in university circles poses this question many times over.

She said, 'This was a major problem when I was growing up because I wanted desperately to be liked. In my first year of teaching the major thing I learned was how easy it could be to get everybody's love and it scared the shit out of me. It's manipulation. It's terrible. I think I'm more on top of it now, more aware of the siren song of what might be the easy way to do things, and also I'm aware of what it does to me. I really do try to learn how to do the kinds of things where I feel I am not giving up on myself or on my principles. I sometimes do things that I don't like to do because I feel in the long run that it's probably the best thing to do. Most times I have to go my way. That brings me a tremendous amount of pain. The key for me is I've got to know the choice I have made. I am very fortunate in that I have good friends who will help me in that situation to talk it out. It's been one of the major struggles in my life. I'm very aware of the phenomenon of working to be liked in my work in the analytical study of interactions. I'm aware of the fact that some people work all their lives to be liked and are liked, and I am aware that I am very liked. I really hate it when I do things that go against myself. I'm not as gentle with myself as I am with other people, which is another problem. It's very easy to give in and play it the way other people want. But I always know when I'm selling out.'

Leadership, self-respect and liking are moral issues for which, like all moral issues, there are no absolute, black and white answers. Most of us, especially introverts who believe in Absolute Moral Laws and extraverts who do not want even to think about the customs and conventions of their society, much less question them, would like to believe that there are absolute answers, but there never can be when such basic differences exist in how we experience our sense of self and the threat of its annihilation. Even in our reasons for the supreme virtues of Truth and Loyalty we differ.

## TRUTH AND LOYALTY

Introverts always make a lot of fuss about truth and truth telling. Knowing what is true is essential for organizing the universe and keeping chaos at bay. Introvert parents often harass and punish their children for lying when the children are, as children do, experimenting with fantasy and seeing where, in a world where truth telling is not always appreciated, they can get away with lying. As an introvert I used to condemn lying absolutely, but I came to realize that I was not so much maintaining a high moral code but trying to make myself feel safer. Now I hold the view that, provided you have a good memory, lying to others can on occasion be done sensibly and effectively. However, the one person you must never lie to is yourself. Do that and you are in trouble. Unfortunately, lying to oneself is the most common form of lying.

Extraverts usually have a more permissive attitude about truth and truth telling because they discovered early in their childhood that truth telling can make you very unpopular. Some extravert children become very wise in knowing in which situations the truth can be safely told and in which situations it is best to lie. Discovering this requires a certain self-confidence and a will to survive. Many extravert children are so punished and threatened with abandonment (as in mother to dawdling four year old in supermarket, 'If you don't hurry up I'm going to leave you here', or father to disobedient six year old, 'There are children's homes for kids who don't do as they're told') that they lose their self-confidence and even come to doubt that they have the right to exist. They grow up believing that to survive they must not ever upset anyone, and 'not upsetting' can often mean not telling the truth. As adults they despise themselves for their lying and weakness, and they find themselves leading inauthentic lives of great emptiness.

Wise extraverts know that relationships where the truth cannot be told are relationships without strength and reliability. One of my clients, John, who agonized for months about whether to accept a promotion to a very senior post, knowing what criticism the holder of such a post incurs and needing so desperately to be liked and accepted, said to me, 'Truth is extremely important to me because it's only by being truthful that I can form a good, worthwhile relationship with others.' John, when he accepted the new post, set about adapting his witty, charming, unthreatening way of telling the truth to the needs of the job, and succeeded.

Loyalty is valued by both extraverts and introverts, but for different reasons. For extraverts loyalty is the maintenance of relationships, while for introverts it is the maintenance of an organized structure which links the introvert to external reality. Disloyalty extraverts experience as abandonment, and introverts as chaos and the loss of adequate contact with external reality.

We extend our loyalty not just to other people but to things. Sometimes the things are reminders of other people to whom we have great loyalty, and sometimes they are so like people in themselves that we feel we cannot reject or abandon them. Objects to which we are greatly attached become part of that kind of fantasy making which Freud called 'projective identification'. In this we unconsciously take part of our experience and impose it on another person or object, and then consciously identify with what we have assumed that the person or object is feeling.

Thus, an extravert and an introvert might each feel great loyalty to their car and be reluctant to sell it even when common sense dictates that a new car is necessary. Unconsciously, the extravert has imposed on his car his own fear of abandonment, and then consciously feels pity for the car which is threatened with abandonment. Unconsciously, the introvert has imposed on his car his own fear of disorganization and the loneliness of his internal reality, and then consciously feels pity for the car left lonely and confused.

If we fail in adult life to make ourselves aware of how we project on to other people and things our own experience of the sense of existence and the threat of annihilation, we can find our lives cluttered with irrational loyalties and unnecessary possessions, and our attempts to rid ourselves of any of these impeded by shame and guilt. Once we have become aware of how we have formed loyalties to certain people and things out of the way we experience our sense of existence and the threat of annihilation, we are free to decide which of the loyalties we still need and which we can let ourselves outgrow.

We should not give up our ability to project our own experience of life in all its fullness on to other people, for the imaginative use of this is empathy, and it is empathy and love that makes us human, and not merely animated objects. It is an essential part of our concern for others.

## CONCERN FOR OTHERS

Often when I talk and write about how introverts and extraverts differ in their experience of their existence I feel that I am giving the impression that extraverts are invariably warmly concerned about other people while introverts go coldly on their way. There are, of course, introverts and extraverts who fit this pattern, but it is not invariable. We all need other people, and so most introverts, like most extraverts, are extremely concerned about other people. What differs is in how they experience and express this concern.

We all like to think that the concern we feel for others is altruistic. We do good to others for their sakes, not for ours. However, in truth we cannot be completely altruistic unless we feel so secure and worthwhile in ourselves that there is nothing we need from other people in order to maintain and to elaborate our sense of existence and to protect ourselves from the threat of annihilation.

Few of us ever experience such security, and none of us in the entirety of our lives. Most of us do good to other people because we love them and wish them well *and* because their presence maintains our sense of existence and wards off the threat of annihilation. Some of us do good to other people solely, or almost solely, because their presence maintains our sense of existence and wards off the threat of annihilation.

If we value and accept ourselves and have the wisdom to see that the threat of annihilation is an illusion – as extraverts we know that when we are alone we do not disappear and that our inner reality is a haven, not a danger, and as introverts we know that chaos means not danger but freedom – then we can form relationships where affection and concern are freely given, without obligation and guilt. We can love people and wish them well, even though that 'well' does not necessarily include us. We can enjoy their affection, admiration and approval without feeling driven to work hard to gain and to hold on to their positive regard.

If we have not perceived that the threat to our existence is an illusion, our relationships with others are always fraught with danger, for we see other people as having the power to annihilate us. So we try to protect ourselves by confining and regulating our affection and concern for others. Some people follow the rule, 'I never love anyone completely, so that I can protect myself against the pain of inevitable rejection.' Some people follow the rule, 'I give my love only when people please me, and I withdraw it when they do not.' Some people follow the rule, 'I give my love in exact proportion to the love I am given and that way I avoid feeling cheated.' Not surprisingly, the people they love often feel unloved.

Introverts know that it is the people they love who tie them to external reality. Without such people they fear they would be adrift on their own empty ocean. Part of the passionate love introvert mothers have for their children is that the child is experienced as part of both the mother's internal and external reality, and the child thus keeps the mother in contact with external reality. Having part of herself in external reality can help the introvert mother grow stronger and more secure in herself, as many introvert women do in motherhood. However, introvert mothers who remain feeling weak and in danger of disintegration can feel threatened by the way their child grows and changes, especially when the child becomes an adult, and so the mother seeks to keep the child as a child. Some introvert mothers who feel in extreme danger of disintegration will choose one of their children to be their protection against disintegration and their sole, or most trustworthy, link with external reality, and such children have either to fight for survival or sacrifice themselves for their mother.

Extraverts know that it is the people they love who form the group which gives them their sense of existence. Without such people they fear they would disappear like a puff of smoke in the wind. Part of the passionate love that extravert mothers have for their children is that the child forms a relationship which is the strongest the woman has ever known and, as the child is part of the mother's internal reality as well as her external reality, internal reality becomes more real. Feeling more secure about her internal reality can make the extravert mother stronger and more secure in herself, as many extravert women do in motherhood. However, extravert mothers who remain feeling weak and in danger of disappearing can feel threatened by the way their child grows and changes, especially when the child becomes an adult, and so the mother seeks to keep the child as a child. Some extravert mothers who feel in extreme danger of being annihilated will choose one of their children to be their protection against disappearance and their sole, or most trustworthy, means of dealing with their internal reality, and such children have to fight for survival or sacrifice themselves for their mother. Alice Miller has described how the mother's demand for the child's sacrifice can call forth from a small child a maturity of empathy and action way beyond the child's years.[16] Until I read Alice Miller I used to think that I had been blessed with some superior talent for understanding people, but now I recognize that as the child of a depressed and sometimes murderously angry mother it was a skill that had to be developed if I were to survive. (This is another example of how we like to perceive our defences against the threat of annihilation as virtues.)

Because we grow up with this feeling that somehow we are not good enough, not entirely acceptable to other people, we find it impossible to believe that other people will love us simply because we exist. We believe that we have to do things for other people to gain and hold their affection. If we are not too greatly driven by our need to be good, we can, out of our positive feeling for our self, do positive things for other people. As extraverts we can feel that we have an unlimited source of caring and concern from which other people can benefit, and as introverts we can feel that we can use our gift for clarity and organization to benefit other people.

Our concern for other people includes our concern not to hurt other people, for in doing so we activate the threat of our annihilation. For extraverts hurting others creates the danger of rejection and abandonment, while for introverts having hurt someone, or acting incorrectly or unwisely, creates that horrible feeling of having got things wrong and having disrupted the pattern of control and organization consonant with our standards. The fear we feel when we think we have hurt someone is called shame and guilt.

The less we value and accept ourselves, the more we feel driven to work hard to ensure other people's affection, approval and acceptance.

Extraverts who do not value and accept themselves feel that they can never keep themselves in a group by mutual affection alone. They feel that they have to secure the membership of the group by making the other members of the group need them. Thus they become the indispensable member of the team, the totally dependable and unselfish doctor, nurse or therapist, the selfless, self-sacrificing parent. In these roles they may be immensely successful, but they often feel put upon by the seemingly insatiable demands of the people who need them. They look forward to old age with dread, for when one is old how can one be needed? When I was involved in nurse education I found that many nurses had this particular dread of old age. I thought that they were in a particularly advantageous position to see the wisdom of my solution to this problem. As the world is full of people who need to be needed, old and helpless people are greatly needed to be needy, so even in the frailest of old ages extraverts who need to be needed can fulfil the function of meeting the needs of those who need to be needed. To date I have not had much success in promoting this concept, for those extraverts who need to be needed are also those extraverts who think that they are being virtuous only if they are rushing around being busy.

Introverts who do not value and accept themselves feel that, no matter what they achieve, they can never rest on their past achievements but must always be striving to do something more to earn the respect and approval of those people whose opinion they value. They do good to others, and can be very effective in the good they do, but they do it out of a sense of duty and obligation. They maintain the high standards they have set in organization and control. They often feel resentful that what they see is expected of them is that they should do everything perfectly. They look forward to old age with dread, for then they see themselves as being forced to relinquish their control and to put themselves in the hands of others whom they see as incompetent and untrustworthy. They do not see that life itself has a certain pattern, that after years of caring for others, we can let others care for us. Like the extraverts who do not value and accept themselves, they have not realized that it takes much more generosity to receive than to give. We can show concern for others by accepting what they wish to give us.

We cannot want to accept what someone wants to give us because we do not want to be under an obligation to that person, a position we see as arousing in us shame and guilt. Sometimes we do not want to accept what someone wants to give us because what they want to give us is something we do not want. Sometimes what they want to give us is sex, and sometimes sex can seem to us as the greatest threat to our self.

## SEX

Most of us for most of our lives are interested in sex for, as introverts, we can find a heightened sense of individuality and a passionate mingling of our inner and outer realities, and as extraverts, we can find a blissful union which secures our existence. However, there is always a possible threat, the conditions of which I came to know very well in my work with couples.

By the 1970s 'frigidity' in women had ceased to be a virtue as it was for my mother's generation and had become a medical condition in need of treatment. When tranquillizers failed to cure the condition doctors turned to psychologists, and so a long line of unhappy women came through my door.

Sometimes finding out what was going wrong for the woman was very simple. There's nothing like boredom to turn you off sex. Every Saturday night, lights off, same event, is not a recipe for lifelong sexual satisfaction. Sometimes finding what was wrong was much more difficult, for the problem was located, not in bed, but in the way each person experienced his or her sense of existence and the threat of annihilation, and in the degree of trust each had in the other.

Only when we have a strong sense of self can we easily give it up. If we experience our sense of self as fragile, liable to disappear or to crumble, we dare not give it up, even momentarily. For a woman, giving yourself in sex is a matter of relinquishing that sense of self, and that can be done only when there is a sense of trust that your partner will not annihilate you.

Thus, for an introvert woman sex can seem like the loss of control which means chaos and annihilation, and for an extravert woman sex can seem like the loneliness and abandonment which comes with the sense of being treated as an object. For both kinds of woman sex can remind them of those childhood experiences when, weak and totally in the power of adults, their sense of self was threatened with annihilation. For many women this is the lasting effect of childhood physical and sexual abuse by men whom they experienced as totally powerful and ruthless.

Being sexually active is regarded as a proper and necessary masculine pastime, and so many men are reluctant to see that they use sex as a way of reassuring themselves that their sense of existence is not threatened with annihilation.

For many introverts, men especially, the chaos which they fear most is that of emotion, their own even more than other people's. Thus many introvert men pride themselves on their calmness and rationality and, in sex, on being able to get physical satisfaction without relinquishing control of their emotions. When their partner is an extravert, woman or man, the partner feels the lack of emotion, particularly the lack of tenderness, as rejection, abandonment and the threat of annihilation. An introvert partner finds relating to an external reality where an important part of it – emotion – is missing or hidden fearful and confusing.

Many introverts, men and women, who know that they need contact with other people so as to maintain their hold on external reality but who fear personal relationships (for there is nothing more likely to create chaos than other people), use sex as a means of having this contact without making a commitment to another person or putting themselves within another person's sphere of influence. Sex is an effective way of preventing conversation.

Many extravert men, fearful that their need for the closeness and tenderness which maintains their sense of existence is an effeminate weakness, seek to meet their need in the only way they regard as permissible, sex. But a need which is met only intermittently becomes insatiable (psychologists call this in learning theory the principle of partial reinforcement) and so such extravert men experience their need for closeness and tenderness as an insatiable need for sex. They make demands on their partners which the partner may find excessive, or they seek other and many partners.

I remember, years ago, a fellow psychologist confiding to me that his ambition was 'to fuck every girl in the world'. I thought then that this was part of his expression of his *joie de vivre*. Now, having met so many men like him, I know that his joy in sex was mixed with a need to gain the closeness and tenderness which was necessary to maintain his sense of existence, but which he felt was evidence of his weakness of character. He gave great warmth, concern, understanding and help to others, but he had difficulty in accepting the affection others had for him. He doubted that he deserved it. By having many partners he rejected them before they could reject him, thus, in that magical way of trying to control what he saw as inevitable disaster, creating the disaster himself (his marriage after an elaborate wedding was, so he told me, 'the shortest on record'). Also he avoided the possibility of forming a commitment to someone who might be stronger than him and thus threaten him with annihilation.

A sexual relationship can be a very satisfactory way of elaborating our sense of existence, and it can also be, like alcohol, narcotic drugs and nicotine, a way of dealing with the threat of annihilation.

## DRINK, DRUGS AND SMOKING

Alcohol and the different narcotic drugs affect each individual differently, but there are some underlying similarities for extraverts and introverts.

The effect of alcohol and drugs seems to be that the restrictions and anxieties which each of us feels in our less real reality are reduced and there is a sense of freedom.

For the extravert under the influence of alcohol or drugs the restrictions and anxieties of internal reality reduce or dissolve, and there is no longer the fear that something which the extravert fears but does not understand might emerge from internal reality to disrupt one's relationships with other people. There is a blissful sense of closeness and relationship to all other people, and a degree of confidence in being accepted by others that is never obtained in sobriety. But there is also the danger that out of that unguarded internal reality will come the emotions of anger and sadness which the extravert, when sober, is sure that no one will accept. Often he is right.

For the introvert under the influence of alcohol or drugs the restrictions and anxieties of external reality reduce or dissolve. The strain of trying to organize and to hold external reality together disappears, and the introvert treats external reality as he always suspects it is, fantasy. Then he can float, irresponsible, saying and doing what he likes. Sometimes he simply quietly enjoys the peacefulness of not striving to control and organize, and sometimes he talks, pouring out all those ideas which, sober, he is sure that no one will accept. Often he is right.

Nicotine does not release us from all the restrictions and anxieties of our less real reality, but it can give us the courage to face them. Cigarettes can change our image of ourselves. Cigarettes can be our friends.

A human friend of mine, Miller Mair, showed me an excellent way of discovering how attached a smoker is to cigarettes. Miller's question is, 'If your cigarette was a person, what sort of person would it be?'

Stephanie Alexander, reading about this in *Beyond Fear*,[17] wrote to me to say, 'Six months as a non-smoker means I'm still a smoker at heart. I can give a picture of it as an infusion of lean masculinity, keeping threatening other people at bay and providing those qualities – definiteness, angularity, invulnerability – I associate with masculineness, to cover up the softness, vulnerability and get-at-ability of being female and me.'

When Bill Hearld, news editor of the *Yorkshire Evening Press*, interviewed me about *Beyond Fear* we established early on that he was an extravert. He described his need for achievement in terms of being able to care properly for his family, not just in being a good provider but in being able to spend time with them. I spoke of the danger that extraverts perceive when they think they are to be left completely alone, and he said, 'I felt like that when my first marriage broke up. I couldn't stand to be alone. I bought a house close to my parents, and for the first six months I would be out every night. I couldn't stand to be in the house on my own. But after about six months I got used to it. In fact, I got to like it. I thought I might even get to like it too much.'

Being promoted to news editor brought the threat of isolation and rejection again, but by then Bill knew that the loneliness of authority need not be annihilating. He said, 'When I first became news editor with the right to hire and fire I noticed that in the news room, when I went up to a group of people, they would stop talking. I found that a bit difficult, but I talked it over with my wife and I worked out a way of handling it. After all, relationships in the news room don't have to be all that close. They need to be a bit cool and distant.'

While we talked Bill smoked. Towards the end of our discussion I asked him, 'If your cigarette was a person, what sort of a person would it be?'

'A good friend,' he said. 'When I get up at six in the morning, when everyone else is asleep, I know there's a friend waiting for me. I haven't always smoked. It's only in the last ten years. I began when my first marriage broke up.'

He reminisced about how the smell of cigarette smoke reminded him of his father and how, as a small child, he used to sit on his father's knee. He remembered, too, the smell of his grandfather's cigar as the family sat around the table at the end of a meal.

I could see that no campaign about the dangers of smoking would influence him. 'You can't reject a friend,' I said.

He smiled. 'No, I can't do that.'

David Sutton told me how, 'Two years ago I gave up smoking. I felt like a second class citizen. Every time you went to somebody's house you couldn't find an ash tray, and I was always saying, "Do you mind if I smoke?", and other people were always saying how smelly I was and the car was. I needed to choose the right time to give up smoking – when I felt right. We went on holiday to California where I've got a house and before arriving there we had ten days in Antigua. It was my birthday. We went out to dinner with some friends. When we got home Jill had gone up to bed and I just said to myself, "I don't smoke anymore," and I haven't smoked from that day since. I couldn't cut it down. It was that black and white thing again.' (David cannot stand uncertainty and indecision.) 'Either you do smoke or you don't smoke. I just had to stop it like that. The problem was more social than health. People say do you feel better? No. No great sense of taste. Apart from the fact that I'm now carrying two stone more than I was when I was smoking. I'm the world's worst as far as people who smoke now. People around me who smoke, I get very cross with them, very arrogant, I'm afraid.'

I asked him to describe his cigarette as a person. He said, 'A friend, because you can hide behind a cigarette. You can also use it to help your thinking time. In a heavyweight meeting and somebody asks you a question. Often you don't know what to do with your hands. You can doodle with a cigarette or a lighter. I used to use cigarettes quite a lot to help me. A classical example, walking into a room, not quite knowing what's going to happen to you on the other side of the door. I suppose, it's a companion.'

So for both Bill and David a cigarette was a friend, but for Bill, an extravert, a friend who provided the relationship necessary to maintain his sense of existence, and for David, an introvert, a friend who helped him find some necessary social skills. As David learned other skills in dealing with difficult social situations and as smoking became less socially acceptable, cigarettes ceased to be friends and he could give them up. Bill felt a strong loyalty to his friends, cigarettes, and he would not abandon them.

'Friends' as some kind of 'transitional object', a means of

making a transition from one situation to another, and 'friends' as the maintenance of a sense of existence represent two kinds of modes of experience, and here extraverts and introverts differ in many subtle and significant ways.

# DIFFERENT MODES OF EXPERIENCE

Enter Terminal 3 at Heathrow or the International Terminal at Kennedy and you will feel that the entire population of the world is on the move. Nowadays it is unexceptional for people to travel huge distances for pleasure as well as for work or migration. *Travel* now is a common human experience, and, as with all experiences, extraverts and introverts deal with it differently.

For all of us home is the place where we can feel most secure. (Home is also the place where we can feel the most insecure, because it contains the people who have the greatest power to annihilate us.) As introverts, we have at home enough organization and control to maintain our sense of existence, and, as extraverts, we have the people and the things that make us feel a sufficiently secure member of a group. Travel threatens both forms of security. Travelling, we can lose all organization and control, and we can feel a dangerous aloneness.

All my life I wanted to travel and now, over the last ten years, I have travelled extensively and found it marvellously fulfilling, with an increased understanding of other people and places and a development of myself. Yet it can still seem a threat. I deal with the threat of death during my travels by believing that dying within a space of a few minutes in an aeroplane crash is infinitely preferable to a lingering death by cancer or senility. The threat of finding external reality strange and uncontrollable is much harder to deal with, and even after I have drawn up an itinerary and lists of things to take and checked and rechecked my tickets and passport, I can wake in the night feeling frightened and wishing to stay at home. Then I have to remind myself that there is nothing to be afraid of, that most of the places I go to are sufficiently similar to England and Australia for me to find them real, and even when I did enter a world totally different from what I knew – travelling alone in India where I felt like Gulliver on an alien planet – I survived.

New places and new people can be tremendously exciting, and this is why many extraverts enjoy travel. But new places and new people may not provide the relationships necessary for a sense of existence. Stephanie Alexander would dearly love to visit England again, but, as she wrote to me, 'Travel alone is one of my worst things: that is when I *really* do not exist and am prone to be left behind or get lost like an invisible and helpless and terrified parcel. Catching a bus is hell for me, so you can imagine what it is like going around the world and then having to get about on buses and trains at the other end. This is not something I tell people about, actually, and it brings me out in goosepimples putting it on paper here. Travel alone is one long, sweating, thumping, short-of-breath terror during which there is no me at all, just a panic-racked hulk. It's been a recurrent horror since, aged about ten, I got on the wrong bus home in a very Afrikaans part of the Reef (we had just moved) and was conveyed way out of town. As it happened the bus passed my father's factory and the driver kindly directed my sobbing steps, and my father emerged from a meeting and drove me home – and even as I set this down for you it is as if a large rat is dining somewhere in the middle of my chest. Oh, dear.'

Extraverts' need for and delight in stimulation from their external reality is the central part of their experience of themselves. They will create *excitement* for themselves out of every available situation, and, if the situation will not yield the excitement of joy, they will create the excitement of anxiety. Jean Hale told me how, 'There's a little game that people play with themselves which is to make things deliberately harder, so that you can feel more satisfaction. The best example I can give you is – my nephew had asked me to give a talk at his school. I had the address, but I didn't know where it was exactly, and the cab got lost. I got there thirty minutes late, right before I had to start talking, and I spoke extempore. Now to give a talk at your nephew's school, to sit down and write a speech, and find out where the school is, and leave enough time to get there is nothing. Where's the satisfaction in that? But to get there thirty minutes late, and make it up as you go along, and do it brilliantly, is –

good for me. I did a perfectly brilliant job of it. I think, though, as I've gotten older I've done that sort of thing less.'

Introverts never want stimulation for stimulation's sake, but what they do not want to be is bored. Time and time again, in my interviews with successful introverts, they spoke of their dislike of *boredom*, often given as the reason for going on meeting more and more challenges.

Ian Padden has met more challenges, and all of them dangerous, than most of us do. His most peaceful occupation is writing, and that is about the matters in which he has taken part all his adult life – the military and especially military 'élites', espionage, counter insurgency warfare, deep-sea diving, oil drilling and engineering around the world, and flying, especially aerobatics where in his small, dark blue plane he is a champion. When I talked with him he queried my use of the word 'achievement'. He preferred the word 'progression'. He said, 'Progression to me is the satiation of curiosity. Something that I don't know, that I've never experienced, I'm simply curious. Someone says, "Can you do this?" and I say, "I think so. I probably could, I don't know, I've never done it before." There's remuneration to that, whether it's to satisfy my own curiosity or whether it's financial. Curiosity isn't important to me, it's just something that is there. I have a choice. It's amusing. I go along, doing things I enjoy. I like to do something because I'm curious as to whether I can. I'll go and try it to find out. Self-satisfaction. It's something to do. What else is there to do? I've tried hanging around doing nothing, and nothing has an emptiness to it. I'll get plenty of nothing when I'm dead. You cannot control the body but you can sure as hell control the mind. That's where you have all your freedom. If you're a dreamer you can dream.'

Ian acts in order to be himself and to control and elaborate the power of his mind. Quentin Crisp does *not* act, but for the same reason, though he would never use the words 'control' and 'power' in relation to himself. Quentin values idleness. Many people will quote his dictum that if you don't dust a room after four years it doesn't make any difference, but as he explained to me, 'I live in one room and I know where almost everything is. I very seldom lose anything. Order is the way of reducing the process of living to its absolute minimum. I live in such a way that I don't have to think about anything except thinking. I really like doing nothing. During the day I sit around. I never understand people who'll say of some activity, "Well, it helps to kill time." I don't want my time dead.'

When Quentin sits in idleness he thinks, and thinking, enjoying a rich and vibrant internal reality, is what introverts mean by not being bored. What they need from external reality is the stimulation of something new to think about.

The phrase *food for thought* describes exactly what I have always known. Something I have not experienced before, be it exploring a place I had never visited before, listening to a life story told by a client, learning a new skill, writing something I have never written before, reading a new book or the daily paper, becomes a kind of sustenance which I take into myself and digest. I have been keenly aware of this since my earliest childhood when, in a suburban home with a mother whose rigid ideas about how life ought to be lived brought little novelty and new people into my life, I would escape to the beach or the bush and into books and newspapers, undeterred by her threat that all that reading would 'ruin my eyes'. It didn't. It saved my life. Reading showed me that I did not have to live solely among the threats and banalities of external reality.

This understanding of the introvert's need for 'food for thought' helped me to reassure Angela Tilby, a BBC television producer, when she visited me while researching for a programme on a hospice for the dying. (Angela is an introvert, not just according to my reckoning but also according to the Myers-Briggs Type Indicator.) She told me about some of the things she had observed in the time she had spent at the hospice and then, aware of the moral dilemma of whether and, if so, how we should observe another's suffering, she said, 'I suppose I am voyeuristic.' I hastened to assure her that she was not. A voyeur's gaze turns people into objects, thus belittling and humiliating them.

Nancy Banks-Smith, whose work as television critic for *The Guardian* often requires her to observe the suffering of others, holds the view that the one important thing we can do for others is to acknowledge their suffering, to take account of them and their lives. It is the affirmation of another person's existence.

This is what Angela does. She is concerned, not simply with

acknowledging the existence and experience of others, but with absorbing it in order to meditate upon it, to take it into internal reality and there to re-create it and bring it forth in some new form which she shares with others in conversation, or in her books, or in her television programmes. I had seen this process taking place from the day she first came to talk to me about the possibility of making a programme about my work in depression, through the many conversations that followed, through her interactions with the depressed people who agreed to take part in the programme, through the filming to the final product, a compelling film of great beauty. Angela had not simply taken a number of interviews and pictures and combined them into a pleasing and informative pattern. She had observed, absorbed, made what she had absorbed her own, structured and organized it, brought it forth, made sure that her subjects and her team knew what she wanted of us, and created something which was her creation, yet it was not so idiosyncratically hers that it did not speak to and about the experience of others. Her film, *The Mind Box*,[18] is not one woman's view of depression as a moral dilemma but it explores for every man and every woman the universal moral issues which the state of depression both hides from and acknowledges.[19]

Watching Angela work and talking to my friends Ron Janoff, a poet and extravert, and Diana Leidel, an artist and introvert, helped me to understand something of the different ways in which introverts and extraverts experience the process of creation.

Ron's job as Director of the Management Insitute at New York University seems far removed from poetry, but in all the years I had known him I was aware how central poetry was to him. I love his poems, but prefer to enjoy them rather than to comment upon them, for they do not lend themselves to the kind of analysis and appreciation that the poems of complex and subtle thinkers like William Empson do. (Out of all the possible poets who produced complex poems I choose to mention William Empson for I knew him and knew him to be an introvert.) Rather, Ron's poems have that quality of 'thereness', where something is shown, displayed, pointed to, and what is conveyed is the quality of the extraordinariness of the ordinary. It is in the awareness of the extraordinariness of the ordinary that we experience ourselves as alive and aware and amazed and delighted and shocked by the world and the people in it.

One evening I did not just say, as I usually do after reading one of his poems, 'That was great' or 'I enjoyed that', but instead I asked, 'Why is poetry important to you?'

That was a hard question to answer. Ron said, 'It's the most complex thing. It's putting into a small space, packing in, a tremendous amount of design power, and not making it obvious – it's something I really enjoy doing, and doing it well. It has an enormous physical and psychological connectedness to it. It's difficult to describe. It's very essential.'

'Connectedness to what?' I asked.

'I think to being alive. It operates to open into a lot more space than just that your body can operate in. Connectedness, it's connected to my own past or voice or feelings, feeling whole. I see it much more of assembling of elements that are out there and trying to move them almost over myself to find where they are matching. It's a matching process of putting together something outside and finding where it resonates inside. If I go to write poetry I usually turn the radio on, turn the TV on, bring the newspaper along and actually let lots and lots unconnected verbal things happen while I'm doing it. I gather things. I've drawers full of scraps of paper. I'll start out with taping things together. It always surprises me when I'm producing the finished work, how similar the surfaces will come out to be and how true over long periods of time, and recognizable to other people, even though I know that their sources are different. That's kind of a key to that feeling of connectedness, there's some kind of match there. There's so many stages in the process, too. Today I was just finishing some poems I wrote two years ago, putting them together today into final versions. It's assembling, bundling, reducing, reworking and finding a chord much more than something that rises from within and getting put on paper. That seems inside out.'

My experience of writing poetry was that the poem suddenly arrived in me complete. It needed only to be written down, with punctuation and the odd word to be thought about. It always came from some process of change within myself and the images it employed, while they might be drawn from my external reality, were metaphors for something inside me. I can appreciate only in an intellectual way how Ron creates his poems.

I asked Diana how she experienced the artistic process.

She said, 'Drawing or painting is different from writing in that you're not looking for connectedness. What's exciting is that there's energy, rather than connectedness. The intensity, the energy, are the things that make drawing so compelling. By concentrating. A painting involves a little more intellectualizing. But it's surprising every time and it's fresh and new every time, and if it's not, you're not drawing. You're doing something else. The process of drawing is very different from the process of designing. When I design something for the magazine, it's not thinking about what I'm going to do or what my intentions are, it's just sitting and looking at what's available around me and collecting and assembling. I was going to say, almost exactly what Ron does.'

Many of the artistic creations by extraverts and introverts are less than what they might have been because the individual extravert and introvert is too influenced by his or her desire to see the world in the particular way that introverts and extraverts value highly. For extraverts it is *beauty*: for introverts it is *perfection*. (Beauty cannot be rejected: perfection is total control and organization.) Thus many extraverts produce work of cloying sweetness and sentimentality, while many introverts produce work so controlled and organized that all life has gone from it.

There are many extraverts who extol beauty so much that they cannot tolerate *ugliness*, and 'ugly' includes old, sick and handicapped people. There are many introverts who extol perfection and hate *imperfection* so much that they cannot tolerate anything they find to be imperfect, and that includes most of external reality. Such extraverts spend much of their time feeling revulsion, and such introverts spend much of their time feeling angry, uncomfortable emotions which are neither beautiful nor perfect. Such people have not realized that beauty and perfection lie in the eye of the beholder, and that neither can be perceived without the contrast of ugliness and imperfection.

Introverts, as they meditate upon, or digest, their observations and experience, are developing some theory to explain what they have observed and experienced. They find great satisfaction out of developing a total explanation, and can feel satisfied if they can understand and explain a problem, even if there is nothing in their explanation which allows them to solve it. Extraverts get very impatient with introverts over this. Extraverts like to get on and do things. They prefer *action* to *explanation*. This way of seeing things underlies many of the disagreements and misunderstandings among psychologists, psychiatrists and psychotherapists. The introverts among them work on developing theories, be they concerning 'dynamic processes' or yet undiscovered genes, which explain why people behave as they do and, if from the theory comes some way of 'making people better', this is a serendipitous extra and not the whole point of the exercise. Meanwhile, the extraverts among them want to get on and 'make people better', and believe that if something works there is no special need to find out why. It is this differing perception of the sense of existence and the threat of annihilation which causes the arguments about the value of ECT (electroconvulsive therapy) or of psychotherapy to run and run.

Along with their need for explanation introverts have a strong sense of the *need for completion or closure*. Enterprises should have a beginning, a middle and an end. David Sutton recognized this need for closure in himself. He said, 'I get very cross when I say to one of my staff, "Please will you do this", and it doesn't get done. Then I'm angry, but it's only because people aren't doing their job. If the standards are being achieved they won't get a contest from me. It's my way of getting things finished, getting things done.' The enterprise that needs to be completed might be small, like doing the washing, or large, like winning a motor race, but whatever, once it is begun it seems, to some greater or lesser degree, difficult and disorderly, and once it is complete it seems easy and order is restored. Andrew Wallace described to me how to him the only way of completing the task of preparing for a race is to win that race, and that coming second, even if that would win him useful points, would leave him with the jangled, uncomfortable feelings that all introverts feel when a task they have invested themselves in is left incomplete. Andrew said to me, 'Something important to me is that when I get out of the car after winning a race I tend to think that was easy, and that stays with me until the next time I get in the car, and then I think, "This is difficult." I thought it was easy and it's difficult.' Believing that something you have completed was easy is an effective way of maintaining your self-confidence and courage.

The introverts' need for closure and the extraverts' exasperation with the introverts' insistence on finishing something can often been observed at home and at work. At home there is the extravert spouse in the car, impatient to be off, while the introvert spouse is still inside the house, finishing the vacuuming or putting his tools away. At work there is the extravert impatient to get on with the next job while the introvert is doggedly finishing off one job before beginning the next. (On those occasions when the extravert is busy completing a job while the introvert is impatiently waiting the extravert is completing the task not so much to obtain a sense of closure, which is present in part, as to avoid the shame of not living up to what the group, say, the bosses or the neighbours, expect.)

The need for completion with its sense of closure is not just a means of effective organization but also a way of dealing with the introverts' great bugbear, *doubt*.

Introverts are very good at doubting, for, as external reality does not seem to them entirely real, it is rarely taken at face value, and therefore the introvert's relation to it is always open to question, the kind of question which Chuang Tsu asked after he dreamed he was a butterfly, 'Did Chuang Tsu dream he was a butterfly, or did the butterfly dream he was Chuang Tsu?'[20]

Introverts can deal with this propensity to doubt by being sceptical of all statements of fact and intention made by everybody, including themselves, or by being obsessional in checking whether their perceptions are true. Most introverts do both. They doubt what people tell them, and they are constantly asking themselves questions like, 'Did I lock the back door?', and feeling compelled to go and check. The less they value and so trust themselves, the more they doubt, and the more they need to organize obsessively and compulsively to deal with that doubt.

This propensity to doubt and to question can get in the way of *learning facts*, the kind of rote learning expected of students. Extraverts, not doubting the reality of external reality, accept without doubting spelling lists and foreign language vocabulary lists, quickly memorize and reproduce them, while introverts are still asking, 'Why?' and 'Is it really?' Material which is organized into a pattern, like a story or the development of an argument, is remembered equally well by extraverts and introverts.

Untroubled by doubt, extraverts can take life at face value, not wonder about its deeper meaning, and so appear to lead happier lives than introverts. (There is some research which suggests that extraverts are happier than introverts. I doubt this. Extraverts are simply more likely to deny they are unhappy than introverts.) But a lack of scepticism leads many extraverts to be very *suggestible*. They can be an hypnotist's delight, for they can more readily accept what another person tells them than can introverts. But they may not be a delight to themselves, for they can so readily identify with what another person tells them. If another person speaks of joy and happiness, the extravert can feel that joy and happiness, but, equally, if another person speaks of sadness and pain, the extravert can feel that sadness and pain, and imagine that what he feels is his own. Reading a medical textbook can be for an introvert an exercise in scepticism, and for an extravert a pain-racked horror.

What is operating here is not just a contrast in scepticism and suggestibility but a contrast in ways of *dealing with emotion*.

Extraverts value their feelings, for it is through their feelings that they know they are linked with the people and things that maintain their sense of existence. In times of crisis they may say, 'I don't know what my feelings are', meaning, 'I haven't taken the time to sort out my feelings and to label them correctly', but they do not doubt the existence and reality of their feelings. Extraverts show their feelings. It is in times of crisis that introverts can be heard muttering a little verse which encapsulates the introverts' *prejudice* about extraverts.

> When in danger or in doubt
> Run in circles and shout out.

The prejudice which extraverts have about introverts is that introverts have no feelings, for in times of crisis introverts appear to be very calm. They may not be calm – inside they might be a jangled, terrified mess – but outside they appear to be calm, for to show their feelings to others would serve, so they believe, to increase the possibility of uncontrollable chaos.

Since emotion can lead for an introvert to painfully high levels of stimulation, introverts have to develop ways of keeping emotion under control. They do this by separating the emotion from their perception of what gave rise to the emotion, and tucking the emotion away in their unconscious. Wise introverts are aware that they do this and make sure that some time later, in a private place, they remove the barrier to the emotion, and let themselves feel the pain, the anger, and the fear that belonged with what had happened. Unwise introverts, priding themselves on their rationality and fearing the annihilation which they believe such chaotic emotion would bring, continue to hide the emotion away.

But emotion hidden does not disappear. It comes back in nightmares and in fantasies that contain a murderous rage which then has to be guarded against in obsessive and compulsive ways. Hidden emotion, too, wears away at the body, affecting, as is now being increasingly understood, the auto-immune system which, once it begins to lose its efficiency, leaves us prey to all kinds of disease.

The way in which an introvert can think, say, 'My father is preventing me from doing what is most important for me' and not feel the frustration, rage and fear that belongs with that thought Freud called the *defence mechanism of isolation*. Using this defence mechanism introverts can remember unpleasant events from their childhood, but not the emotions that accompanied them. The extravert prefers the *defence mechanism of repression*, where the event is forgotten. Since emotion is not such a threat to the extravert as to the introvert, the emotion attached to the event is not so firmly tucked away in the unconscious, and when events similar to the repressed event come along, out comes the old emotion, but, without the appropriate event to attach it to, seeming strange and inappropriate. Thus the fear aroused by a sexual assault in childhood can reappear in adult sexual encounters while the sexual assault itself is forgotten. Wise extraverts make an inward journey to recover lost events whose emotions still trouble them. Unwise extraverts refuse to make the inward journey, but instead try to find reasons in their external reality for the emotions they feel.

Because extraverts forget events in childhood and introverts forget the emotions of childhood, both can, in adulthood, through their beliefs in the correct way to bring up children, or through their desire to express their violent or sexual feelings, inflict on children the same pain, humiliation and fear that had been inflicted on them. By forgetting what it is like to be a child we can treat children as objects available to meet our needs (including our need to be the perfect parent) and by forgetting what it feels like to be weak, helpless, and in the power of vengeful giants we can declare, 'I was beaten/sexually assaulted as a child and it didn't do me any harm.'

This unfeeling, brutal attitude would be rejected with great revulsion by many extraverts, for they identify very readily with the pain and suffering of others as a way of attaching the emotions they feel from the past to some current event. The emotions they feel are those of a suffering, helpless child, and since, they think, these could not belong to them, a grown adult, they see these emotions as belonging to other people, the sick, the abandoned, the starving. Unaware of the real truth of what they are saying, they cry, 'I know just how you feel' and rush off to save the suffering people. From such projective identification, as Freud would call it, come many acts of great charity, but extraverts who are unaware of this process in themselves wear themselves out in their concern for others, and suffer the pain of the pity they feel for others which they will not allow themselves to feel for themselves.

When the emotion that the extravert feels without the memory of the event which gave rise to that emotion is fear, the extravert looks for something in his external reality which could provoke this fear, and finds external reality full of possibilities. Our body is in external reality as well as internal reality, so it can become the focus for fears of illness and death. External reality contains all kinds of dangerous objects, like spiders and snakes, or it can contain a circle of critical, hostile, rejecting eyes. The possible shame of being the object of such a gaze keeps many extraverts locked in their own homes and weighed down with the psychiatric label of 'agoraphobic'.

It is our *unawareness* of what we do that gets us into the difficulties which bring with them the threat of annihilation. To be aware seems to be the way of protecting ourselves, not just against the unrealistic, cruel demands we make of ourselves but also the unrealistic, cruel demands that society makes of us in our roles as men and women.

# MEN AND WOMEN

Tradition dies hard, and the traditions of what a woman and a man should be has not even fallen ill, much less died. Women are still expected to be mother and men to be the hunters, out there fighting and winning. Even the ambitious career woman feels that she should be 'good at relationships' and 'mother' her staff. In preparing to share the experiences of childbirth and parenting a man feels that he should achieve the status of having the best childbirth and being the best parent. Nora Ephron wrote most unkindly of 'the kind of hopeless father who goes through the whole business under the delusion that it's as much his experience as it is yours. All this starts in the Lamaze classes, where your husband ends up thinking he's pregnant, and let me tell you he's not. It's not his body, it's not his labor, it's not his pain – it's yours, and does any man give you credit or respect for it? No. They're too busy getting in on the act, holding their stopwatches and telling you when to breathe and when to push and taking pictures of the kid coming out all covered with goo and showing them to your friends at dinner parties and saying what a beautiful and moving experience it was.'[21]

The traditional role of the woman is that she should find her fulfilment (her sense of existence) caring for her family (relationship to others) and that if she remains single and childless (rejected and abandoned) she is a person of no account (annihilated). Thus women are expected to be 'people persons', extraverts.

In this way extravert women find it easier than introvert women to fit the pattern that society expects of them, but they may not be able to do this successfully all of their married lives. An extravert woman who has devoted herself to her family and not developed and maintained relationships with people outside her family can find herself alone when her children depart, her parents die, and her husband loses interest in her. Thus many extravert women, after years of being devoted wives and mothers, can find themselves swept by the terrors of annihilation, and live lives of alternations between terror and the cold misery of depression. What little self-confidence they have remaining is undermined further by doctors who dismiss their suffering with, 'It's the menopause', and offer drugs which make the woman too tired to defend herself, much less to do anything effective to change her situation. Wise extravert women in similar circumstances replace ungrateful and absent relatives and household tasks with caring friends and interesting activities.

An introvert woman can interpret the role of wife and mother in terms of achievement – bringing up her children well and providing the home and support that her husband needs. Using her skill in organizing she can make space for her own achievements in a career, a charity, an art or a craft. An introvert woman who manages to live her life this way usually has a clear idea of how necessary it is for her to have a sense of achievement, and, if so, she also knows how much she could have achieved if she did not feel compelled to meet her family's needs before her own. Usually what introvert wives and mothers feel is not so much, 'I could have been immensely successful if I didn't have the family to look after' as 'I could get a lot more done if I wasn't always being interrupted.'

Rebecca West once remarked that a woman's life was made up of interruptions. Because it is, women learn to work in a way which adapts to interruptions. Men working with women are often amazed and aggravated by the way so many women work, having several jobs on the go at once, doing a bit of one and a bit of another, instead of settling down to complete one task at a time. What infuriates some men is the way women working in such an apparently disorganized fashion actually achieve within the time the desired goal.

Introvert women, using their organizational ability, can be extremely effective in working in this way, but they know that doing 'a bit of this' and 'a bit of that' as time and opportunity allows prevents them from using the one skill so essential for achievement, *concentration*.

(I do not wish to suggest that extraverts are not capable of intense and prolonged concentration. I am trying to describe, in part, what introverts do when they are being effective in their internal reality. It is easy to see extraverts being effective in their external reality. I often think that when I am absorbed in writing on a train or in a library I must appear rather peculiar. I stare at people without seeing them, and I suspect that from time to time I mutter or gasp. It is no wonder that introverts are more likely to be classified as mad than are extraverts.)

If what interests you most is in your internal reality, if you can withdraw easily from external reality, and if you can control your emotions, then you are well equipped to operate in the state of concentration which is essential for the creative process, be it creating a symphony or devising a business strategy for the next decade. Some introvert women will battle to make for themselves the time and space necessary to allow them to use this skill of concentration, but others, believing that they must put their family's interests before their own and/or that personal achievement is unfeminine, will not organize their lives so as to do the things which will give them the sense of achievement, clarity and authenticity so necessary for their sense of existence. Thus many introvert women, even as they survey their well-kept home and family or their career of service to others, feel a sense of *waste*, and with that a feeling of sadness and guilt all too hard to endure. If the sense of waste becomes a sense of futility and if with that comes bitterness and a destructive envy of those who can achieve, then the introvert woman becomes a very lonely woman, whose loneliness can then be compounded by the utter loneliness of depression.

It is not just by chance that the best descriptions of this power of concentration by introverts I was given in my interviews with successful people came from introvert men. Ian Padden said, 'I can steer my mind in any direction. I can set my mind to doing that and I won't be distracted. By concentration I can totally ignore everything that's going on', and then told me, when my tape recorder was switched off, about how he had been a subject in sensory deprivation experiments and in experiments in inter-rogation techniques where the aim is to obtain information irrespective of what happens to the person being interrogated. Ian described to me how he used his power of concentration to withstand the effects of sensory deprivation and his interrogators. By setting himself complex mental tasks he could ignore the altered states of sensation and perception and the suggestions and coercions of his interrogators.

What Ian was describing was concentration as a near total withdrawal into internal reality where the introvert feels safe and at home. Sometimes the introvert uses this concentration as a way of achieving an effective, active relationship with external reality. This is what is meant in the Zen teaching about paying attention to what you do as you do it, and in what is taught as 'walking meditation'. When what you are doing is a game, then such attention is 'the inner game', as in 'the inner game of tennis', or, as Andrew Wallace described it to me, the inner game (though he did not call it that) of winning a motor sport championship.

Andrew said, 'I can remember one race last year in Belgium, when I had to win the race to win the championship. I was comfortably out in front, and there was half the race still to go. I knew it was an important race for me. I had to win. I mustn't make any mistakes. Suddenly driving round the circuit, I almost switched off to that. The car was almost driving around on its own. I was just sitting in the car and I began to think to myself, "This is great. I like sitting here. Everything's going really well. Nothing can possibly go wrong." I almost didn't drive the car. It was almost as if somebody else was doing it. When I think back, you have to be doing everything right for it to work. You have to have braking exactly at that point, and changing gear exactly at that point, and checking in the mirror and checking the temperatures, but I was never aware of doing any of that. It doesn't happen every time. It just happens when everything's going perfect. Out of twenty-one races it probably happens five or six times at the most. In Belgium we won the race and won the championship and it was an amazing feeling!'

Not all introvert men intent on winning have the sense to develop this power of concentration because their natural desire to keep their emotions in order has been compounded greatly by their traditional upbringing which taught them that all emotions (other than those of aggression, sex, envy and greed) are despicable, feminine and irrational. As Ian Padden said, 'When emotions come in the door, common sense and reason go out the window.'

The introvert man, as a calm, rational, achieving individual, is an embodiment of the traditional role of men. Accepting this traditional role without question damages the introvert man, for it prevents him from recognizing that isolating emotion from cognition should be merely a temporary defence, not a lifelong practice, for unless we keep our experience whole, that is, what happens to us with what we feel about what happens to us, we cannot understand and so master what happens to us. By *mastering our experiences* I mean absorbing our experiences in such a way that no matter how much we are shaken by them, and how much our sense of self is threatened by them, through our actions and through our meditations upon our experiences, our sense of self emerges, whole and strengthened. The introvert man who fails to do this is left divided and diminished, unable to form the satisfactory relationships which he needs to sustain him, and so becomes increasingly isolated, a prey to his fears and his obsessions.

Similarly, the extravert man who seeks without questioning to fulfil the traditional role of men by being an 'action man' (living entirely in external reality) and a good 'team man' (being a member of a group) is damaged, for by not daring to enter his internal reality in order to meditate upon his experiences and his feelings about his experiences and so understand them, he fails to master his experience. He is left with a sense of emptiness which he experiences as anxiety and often expresses as irritability. The persistent irritability of chronically anxious extravert men makes the people they depend on for their sense of existence withdraw from them, thus increasing the extravert man's anxiety. Unable to acknowledge, much less express, their need for tenderness, they bully and manipulate their wives and children and become crabby, selfish, unlovable old men.

Women and men, as they struggle with their own sense of existence, the threats to it, and the demands of society, commonly seek a solution which, in the long run, adds to their problems. They are drawn to their opposite, extraverts to introverts, introverts to extraverts, and then they discover that at close quarters extraverts and introverts do not always get along well together. Opposites attract – and they repel.

# 5

# Opposites Attract – and Repel

When we fall in love it is with someone who has, or who we think has, attributes which we admire but lack in ourselves and see ourselves as not capable of possessing. The object of our love fills us with wonderment and awe, and with the joyful possibility that now we shall have access to ways of being and behaving from which we thought we were always excluded.

If the object of our love does not return our love, we suffer a double loss, the loss of the object of our love and the loss of what we ourselves might have been.

If the object of our love does return our love, and if there are no obstacles to prevent us from becoming a couple, we then, over the following years, may pause to ponder what George Bernard Shaw said,

> 'There are two tragedies in life. One is to lose your heart's desire. The other is to gain it.'

Some couples fall out of love as quickly as they had fallen in, and either separate or remain together in mutual distrust and dislike. Some couples progress from falling in love to loving, and this is a very painful progress, full of misunderstandings and disappointments.

Some of these misunderstandings and disappointments come from the different outlooks and expectations that men and women have, or from different beliefs stemming from the different classes, races or religions to which each member of the couple belongs. However, underlying all these different beliefs and attitudes are two profoundly different perceptions, the experience of the sense of existence and the threat of annihilation.

All marriages, including those relationships which have the attributes of marriage except the legal sanction, are, it seems, made up of an extravert and an introvert. Presumably there are exceptions among arranged marriages, though I suspect that parents concerned with their children's happiness and not just with financial advantages, choose partners for their children with some awareness of the attraction of opposites. So far, and my researches among family, friends, clients and acquaintances extend over many years and many couples, I have not come across a couple made up of two introverts or two extraverts. I have met couples who thought they were two introverts, but who, when they considered it, realized that one of them was a shy extravert, or an extravert who had developed a passionate interest in his or her internal reality. I have met extraverts who thought that their partner was also an extravert, but was in fact a socially skilled introvert.

**It is the different ways of perceiving the sense of existence and the threat of annihilation that draws a couple together. It is the different ways of perceiving the sense of existence and the threat of annihilation that pushes them apart. Only by being aware of the differences and accepting the other person's perceptions as valid and as valuable as our own can we reconcile our differences and love one another fully.**

# ATTRACTIONS

How often, as we see our friends and relations forming marriages and alliances, we say, 'What on earth does she see in him, or him in her?' This is usually a rhetorical question requiring no answer, for by it we are saying that the marriage is a mismatch.

So it may be, from our point of view. But from the participants' point of view it is not, for each partner has what the other needs, access to a less real reality.

Introverts see in their extravert partner the ability to move freely and securely in external reality. The extravert in question may not feel particularly free or secure, and so may not appreciate that he or she possesses an understanding of external reality which the introvert does not. This understanding may relate to doing practical things, with many introvert wives seeing their extravert husbands having some natural affinity to electric plugs and hammers and nails, and many introvert husbands seeing their extravert wives having a natural affinity with pots and pans and food. More often the special understanding has to do with getting along with other people. In so many couples it is the extravert who faces the social world, dealing with people, making new contacts, and maintaining old ones, while the introvert follows and shelters behind the extravert.

Here the extraverts are doing something which they have done from their earliest days. They can see how social groups work, and, if they have sufficient self-confidence, they can use this knowledge to their own advantage. Even before they start school children can categorize other children as popular or unpopular. Psychologists using these categories of popular and unpopular have studied how easily such children join a group of other children engaged in some activity, and found, not only, as expected, popular children joined more easily than unpopular children, but how popular children achieved this. This has been described as follows:

> 'One secret of the popular children's success lies in their ability, displayed both verbally and non-verbally, to understand the structuring of the group's activities, to recognize what is going on, and to produce well-timed entry bids that accommodate to the group's involvement, thus minimizing any disturbance of the ongoing action. They have learned, in effect, the following guidelines. The don'ts: don't ask questions for information (if you can't tell what's going on you shouldn't be bothering those who do); don't mention yourself or state your feelings about the group or its activity (they're not interested at the moment); don't disagree or criticize the proceedings (you have no right to do so, since you're an outsider). The dos: be sure you understand the group's frame of reference or focus (are they playing house?); understand the participation structure of the activity; slip into the ongoing activity by making some relevant comment or begin to act in concert with the others as if you actually were a knowledgeable member of the group; resist making suggestions or attempting to redirect until you are well into the group.'[1]

These rules are much more easily understood and followed by extraverts than introverts because they relate to what is actually going on in external reality and to being a member of a group rather than an individual. Unpopular extravert children, that is, extraverts who have had their self-confidence undermined at home and/or at school, can understand these rules and, once given the chance, follow them successfully. Popular introvert children allowed into a group will remain popular only if they keep their self-confidence within bounds, do not give too many orders and insist on games which relate to their idiosyncratic interests and not shared common interests.

So in adult life it is the self-confident extravert wife, knowing the rules of joining a group, makes the contacts with the local church, the parent-teacher association and other community groups, while her introvert husband follows her or remains at home, and the self-confident extravert husband who joins Rotary, or the pub darts team, or the local cricket team, while his introvert wife follows him or remains at home. In many marriages the introvert finds that the contact with other people mediated through his partner is sufficient to meet his need. However, if his partner dies or defects, the introvert who has not developed his own circle of friends is threatened with the isolation all introverts dread, a self alone on a seemingly empty planet.

Meanwhile, extraverts see in their introvert partner the ability to move freely and securely in internal reality. The introvert may not feel particularly free or secure, and may not appreciate how the extravert always has this sense of internal emptiness or potential emptiness. Just as extraverts find it very difficult to envisage how external reality could ever seem unreal, so introverts find it very difficult to envisage an emptiness inside. An introvert under stress may feel fragmented, or drained of emotion, or reduced to feeling 'two-dimensional', but there is still some kind of a sense of being filling this internal reality. Introverts find it very hard to conceive of a sense of existence which is experienced as a façade turned outward to the world with nothing, or the possibility of nothing, behind that façade. Hence they do not always appreciate that their partner, who moves so confidently in external reality, looks to them as an anchor, a fixed point in a changing world, a provider of internal stability which the partner feels he cannot provide for himself.

It is not just this sense of *thereness* which the extravert appreciates in his partner. It is the regular habits of the introvert which give such a sense of security. If you always have a need for other people to be present in your life and a more or less conscious anxiety about being left entirely on your own, it is very comforting to have as a partner someone who can be relied on to arrive home at seven every evening, or be putting the children to bed at that time every evening. If you have a tendency not just to get excited, which you enjoy, but to get somewhat over-excited, it is very comforting to have as a partner someone who, by his calmness or by her sensible attitudes, places limits on your excitable behaviour.

Thus an extravert and an introvert together can achieve a structure in each person's two realities which they could not obtain on their own. However, for this to work effectively the couple need to do more than love one another. They have to trust one another.

This came out in my conversation with Judith Stamper and Harry Gration. Judith is the introvert and Harry the extravert. They are not a couple couple but a working couple, presenters of the BBC TV news programme *Look North*. It is a television tradition to have such a programme presented by a man and a woman (in the USA there is usually an ethnic contrast as well) and for there to be some conversation between them which is a mixture of teasing and flirtation. Most of such conversations leave the viewer squirming with embarrassment, but with Judith and Harry the conversation is so amusing that most viewers watch *Look North* not for the news but for the pleasure of seeing Judith and Harry together. It was not always so. I remember when they started working together nearly four years ago Judith did not seem to find Harry's teasing remarks at all funny, whereas now she seems greatly amused and returns tease for tease. I wanted to ask them whether over the years they had actually drawn closer together or whether they had simply become better actors.

Judith said, 'I've always been used to a kind of competitive element, especially on television, and so I'm always on my guard, and somebody who immediately starts to insult you, I'm slightly suspicious of. It was like this when we were first put together. After a time I really got to like him – God knows why – as a person, and that came through work. I can – and I think we both feel the same about it – I can trust Harry in *any* situation in the studio to get me out of a tight spot and vice versa. And if we're both in a spot, we just laugh it off. There's no element of competition or rivalry. If you're playing for yourself you tend to play a card for you to win. If you're playing two together you're bound to win even more. So we're not acting selfishly, we're acting selflessly for the benefit of the whole, because of our personal relationship which is very good. We know each other quite well. I think we are equally competent. Looking at other people, I think we are very good. Each of us has a cracking ego. But somehow our two egos are able to live together well, partly because we complement each other. Another thing that's cemented the relationship is that we have the solid defence of the two of us together against the rest. We know we're both in the same boat doing the same thing, both with the same interests so everything from the latest pay deal through to gossip in the office, we can combat together. That feels better than being alone.'

Harry agreed. 'I think that the basic reason it works is that the competitive element isn't there in any shape or form. In many duos on television there's an element where they're trying to outdo each other all the time. We can say with our hands on our hearts that we have never once fallen out. We've never had a cross word, and that's socially as well, because socially we see a lot of one another.'

However, Judith and Harry are not married to one another. If they were they might find the problems that Ron Janoff and Diana Leidel do. They talked to me about how they had been drawn together by collaborating on some projects and that these experiences of collaboration were one of the most enjoyable parts of their relationship. Ron told me, 'It's very pleasurable to us to have an activity, especially when it involves some kind of presentation, arranging it together and playing off against each other's sense of what it should be.' Each is ambitious. Ron said, 'We both want individually to succeed and for the family to be a success. There's an element of competition between us that's very strong, as sort of keeping equal to one another in terms of levels of responsibility in our jobs and in our incomes.'

When they were first married such collaboration enabled them to 'define our roles around the project, to make the gender role more neutral and go after the part of the role you're more comfortable with. In a sense there isn't woman's work or man's work, or my role or her role specifically.' However, when they launched themselves on 'the joint project of child rearing' such collaboration was no longer so simple. Diana said, 'For Ron to take care of his career and me to take care of the domestic life, I would become terrifically angry. I think that's a very destructive way for a woman to live.'

Fortunately, they are both good organizers and committed to the belief in sharing the care of their son and the household chores, and dealing with issues such as the fact that Ron's job takes him away from home in attending conferences whereas Diana's job does not, thus leaving her with more domestic responsibilities, and the fact that both of them hate doing the laundry. They try to solve the first of these problems by planning their travel in conjunction with Ron's conferences and, according to Ron, buying new clothes instead of washing old ones. Not all such collaboration is to their own good. Diana said, 'If there's one place where neither of us has expertise, like in financial affairs, there the collaboration works against us, for we both collaborate in avoiding it.'

Successful collaboration between a couple consists not just of doing things together but in understanding and supporting one another.

When I talked with Milta McLean Dennis I wondered how her husband, Vernon, felt about his wife being so ambitious and so successful. Milta explained, 'My husband was an only son. His father always placed his mother on a pedestal. His father always used to say to him, "If you find a good woman hold on to her. Your woman is a reflection of you." That's why he lets me be the person that I am. He really does not try to stifle me, because he realizes that I am a reflection of him and I'm good. I'm a good woman. He does not feel threatened by me. In conversations with his friends I can sense that if they were in his position they would feel very threatened.'

Nevertheless, when they were first married they did differ on the importance of having children, and at first Milta did not realize this. 'I wanted to establish my career. I felt that a child would hinder me. I would have to assume the same responsibility that I had been assuming all my life. I wanted to wait, and I wanted to acquire some of the materialistic things I always wanted. Vernon couldn't understand that. His reason for being in existence from a personal standpoint was to have children. All those things we acquired, it was important to him to leave that behind for somebody else. I had never thought about that. I realized how important it was to him. It was all about family and building a family. It was just as important to him as achieving is to me. I could not understand that for a long time. I am at a point now where I would like to have children, because I am confident about my career and I have acquired enough now where I don't need a lot of materialistic things in my life. The difference between my husband's childhood and mine, if he had a candy bar he had it all to himself. If I had a candy bar I had to split it three ways. That was what we had to understand about one another. Those things he took for granted, I didn't. I decided very early in life I was going to get those things for myself and that no one was going to keep me from doing that. But now I've reached a point where I feel confident in raising a child.'

Milta had realized that until we meet the important needs we bring into adulthood from childhood we are not ready to take on the responsibilities of bringing up a child. The main reason that parents do so badly in bringing up their children is because they have entered parenthood with many unmet needs, unmet, perhaps, because society did not provide an opportunity for those needs to be met, or because they believed that they did not have the right to have needs. There are many introvert mothers who lead miserable lives (and so do their children) who will not allow themselves to acknowledge that what they need is to achieve something for themselves and to take pleasure in that.

Milta and Vernon are collaborating so that each can meet the needs arising from their preferred reality, she to achieve and he to have a family, and by understanding each other and allowing each other the right to have these needs their collaboration is successful. Sometimes a couple's successful collaboration is in overcoming the limitations of their preferred realities.

I sat in a garden in Brooklyn and talked to Michael McTwigan, writer and designer, and an introvert who believes that, 'There are immutable laws which you can count on to be true. One of the strongest is the belief that you can solve problems, that you can work things out and come to some solution. Life is a series of goals, a series of questions, a series of events, that must be dealt with.' I described the contrast between the extravert and the introvert. Michael said, 'As we have been talking I have been thinking about my wife, Maria, and how she fits into the extravert mould. Maria forces me to be more social than I would be on my own. I don't mind. I enjoy it. I do enjoy people. It's just that left to my own devices I mightn't see anybody. Not quite that extreme, but almost. A lot of my life is more introspective than Maria's is. I've been that way as long as I can remember.'

Later I talked with Maria who said, 'Other people are tremendously important to me. There are times when I need people too much, and Michael's gift to me is to remind me that I can step back, and that I don't need to be loved or be in touch with all this external world so often. If I just return into myself and to some inner resources which I have, the answer lies also there. Because I love him and trust him, and because he's not a big advice giver, I can take his advice. Likewise, he will retreat. He will simply be so enthused with his love for his family and a few close friends that he is satisfied. But when you have such a small world you lose an openness. That part of Michael which is really free is unconventional and doesn't know the social rules. I remind him that he should just step out a little, step out of the house, break ranks, and because he sees me with this incredible sprinkling of friends he realizes that there can be joy in that. It doesn't have to be serious like all his friendships are. There can be lighthearted acquaintances. I think he gets strength from that. I give him freedom to break from his condition, and he gives me the freedom to break from mine. It's a sweet example of opposites attract. That's the good side. The bad side is that I'm sometimes lonely. I sometimes want a rolypoly extravert of a man. But I would have never married that kind of man. I never even dated that kind of man. So I never really wanted that kind of man. Maybe it's just part of a fantasy.'

A couple's successful collaboration involves not just supporting and promoting each other's good feelings. It means tolerating each other's bad feelings. The fact that Maria could talk of the fantasy she had of 'a rolypoly extravert of a man' in Michael's hearing meant that she had talked about this before and that he had accepted it. The bad feelings that require tolerating most frequently are not those of disappointment but of anger and fear.

The way in which Harry and Judith deal with anger and fear is, I have found, typical of an extravert and introvert couple. When a couple does not understand and accept their differences about handling anger and fear they cause each other a great deal of misery. When they do understand and accept each other's typical way of handling anger and fear they share the problems of life between them. This is what Harry and Judith do.

Harry said, 'Normally I crack a few jokes before we go on air, but if I'm particularly nervous about something I'll say nothing. Judith likes to know precisely what is expected of her professionally when the going gets tough. I tend to let Judith do that, and I accept that she's the boss in the situation. It goes back to the old business of trust. I'm perfectly capable of getting myself out of messes, but she will clear the way, and she probably doesn't realize that's happening.'

Judith replied, 'No, I didn't really, but when you said it I identified with it. In small things I get very annoyed and it's all on top, I wear it on my sleeve, whereas Harry's very silent about it. I may tell people off and I go into what I call a "red mist". But about big things I tend to be very calm and I'll calculate how I'm going to get around it. Harry's the other way around. He worries about big things, thinking the world's going to fall in, and I'm saying, "Don't Harry, you've got to take it step by step. Let's talk about it. It's going to be all right." Whereas about small things, like something going wrong in the programme, I'm all over the place and he's just sitting there saying absolutely nothing.'

I put it to them that Judith did not mind being angry but did not like being frightened, whereas Harry did not like being angry but did not mind being anxious. They both agreed. Harry commented that he always got anxious when the end of the year came around and contracts had to be renewed.

This led us on to talking about hard work. Even though many of us have been brought up with the adage 'self-praise is no praise', there is one piece of self-praise we always allow ourselves, and that is that we work hard, indeed, harder than anyone else we know. What is implied here is that by our hard work we are nobly self-sacrificing. Competition to be seen as the hardest of hard workers is very keen, often between partners. If the couple do not understand why they each work hard, not the specious reasons of 'I have a family to support' and 'Who would look after you all if I didn't?' but the real reasons of being an extravert or an introvert, grave misunderstanding can arise.

Judith and Harry both work extremely hard and both know why. Harry said, 'I am very conscious that we are a commodity that they are using and if they don't want it, they'll get rid of it.'

I asked if in his worrying about the contract there was an element of being rejected.

Harry said, 'Yes, very much so. This is probably the biggest problem in my life. I have always had this feeling that people want to turn against me. I can't explain that, I've had it from the word go. I've always felt the worst about people and I've sometimes acted in a way that would make them feel the worst about me. It's the one thing in my character that I'm trying, even at the tender age of thirty-six to change. And I think I am doing it, actually.'

Judith patted him and said, 'I would never reject you. You'll be all right. You'll always have me.' Harry responded with 'You've boosted my confidence' and went on to say, 'I love to work. I used to work to such an extent that I lost sight of everything. Values. Friends. I always felt that I wanted the people I worked for to say about me at the end of the day, "If there's any doubt about this guy, we can't fault his appetite for work, his ability to go out at any time and any place." That has been my downfall. I have been too soft. Judith told me this many times. You have to learn occasionally to say no, otherwise people won't respect you. I've stood up for myself a little more recently, but I'm still a workaholic.'

Judith said, 'I can really look forward to a weekend off, and when it comes I wish I was working. I'm so restless, wanting to do something constructive. I hate wasting time. I'm also a workaholic, but for different reasons from Harry. I think I have to discriminate and insist on doing the things that I really want to do and I know I can do well, rather than doing it for the sake of doing something.'

As Ron and Diana, and Judith and Harry, show, competition between partners is exhilarating and satisfying when the competing couple love and trust one another. However, when the competition is mixed with envy, the relationship becomes destructive. Jennifer, a splendidly dramatic artist, told me how her introvert husband envies her. 'Both of us,' she said, 'want to be the centre of attention.'

When envy is present in the relationship it is because the envious person is not content with sharing the other person's talents but wants to own them. Envy is 'You have what I wish to possess'. Jealousy is 'You have what is rightly mine', and this occurs in a couple when one person sees the other doing something which he feels capable of doing, would like to do, but dare not do. Thus an extravert husband might envy his introvert wife's ability to be a creative writer, while believing that such creativity is totally outside his range of ability. Or an introvert wife might be jealous of her philandering husband because she has passionate sexual desires and curiosity, but she would not dare to undertake any sexual adventure, or perhaps even dare to acknowledge to herself that she would like to undertake such an adventure.

We get into these tangles of envy and jealousy because we create for ourselves such limited roles. So many introvert women, intent on being good and doing good, construct for themselves lives of moral rectitude, work and duty, with no time to play or be irresponsible, and then find that such a life is rather joyless. Instead of providing for themselves the joy of being irresponsible and playful, they expect that someone else will do this for them, and they fall in love with fascinating extravert rascals. Such a woman either endures the humiliations heaped on her by these rascals, or even a series of these rascals, who, fascinating though they may be, are not good husband material, or the woman makes an equally great mistake of trying to reform the rascal.

Either he resists, causing her much aggravation, or succumbs, whereupon she despises him for being weak.

Many extravert women, wanting a man who is strong, reliable and exciting, 'a buccaneer with a nine to five job', as a wily old American psychologist Robert Claiborne once described this fantasy figure. There are strong, reliable, exciting, introvert men, but their strength and reliability are more likely to be applied to their own interests and achievements than to the extravert woman's desire that he provide her with the necessary level of stimulation and be the fixture that keeps her self secure.

If we do not allow ourselves to know what our needs are, and if we do not allow ourselves the right to have needs, we get ourselves into relationships where we are expecting our partner to do for us what we should do for ourselves. It is like blindfolding yourself to steal apples off a tree so you can pretend to yourself that you are not a thief.

We might be drawn to our opposite like iron filings to a magnet, but unless we are aware of the nature of the attraction we soon find ourselves pulling apart.

# REPULSIONS

I could write a very large book about how an introvert and an extravert as a couple can disagree. Whenever a couple argue, separate, divorce, whenever one of them becomes depressed or agoraphobic, obsessional, manic or schizophrenic, whenever one murders the other, or commits suicide, whatever issues they fall out over, fidelity or money, careers or holidays, friends or relatives, the basic cause of their disagreement is that each does not understand and take seriously that the other has a different perception of the sense of existence and the threat of annihilation.

Often the disagreements and misunderstandings arise simply because each does not appreciate that the other requires a different level of stimulation. The couple where the extravert wants to be out partying and the introvert wants a quiet night at home is commonplace. It is not just that introverts find too much stimulation painful, but that what stimulation they do enjoy they deal with differently. Jo Brans met her second husband when they were both teaching. Now he is still teaching while she stays at home writing. She told me, 'When we were teaching we realized that at the end of the day I would want silence and he would want to talk. Now he is an active arts consultant, often commuting between cities, while I stay at home writing. When he arrives home of an evening he'll say, "Tell me what you did today." If I've had lunch with a friend he'll say, "Now I want you to tell me everything that you said." I just have no desire at all at that time of day to keep going. I can take one encounter and just brood over it for three days. Replay it, play all the parts, what I would have said. If you're still working over an encounter you don't want another one. Lots of times when Willem wants me to tell him everything that was said, I'm not quite ready to talk about it. I'll bring it out later when I've come to some sort of conclusion about it or have something to say about it. Willem's always waiting for me to drop something. It's nice because it means that he's really interested in what I have to say.'

Unfortunately, not all extraverts are so interested in the introvert's ruminations. By the time the introvert is prepared to comment on something, the extravert has lost all interest in it or forgotten it. Without a positive response, the introvert ceases to offer his or her observations and becomes increasingly silent.

As a couple cease to be enchanted with their differences and find such differences aggravating, the prejudices that extraverts and introverts have about one another come to the fore. The calmness and silence of the introvert the extravert interprets as having no feelings, and, since the extravert values feelings, a lack of feelings can be regarded only with contempt. The extravert does not realize that behind the façade of calmness and silence the introvert can be in emotional turmoil, a state which the introvert finds very frightening. Meanwhile, the extravert's display of feelings the introvert regards as insincere and exaggerated histrionics. The introvert can be aware of an emptiness behind the extravert's performance, but instead of feeling sympathy for the terror of an empty internal reality which the extravert feels, the introvert is contemptuous.

I have met many couples who have suffered a great tragedy and who are unable to mourn together. The extravert will say, 'She's got over it. She hates it when I get upset', when in fact the introvert has made no progress at all in coming to terms with the tragedy and is terrified of losing control and shattering, something which her husband's distress threatens to do to her. The common pattern where the wife, an extravert, is agoraphobic is that the wife is trying to get from her husband a response which shows that he has got feelings other than anger. He, under the guise of being the calm, rational, sensibly concerned husband, is terrified of losing control, and, despising her histrionics, retreats further behind his calm front as she, more and more terrified of being left alone, behaves increasingly outrageously.

The prejudices which extraverts and introverts have about each other prevent them from taking seriously the other person's belief in the purpose of life. Couples rarely say to one another, 'My purpose in life is to achieve', and, 'My purpose in life is to be in close contact with other people.' Instead they fight over things like holidays. The introvert is against holidays. 'When you get back from a holiday there's nothing to show for it.' The extravert is for holidays. 'It's important to do things as a family.'

When there is little understanding and acceptance of one another's unstated but powerful point of view, the disagreements are deeper than just over holidays.

If the man is the introvert and the woman the extravert, he can become very weary of her need for other people. He wants a quiet home, and she fills it with family and friends. He wants her to pay attention to him and minister to his needs, while she is caring for all and sundry. He wants her to stay quietly at home and she is out gallivanting around. Unable to say, 'I need you, I am jealous of the attention you give to other people, and I am frightened that you will go away one day and not come back', he becomes cantankerous and difficult to please. If, as well, he feels that he is not achieving, that life is passing him by, and that he has done nothing of note, then he finds himself dangerously alone, and chaos threatens. If, on the other hand, he is achieving and more success is possible, he can find that she does not appreciate his work as *his* achievement, but only a source from which she can acquire resources to maintain her involvement with other people. Instead of telling him how wonderful he is, she invites her relatives to dinner. Worse, she may look at what he has achieved and say, 'We've got all we need. Take things easy. Don't work so hard. You're too ambitious.' She means it kindly, even though her words are motivated by the fear that his ambition may force her to leave her family and friends, and that over-work on his part might result in his death, and the possibility of such aloneness terrifies her.

When there is little understanding and acceptance of one another's point of view and the man is the extravert and the woman the introvert, the man may meet part of his need for being a member of a group by being a good team man at work and in some kind of team sport in his leisure, but along with this he has the extravert's romantic and conventional notion of what family life should be. He wants a family life, but he expects his wife to carry out all the work that family life entails. She is the one who should send birthday presents and Christmas cards; she is the one who should keep the cake tins replenished and the house sparkling clean; she is the one who should bear the children, visit his great-aunt, sew buttons on his shirts and make a good cup of tea. His introvert wife, as much as she loves her children, enjoys running an efficient household and meeting her duties to relatives, does not wish to be enveloped in family life so much that she cannot achieve anything for herself. One of my introvert women colleagues, whose marriage has all the outward signs of immense success and happiness, told me that the two happiest years of her life was when her husband was posted abroad, her children were married and living elsewhere, and she could get on with her research. 'Peace, perfect peace, with loved ones far away.'

Extravert husbands will often protest that they understand how their wife needs 'an interest' outside the home, but they see this interest as something not very important. (Only men have interests which are important.) The woman's 'interest' can easily be put aside for something really important, like the football club dance. Some introvert women spurn such 'interests', knowing that they cannot provide a sense of achievement and so are not worth the trouble of making time for them. Some introvert women know, or discover, that if they acquire 'an interest' which becomes an absorbing passion promising real achievement, their extravert husband will not be pleased.

Jo Brans told me how, when she married for the first time, she stopped writing. After having two children she decided to go back to school. 'My mother said, "If you do this it's going to destroy your marriage", and she was absolutely right. I went back to school. My responses to him were different, and he just couldn't handle that. My self-confidence suffered a lot in that marriage. He did a number on me, without really meaning to. He used to tell me that I was not good with people. He told me I was shy, and I had never thought of myself as shy, but he told me that I was. He didn't say it loud and clear, but in all sorts of ways he made me feel that I had to hide behind him. So I saw him as this extravert with lots of social skills which I thought at the time I didn't have. He constantly summed me up as being a kind of needy person. Eventually I didn't believe those things about myself, especially when I went back to school. I did very well at school. I made good friends. I don't want to say he did it, because you only accept what other people tell you about yourself if you're willing to accept that, but I had come to think that I wasn't a good member of a group, and I went back to school and I saw that I wasn't this shy, lone person that I had begun to think I was. He was very shocked when I went away. He was very unhappy. I don't think it was because he was so madly in love with me. I think it was because it must have threatened his whole world view when the worm turned. We've stayed friends. If I had been smarter and grown up at the beginning of the marriage and said, "I'm going to do this and do that," I'm sure it would have been fine. I'm sure he would not have objected. I'm sure he became tyrannical – that's too strong a word – because he got used to seeing me in a certain way, whereas, when I married Willem, we met as equals.'

An introvert woman who does not accept her need to achieve can try to meet her need to achieve without admitting that she has it by marrying a man who she hopes will do her achieving for her. However, her partner, an extravert, may want to achieve so as to secure his membership of a group, and he may be extremely successful at that, but his success can never be her success, for reflected glory is no glory at all. If he does not succeed she is left frustrated, shamed and resentful with a man she despises. I saw this enacted one day when I was in a line at a supermarket checkout and ahead of me was a well dressed, middle class, elderly couple. The wife stood with her cheque-book ready while he filled the trolley. When this was complete he said to her, 'Shall I put this in the car?' 'Do,' she commanded, and, as he went off, she turned and said, mainly to the world at large, but partly to the girl at the till and me, 'I can get the shopping done in half the time, but he will insist on coming. He thinks he's helping me, and I have to let him think that he is.' The written word cannot convey the contempt with which she said this.

What was being played out here was another scene in the misunderstandings between a couple, he, in this case, being the extravert, wanting to help, wanting to be useful, hoping to be needed if not loved, and she, the introvert, the organizer, the controller, the leader, he fearing her anger, and she despising his fear.

The misunderstandings are based on the differing perceptions, not just of the sense of existence and the threat of annihilation, but of anger and fear.

Thus, for Ron and Diana, though they can laugh about it, the problem of the laundry rests on this basic difference. Diana, the introvert, experiences having to do the laundry as an impediment, something which prevents her from getting on with her projects, not just those in her art and work, but in developing herself, finding challenges and meeting them. Whenever we are prevented from fulfilling the necessary conditions of our existence, however briefly, we become frightened. This fear can, without being noticed as fear, in a millisecond be turned into anger. Ron, being an extravert, dislikes anger for it is the emotion which disrupts a group and threatens rejection. Even though he knows that their relationship is far too strong to be disrupted by the necessity of doing the laundry, he still experiences a sense of danger. So he tries to circumvent the whole issue, even to the point of rushing out and buying new clothes. How often he has done this, I do not know, but he does seem to have a seemingly endless array of splendid clothes.

Because they understand one another's different responses to fear and anger, Ron and Diana, like Judith and Harry, are able to work out ways of dealing with their responses which do not disrupt their relationship.

Without understanding and accepting no such reconciliation is possible.

# RECONCILIATIONS

The starting point is recognizing that your partner does not see things as you do, and that a different perception is not evidence of madness or badness. Not everyone wants to achieve and win, and not everyone wants to snuggle into a group. Nor is there any overall advantage or any kind of superiority in being an extravert or an introvert. The advantages of being one are balanced by the disadvantages, and a world composed solely of extraverts or of introverts would be a crazy place.

Somehow, we have to allow our partner the right to see things differently from us, even though we cannot appreciate fully what that perception is. We need to understand our partner, but we also need to understand that we can never understand fully. Whenever we say, 'I know just how you feel,' we are mistaken. We can never know exactly and totally how another person feels. Our perception of what another person is feeling can be right *up to a point*, and just as we can never know what it feels like to give birth until we actually give birth, so we can never know what it is like to be an introvert unless we are an introvert, or what it is like to be an extravert unless we are an extravert. Thus in a couple there is always a gap in one another's understanding.

Over the years I have made a tremendous effort to understand what an extravert means by a sense of internal emptiness or potential emptiness, and why the absence of loved ones should be more devastating than simple longing and loneliness. I think I understand, but it is an understanding in my head, not in my heart, such as I feel when an introvert says, 'I can't get it together. I've achieved nothing and everything is going out of control.'

Extraverts have the same limitations in their understanding of introverts. When I laddered Molly with her husband Mark listening, Mark said, 'I think I would have expected different responses from Molly. I may have misread her, but I think that going through life, attempting to have a clear view of your world and your life, is very subjective to Molly, which is all right, but it has to be restricted to her subjective view of what's clear. Molly changes her mind about what's clear. What's clear one day might be something entirely different the next. Molly's a little flaky about things.' What Mark had not picked up was that the clarity for which an introvert strives is an evolving clarity. Introverts who lack self-confidence like to feel that they possess the Absolute Truth and Absolute Clarity, for in their desperate need for security they are prepared to lie to themselves. Introverts who value themselves accept that we can never have absolute certainty and absolute clarity, but that we can, day by day, gain increasing clarity, and that the process itself is very satisfying.

In realizing that there are limits to our understanding we can come to see how important it is to have access to different perceptions of reality, both external and internal. Our partner's different perception can illuminate aspects of reality to which we are blind, and provide solutions which lie outside our range of competence. Thus through our partner we can elaborate our sense of existence.

To be able to do this we have to be in a relationship of two equals, two adults, and not in the power struggle of one trying to control the other.

If we are more concerned with warding off the threat of annihilation rather than elaborating our sense of existence, we see our partner's function as being part of our defence. Then we cannot allow our partner to act freely. We have to try to control our partner and turn his actions into those which we desire. Extraverts want their partner always to be there, warding off isolation and abandonment. Introverts want their partner to fit into their structure of control and organization. Some couples evolve a balance of power consisting of 'I will always be here so long as you do what I tell you: I will do what you tell me so long as I know exactly where you are every minute of every day.' Such a couple are prisoners bound by self-imposed chains of fear and weakness. Some couples, in their attempts to make their partner meet their needs, fight a war of attrition, where there is no weapon which they would not stoop to use. Guilt ('After all I've done for you'), touchiness ('Now you've upset me'), blame ('You've made me ill'), threat ('I won't be responsible for what I do'), blackmail ('Unless you do what I want I'm leaving'), counterblackmail ('If you make me do that you'll be sorry'). They are eternal children, eternally fighting.

In such couples, seeking to control one another, the word 'love' is frequently used. 'If you really loved me, you would do what I want.' 'Because I love you you must do what I want.' Love as a means of control is not love at all. It is just a commodity used for rewards and punishments.

If we truly love someone, we love that person simply because the person exists. The person may, incidentally, meet our needs, or help keep the threat of annihilation at bay, but these are serendipitous bonuses, not the purpose of our love. In love we wish the object of our love well, and, if that 'well' does not include us, we can feel sad for ourselves losing such joy, but not anger and resentment, for the fact that we love a person does not put that person in our debt. We can feel anger and resentment because that person has used up our precious time or squandered our financial resources, but not for having been the object of our love. Love is a free gift.

This is not the concept of love which has been presented by Hollywood and its followers for as long as I can remember. In this tradition, when one character says, 'I love you', the character to whom this is said has to respond with, 'Then I'll do what you want,' or else feel guilty. It is as if 'I love you' evokes some universal and immutable and totally commanding law which all must obey and which provides an excuse for whatever bad behaviour which might follow. 'I love you and therefore you must do what I want.' 'I love you, but if you don't do what I want I will stop loving you.' 'I love you, and so I shall desert my partner and our children.' 'I love you, and if you don't love me in return I shall get drunk/kill myself, /murder you/steal/make you feel guilty.' All this makes stories for films and television, but instead of these stories being seen as an account of how insecure and childish adults try to control and manipulate one another, it is taken as a faithful reproduction of the course of true love.

If the course of true love does run smooth, then, according to the myth, the couple live happily ever after. This 'happily ever after' used to mean that the man did manly things and the woman did womanly things, and that there were areas of mutual incomprehension. Men were not supposed to understand everything about women, and women everything about men. Then, in the 1960s, along came popular psychotherapy, and with that the notion that two people could understand one another totally and perfectly.

The desire to be understood can be simply the desire to be accepted as the person that we know ourselves to be. We do not expect the other person to know why we are as we are, just that we are as we are. However, some people, particularly those who doubt their own value and worth, express a passionate desire to be understood which is not so much a desire to be accepted as a desire to avoid further pain. It is an attempt to control the other person by manipulating that person's sense of guilt and goodwill. It is, 'If you really understood me you would know what hurts me and you would not do it ever.'

Thus the words 'love and understanding' come together as a romantic myth that states, 'Because I love you and you love me you will do what I want and you will never hurt me.'

When in childhood we try, and so often fail, to follow the rules and regulations that adults place upon us, we comfort ourselves with the thought that when we grow up life will be better. Indeed, this is what adults promise us. If you are good, Prince Charming will rescue you, the Sleeping Beauty will awake into your arms, and you will live in love and understanding for the rest of your life.

So, in adult life, when Prince Charming refuses to do what you want, no matter how much you love him, and Sleeping Beauty is as dozy as ever, without any idea, or any interest in any idea of what you really are, you feel cheated. 'I've been good. Where's my reward?'

Our belief in the myth of love and understanding prevents us from realizing that the very conditions which attracted us to our partners are the conditions which prevent us from understanding our partner fully, or our partner understanding us. Many people do not wish to realize this, for in doing so we have to confront the essential loneliness of the human condition. We each have to live in our own world.

Yet, if we do not confront the essential loneliness of our condition, we can never establish the kind of relationship with other people which gives unthreatening warmth and contact while allowing us to enjoy the freedom of our aloneness. Such a relationship cannot be created by a couple who are engaged in being two good children playing house, yet this is what so many couples do, still trying to prove to their parents that they are good. (So much of our interest in sex has nothing to do with love, but with being naughty, which good children must be if occasionally they can be themselves and so preserve their sanity.)

When we live a life where love is seen as a commodity to be given as a reward or withheld as a punishment, we become very lonely and very threatened. Under such threat we may feel forced to use the most desperate of defences, madness.

# 6

# A Choice of Madness

In the creation of the Successful Self it is necessary to know how we experience our self, not just whether as an extravert or an introvert, but as good or bad. Experiencing oneself as bad can force a person to use those desperate defences which psychiatrists call the symptoms of mental illness. Many people waste much of their lives locked into such defences, but others use such a situation as 'the dark night of the soul' out of which liberation comes.

When I lead a workshop for people who are in some way involved in 'the caring professions' I usually ask them, 'Do you experience yourself as being essentially good or essentially bad?'

Some of the people look puzzled and say, 'Well, I've never thought about it', and, having thought about it, decide, 'Good, I suppose.'

The others respond quite differently. They know immediately and precisely what my question means. Their belief in their essential badness is central to their awareness of themselves, and all they have to decide is how to frame their answer for an audience. Some will say, 'Bad, of course.' Others will say, 'Not so much bad as not acceptable. That's what I feel.' Whether they use 'bad' or 'unacceptable', they reveal in other places in the group's discussions that they work endlessly at overcoming their sense of badness and unacceptability and are therefore exceptionally good, and that at periods in their life they have experienced depression and perhaps some of those other states which psychiatrists call mental illness. They are all good, fine, caring people, but only those who know them see this. To themselves they are not good.

This sense of being 'not good' ranges, so I have found, from feeling unacceptable, through a sense of essential badness, to a conviction that at the person's core is something so evil that, if it were revealed, other people would not only reject and scorn it but would be harmed by it. Thus some people will say, 'I always feel there is something wrong with me.' This 'something wrong' can be felt as being in every situation and in every way unacceptable to oneself and to other people. Or the 'something wrong' can be felt as a badness, a propensity to do bad things, to give way to bad impulses and bad feelings, which are always to do with anger. Or the 'something wrong' can be felt like a black, filthy rottenness.

This black filthy rottenness can be felt in two ways. Sometimes it seems to be stuck to the outside of our self, as if the filth had been thrown by someone and stuck to our soul. This kind of feeling can come upon us when, in adult life, other people treat us badly, rejecting us, shaming us, dragging us down, involving us in acts which we knew were wrong. It is no wonder that so many religions have rituals of washing away sin.

However, some people experience a sense of badness which no amount of spiritual washing will remove. They feel that their very self is impregnated with filth, an evil which can never be removed. Every day they are locked in a battle between good and evil. Some such people are psychiatric patients, but many more are people holding down responsible jobs, caring for others, and achieving levels of sheer goodness never achieved by those of us who live comfortably with our self.

If you feel good about yourself, you don't have to think about being good.

But if you believe that you are bad, evil, unacceptable to yourself and to other people, you have to work hard all the time to be good.

**If you believe that you are bad, evil, unacceptable to yourself and to other people then, if you are an extravert, you believe that if people discover how bad you are, you will be rejected, or, if you are an introvert, you believe that you can never achieve, never get things right, never keep things under control. Thus, believing that you are bad means that you are always threatened with annihilation.**

Why do people place themselves in this jeopardy?

# 'THERE IS SOMETHING WRONG WITH ME'

Babies do not come into the world believing that there is something wrong with them. They arrive, pleased and curious, and ready to complain when something is not to their liking. But soon it is made clear to them that their complaints are not acceptable. Babies find this unfair, and then it is made clear to them that they themselves are not acceptable.

The belief 'I am bad' is a conclusion which a young child, often no more than two or three, draws from a very painful experience. The child (and this applies to girls as well as boys, even though here I use the masculine pronoun) finds himself in a situation where the adults on whom he depends, usually his parents, are inflicting great pain on him, and he cannot escape. Often it is a tussle over toilet training. His small bladder or bowels have shed an impossible load, or, empty, have failed to produce what the parent has ordered to be produced. Often it is about food. His small stomach is full and his parent insists that he eats. Or his distended stomach is empty and his equally starving parent ignores his demands for food. Sometimes the reason for the punishment is beyond his comprehension. His parent is angry with someone else, but takes his anger out on the child. Sometimes the child is being blamed, or he thinks he is being blamed, for some disaster, like a parent dying or deserting the family. Sometimes the child feels frustrated, or unjustly treated, becomes angry, and is punished for being angry. Sometimes the child is used as a sexual object, threatened by the user, and unprotected and betrayed by those who should have cared for him.

The child's correct assessment of any of these situations is, 'My bad parent is inflicting pain on me.' He might not have the language to think a precise thought in words, but he knows that he is the victim of a bad parent.

But even as he thinks this, he realizes that he is in even greater danger. The person on whom he depends has become his enemy. He is rejected, alone, and all that formed his security has crumbled and vanished. He is completely helpless. He is faced with the annihilation of his self.

It is the sense of complete helplessness which is so devastating. Faced with great danger, so long as we feel there is something we can do to protect and support ourselves – bar the door, hold the hand of a friend – we can be terrified but not annihilated. But when we are alone and prevented from all action, the state of helplessness can become the state where we believe our self will be wiped out.

And so we act. To preserve our sense of self we will sacrifice whatever is necessary. Sometimes it is our body. The only act of self-determination left open may seem to us to be that of suicide. Sometimes what we sacrifice is our self. We give away something of our self in order to save our self.

This is what the child helpless in the power of a dangerous parent does. He does what people often do. When we cannot change what is, we change how we define what is.

The situation of 'My bad parent is inflicting pain on me' is redefined. It becomes, 'I am bad, and so deserve the pain my good parent is inflicting on me.'

Now the child is no longer helpless. He is the author of his own disaster. His parent is still his good parent. Order has been restored.

For some children the situations which produce such helplessness and require such a redefinition occur only once or twice. However, for some children, indeed, many children, such situations occur again and again, and with such ferocity that the child is forced to perform an additional act of redefinition in order to hold the first redefinition in place. 'I am bad, and so deserve the pain my good parent is inflicting on me,' becomes, 'I am bad, and so deserve the pain my good parent is inflicting on me, and when I grow up I shall punish bad people in the way that I was punished.' Thus can the child, when adult, force his children to see themselves as bad in order to make them good. He can say, 'I was beaten as a boy and it never did me any harm', without realizing that the harm it did him was to think that there was no harm. Now he has acquired the right amount of insensitivity to other people's pain to be able to perform, when called upon if required by those in authority, and he respects authority, the tasks of a soldier, a policeman, a prison warder, a concentration camp guard, a torturer, an executioner.[1]

Knowing yourself to be bad gives an illusion of control and security. If we believe ourselves to be basically bad (while, of course, working hard to be good) we can believe that disasters do not occur randomly, by chance. They occur because we are bad. We deserve them. If we are bad and work hard at being good, we can prevent disasters occurring to us and our loved ones.

We hang on to this illusion of control and security because we cannot, so we believe, bear to re-experience the sense of helplessness we knew as a child. By our diligent goodness aeroplanes will not fall out of the sky, winds will not turn into hurricanes and cells into cancers. Our fear of helplessness is compounded by our love of magical power, and so we stop our ears when someone says, 'You're not bad. You should value and accept yourself, and that means every part of yourself.'

We can be so frightened of the sense of helplessness we experienced as a child that we do not even allow ourselves to remember it, much less contemplate it and so realize that we felt that helplessness *only* because we were a small child and dependent on others. As an adult we do not have to be dependent on other people. We can look after ourselves. Other people in the guise of nurses and doctors, or police and prison warders, or muggers and rapists, or terrorists and kidnappers, may take charge of our body, restrict our movement and deny us choice, but they cannot take over our minds *unless we let them*. Being in a situation of physical powerlessness is hugely unpleasant, and being tortured and threatened with death is even more so, but even these extreme situations need not threaten our sense of self. Reports from those people who survived such extreme situations show how they had not given their kidnappers and torturers the power to annihilate their sense of self.

However, many of us give this right to just ordinary people. The man who believes, 'If my wife leaves me I'll be finished' has given his wife the power to annihilate him which his mother had when he was a little boy. The woman who says, 'I'll do anything to stop my father criticizing me' has not withdrawn from her father the power he had to annihilate her when she was a little girl.

Often we do not withdraw the gift of this power because giving other people the power to annihilate us seems to be one way of holding on to them. Becoming indifferent to another person's anger or criticism can seem like becoming indifferent to that person, especially when their anger and criticism was the only evidence we had that they were not indifferent to us, and we did so much want them to care for us. One of my clients, telling me about how her mother was always wrapped up in her own affairs, said, 'I always wanted to give my love to my mother but she has always ignored it. That just makes me feel like a nothing. What have I got to do to her to love me?'

What most of us felt as children that we had to do to get our parents' love was to obey them and to be and to become the person our parents wanted us to be. If we were lucky we had parents who did not issue many orders or impose many punishments, and who wanted us to be a person not very different from the person we already were. Very few of us are so lucky.

Most of us spent our childhoods trying to please parents who were very difficult to please.

Some of us become so good at pleasing our parents that we did not realize that we were very obedient. To disobey was unthinkable, and so we never thought of it. In adult life we say, 'I had a happy childhood. My parents were the best parents a child could have.' I often meet such people when they come as clients, distraught and complaining of those miseries which psychiatrists call the symptoms of mental illness.

One was Marie, locked in the frozen misery of depression. Her childhood, so she told me, had been happy, her parents, especially her father, were wonderful. As the wife of a lawyer and the mother of three children, she showed all the signs of being an obedient, well brought up daughter.

'Did you ever disobey your parents?' I asked.

She said, 'I'd argue with my mother. Never with my father. One look from him was enough.'

'What if one look had not been enough? What if you had persisted?'

She looked puzzled. 'I don't know. I've never thought about it.' This is the ultimate in obedience, to obey and no longer be conscious of the punishment for disobedience.

At that point, our first meeting, it would have been cruel to press her, for that meant asking her to remember that in her childhood she had felt the fear she was feeling now, the drenching terror of annihilation. The look with which her gentle father controlled her was the look which reminded her that if she broke the strict and rigid rules of her family she would be unacceptable to the family, and so she would be cast out of family life and into a dark and dangerous chaos.

Not all parents manage to control their children with a look. Many resort to endless, carping criticism. Such criticism has an additional advantage for the parent. It provides a vehicle for the expression of the parent's frustration, anger, resentment and envy of people other than the child.

When a couple set a pattern of communication which includes massive and continual mutual criticism their children, as they each learn to speak, learn this critical interactive style which they then use on one another. This family style of continual mutual criticism is displayed nightly on our television screens in soap operas and situation comedies, and we watch with interest and laugh. In real life it inflicts on all the family members continual and appalling misery.

Because this style of communicating within the family is continual, it becomes like the air we breathe, and thus many people do not consciously realize that they are continuously under attack, involved in a war of attrition which wears them down and fills them with that sense of badness and unacceptability.

To maintain this continual criticizing style and to defend oneself against the attacks made by other family members it is necessary to see all unacceptable behaviour as arising from a fault within the person and having nothing to do with the relationships between that person and other members of the family. Thus, many mothers write to me at *Chat* magazine and ask, 'How can I control my naughty child?' without recognizing that the child's naughtiness is a response to people and events. One mother gave as an example of her six year old son's naughtiness the fact that he refuses to wear the glasses that have been prescribed. She does not recognize that six year old boys wearing glasses can be seen as figures of fun by their classmates and that there is something strange, even frightening, in knowing that your surroundings appear different when you look at them through glasses. Instead of seeking the cause of her son's behaviour in the relationship between him and his world, she locates an evil cause within him. In essence he is bad, and so, as I gathered from the rest of her letter, he has accepted his mother's definition of him and he acts in accordance with her expectations. Treat your child as if he is bad and, to satisfy you, he will act as if he is.

Caroline, for as long as she can remember, has been told by her parents that she is both mad and bad. Why any parent would see madness and badness in an enchantingly beautiful tiny daughter seems crazy until one knows that the craziness lay in the marriage of two people who were each desperately unhappy and who, rather than confront the source of their unhappiness, their own difficult childhoods, took their bitterness and anger out on their child. As in many families, a child was selected as the scapegoat, the cause and the bearer of all the family sins. In biblical times the scapegoat, having been loaded with the tribe's sins, was turned out into the wilderness. Children as scapegoats are not so fortunate. All they can do to escape from their family is to go mad or die.

Children who are scapegoated in working class families might, if they are beaten sufficiently, be rescued by some outside agency, but scapegoated children in middle and upper class families are not so lucky. The maltreatment of such children rarely comes to light, and when the child responds to the parents' maltreatment with the required madness or badness the legal and medical authorities conspire with the parents to locate the madness or badness in the child.

This is what happened to Caroline. Her father held a high position in the county and was very well known and respected. What was not known was that he frequently beat his daughter and did not speak to her except to belittle her. Nor was it known that his charming wife, so respected for her charitable work, neither protected Caroline from her father's brutality nor supported her with love and praise. She cared a great deal for Caroline, but that did not stop her inflicting on Caroline an endless stream of criticism.

Caroline is a talented artist, and an introvert, but she has never been allowed to achieve, or even think that she is entitled to achieve. She blamed herself for the disasters in her life and for her inability to work.

The main problem she had about working was her sleep pattern. She found it hard to go to sleep, so she went to bed late and then could not wake up before noon. She presented this to me as an example of her incorrigible faults. When I asked her to describe just what happened, she told me how she feared to sleep because her dreams were of pain and punishment, and as she woke she was filled with a massive, overwhelming sense of guilt.

If, from earliest childhood, you have been told by your parents that you are the cause of their every discomfort and disappointment, you acquire a very powerful sense of guilt and damnation. This sense of guilt and damnation will prevent you from realizing the injustices which your parents heap upon you, because merely to think that your parents are unjust is evidence of your own weakness and wickedness.

So it was very difficult for Caroline to tell me of the lifelong injustices she had suffered. She preferred to tell me about all the wicked things she had done, evidence of her own essential badness. Gradually, however, she allowed herself to acknowledge what she knew, that her behaviour which had been labelled by her parents and psychiatrists as 'mad' and 'bad' was a response to the way her parents persecuted her. She could then acknowledge that she felt much better whenever her parents were away.

However, she could not separate herself entirely from her parents, for she knew that her mother needed her as a support in her lonely marriage. I wondered whether it would be possible for Caroline's mother to change her behaviour towards Caroline, so when she visited me to ask about Caroline's progress I, in telling her how the core of Caroline's problems was her lack of self-confidence, risked suggesting that she should refrain from criticizing Caroline but only praise her. This proved to be a total failure. For some weeks after that she prefaced every criticism of Caroline with, 'I know I'm not supposed to say this.' 'I know I'm not supposed to say this, but your room is a pigsty. You've had those dreadful friends of yours here again. You've ruined my life . . .' and so on.

The only way to deal with such a parent is to laugh at her, and this Caroline was increasingly able to do. As well, she set about the task of giving up taking the anti-depressant drugs which her psychiatrist had been prescribing for some ten years. When she first took this drug Caroline had been eager to accept the psychiatrist's opinion that she suffered from a mental illness. That way she did not have to confront the issues of responsibility and justice. When the drug initially made her feel much better, indeed, extremely active, she was greatly pleased, but when she abruptly stopped taking the drug she plunged into a near immobile depression. She resumed taking the drug and, when capable of action, she went to the library to find out about the drug. It was a monoamine-oxidase inhibitor and, like all the anti-depressant drugs constructed to this pattern, has a chemical structure very similar to amphetamine. Caroline was familiar with 'speed', and so she recognized why this drug made her feel impelled into activity and why stopping taking it suddenly was so devastating. She knew that she would have to come off the drug, and that that would be difficult.

There ought to be bravery medals for people who manage to end their addiction to tranquillizers and anti-depressants. It requires great courage and persistence, and the life they save is their own. Caroline managed to end her addiction and to venture back into the world of work. She found that the hardest addiction to end was to cigarettes who were, as she told me, 'loyal, constant, warm, loving, accepting friends', something her family had never been.

Often the criticism which parents heap upon their children contains 'the shadow of the ancestor',[2] that is, the child is seen as having inherited 'madness' or 'badness' from some shameful, despicable ancestor. Belief in inherited characteristics is another form of the refusal to accept responsibility for one's own actions but rather to locate the cause of one's displeasure as a badness within another person. National leaders do this to their country's enemies, psychiatrists to their patients, and parents to their children.

Families construct their stories, their family history, which defines who they are and, therefore, what they are allowed to do. Children born, say, in Belfast to a Catholic family with a long history of service and sacrifice to the cause of Free Ireland will find that their family's story, as interpreted to them by their parents, will include the expectation that they will show service and sacrifice to the cause, and not scamper off to England for a life of ease and safety. Similarly, children born into a family whose history includes 'a black sheep', an uncle in a psychiatric institution, a grandmother's 'nervous breakdown' will find that their family's story, as interpreted to them by their parents, may include the expectation that they will take on one of these roles.

To study how a family creates and interprets its own history and uses its interpretation to predict the future of its children is very difficult. The shared meanings that a family create are subtle and complex, and difficult for an outsider to observe and understand. It is infinitely simpler to draw up a family tree, mark in black any family member who showed, according to the family history, some 'mental instability', and to explain the resulting pattern in terms of some yet unidentified gene.

If, as a child, you hear your relatives speculating as to whether you have inherited the gene which made Uncle Henry go mad, you will not feel comforted, but, rather, frightened and helpless. There is nothing we can do about an inherited gene. Believing that you are fated mad or bad becomes a self-fulfilling prophecy.

Sometimes the message that a child gets about an inherited madness or badness is more subtle. My mother used to warn me against becoming like my father's sisters, with the implication that I had already begun to err in that direction. I never did discover what dread thing this group of fine, strong women possessed, and in adulthood I suspected that the danger related more to my mother's sense of her own inadequacy rather than to some undesirable trait possessed by my aunts, but as a child the thought that I might already possess some profound, unacceptable vice was something that sapped my self-confidence.

Thus, out of the way our family defines us and our own childish need for their love and acceptance we can construct for ourselves a sense of existence which we feel is bad, evil, unacceptable to ourselves and to other people.

Once we have done this we have made ourselves vulnerable to the threat of annihilation. As extraverts we see ourselves as deserving rejection, and as introverts as incapable of keeping chaos at bay. We have to defend ourselves against this threat. As extraverts we think, 'If I can't make people love me, I'll make them need me,' and so we work very hard at being needed, loading ourselves with endless burdens, coming to resent the demands that those who need us make upon us, but frightened to express this resentment lest our anger drives people away. We are immersed in anxiety. As introverts we think, 'Even if I cannot achieve what I would like to achieve, I can make control and organization my achievements', and so we work endlessly at controlling and organizing every aspect of our lives, intolerant of disorder, demanding perfection, angry with imperfection, fearful of our anger and our powerlessness to impose complete control. Fear rules our lives.

Such extraverts and introverts, provided that they are strong and healthy and that life does not deal them too many blows, can appear to outside observers as successful people. Only they know the sense of emptiness or disorder within. But anxiety and driven activity take an immense physical toll, while the body's normal ageing means that we cannot be as active at forty as we were at twenty. No matter how hard we work, people can cease to need us as they grow up, or die, or have their needs met, and no one person can control the universe. Thus extraverts and introverts, convinced of their own essential badness and working hard to be good, become less and less able to perform the feats of goodness seen as necessary to ward off the threat of annihilation. So the threat becomes greater and the fear more immense.

Desperate defences are needed against such a threat and such a fear. These defences psychiatrists call the symptoms of mental illness.

## DESPERATE DEFENCES

Whenever we feel threatened we move to the position of greatest safety available to us. If the threat is a hurricane, we move inside a building we hope is strong enough to withstand the wind. If the threat is bombs and shells, we move inside a shelter which we hope is strong enough to withstand the explosions. If the threat is those conditions which we fear will annihilate our self, we move inside a reality we hope is strong enough to hold our self together.

Thus, under the greatest threat, introverts retreat into internal reality, and extraverts rush into external reality. They construct their defences in their preferred reality.

Introverts build their defences in their thoughts, first as systems of organization and control which are expressed as obsessions and compulsions, and, if these are not strong enough to hold chaos at bay, they retreat totally into their internal reality, develop their own idiosyncratic way of interpreting events, and display the behaviour which is called schizophrenic.

Extraverts build their defences in the external world, locating the cause of their immense anxiety in fears of things (phobias), fears of being in some special place (agoraphobia), and in the body with fears of illness and dying. If the dread of annihilation cannot be contained within these things, the next line of defence is a massive denial of the fear, that is, a denial of the experience of internal reality, achieved by increasing activity in external reality, the unmeditated rushing around which is called mania.

*Sanity* is the process whereby we maintain a truthful awareness of both our realities, not denying the existence and meaning of the contents of both, and trying to create a coherent total meaning which encompasses both realities and which relates to the meanings which other people create. When we deny the existence of one of our realities, or abandon any attempt to make sense of our realities in a way which is shared by other people, we cease to be sane. Thus the final line of defence by both extraverts and introverts is called insanity, psychosis, or *madness*.

The one form of defence which is available to both extraverts and introverts, and is therefore extremely popular, is depression. Historically, under threat, we have rushed into the castle and pulled up the drawbridge, or into the stockade and slammed shut the gate, and, even though our sufferings inside the enclosure might be great, we hoped that the stones of the castle or the logs of the stockade will withstand the onslaught by our enemies. So in depression we have withdrawn inside an enclosure whose walls are invisible but real and palpable to us and to those who try to reach us. Inside, our sufferings are great, but if we build the walls strong enough we can withstand the onslaughts of the hostile world, and the guard at the gate will let no one in, nor us out, for the guard at the gate is our self.

We can employ the defence of depression on its own or in conjunction with the other desperate defences.

The need to employ a desperate defence comes from the interaction of two factors, our own belief in our essential badness and a failure on the part of those people to whom we relate to affirm that we have value and significance in our own right.

Under the threat of annihilation which defence we choose is a function of three elements, whether we are an extravert or an introvert, what degree of badness we see ourselves as possessing, and the degree of criticism and negation which other people direct at us.

## ANXIETY AND PHOBIAS

Many extraverts spend their life being anxious. They tend to explain this in terms of some inherited personality trait. 'I'm an anxious person. My mother's just the same.' They rarely pause to consider that anxious mothers *teach* their children to be anxious. They define the world to their children as a dangerous place. 'Don't eat that. It'll make you sick.' 'Keep away from the fire. You'll get burnt.' 'I've always been frightened of the dark.' 'Urgh, a spider. Don't touch it.' 'Be careful crossing the road. You might get killed.' 'Don't talk to strangers. You never know, they could hurt you.'

With all these premonitions and predictions of danger around you all the time, it is no wonder that you grow up being continually anxious.

If you absolutely dislike being anxious (as introverts do) you will work hard at finding ways of obviating the effects of your mother's anxiety (such as becoming obsessional and/or very rational). However, for extraverts anxiety is useful. When you cannot obtain stimulation which is joyful, you can always find stimulation which is anxiety creating.

Whenever an extremely anxious extravert is telling me about how intolerable this persistent, encompassing anxiety is, I always, at some point, ask, 'If I had a magic wand that I could wave over you which would take away this anxiety and ensure that you would never be anxious ever again, would you let me wave it

over you?' The anxious extravert always answers, 'No.' To such
an extravert never being anxious means not being alive. It means
being an insensitive vegetable. (By contrast, many introverts pride
themselves on never being anxious.)

Extraverts would rather feel and so suffer than not feel at all.
One very charming and competent extravert woman, Geraldine,
came to tell me about the intense anxiety and depression she was
experiencing ever since she had been deserted by her lover in a
particularly ungrateful and demeaning way. Her friends told her
she was well rid of him, but she longed for him constantly and
made fruitless and shameful attempts to get him to acknowledge
her existence and the good times they had had together.

Geraldine told me her story very forcefully and dramatically,
and I did not interrupt. However, when she said, 'It's very
important to me to feel passionate,' I had to ask, 'Why?'

She said, 'I can't let go of him. There would be a void. I'd
become a plain, dull, middle-aged woman.'

The belief that it is necessary to feel anxious in order to feel
alive is held by many extraverts. Some keep their anxiety at
pleasurable, useful levels. It makes them feel energetic and enthu-
siastic, and life exciting and challenging. However, for many
extraverts their anxiety mounts to levels which are painful and
which prevent them from coping adequately with their work and
their relationships. Such extraverts rarely look inwards to see
where the anxiety comes from.

If they did, they would see that there is one emotion which they
cannot tolerate at all, and that is anger. As children they have
been punished for being angry and have seen terrible actions by
angry people (seeing your sibling being given 'a damn good
hiding' can be as terrifying as being given one yourself). As
adults, the feeling of anger within themselves and the expression
of anger by others makes them frightened, and this fear is
compounded by the knowledge that anger can destroy the
relationships on which their sense of existence depends. So they
deny the anger which naturally follows frustration, and adult
life is full of frustrations, and they allow themselves to be
humiliated rather than to oppose the people who treat them so
badly. So their anxiety mounts.

Instead of looking into their internal reality to find the cause and meaning of their anxiety, they look to where they feel most at home, external reality, to find the cause and meaning there.

External reality is full of objects which can be dangerous. One way of dealing with this overwhelming, nameless dread is to package it and put it on some dangerous, or quasi-dangerous object. Snakes and spiders are very suitable. Then you can feel terrified of a snake or a spider and do your best to avoid encountering one. Unless you live in the tropics you won't meet too many snakes or spiders, and so you won't be too inconvenienced by their presence. When one does come along, you can ask someone else to deal with it for you. In fact, you can train your family to come running every time you shriek, 'There's a spider in the bath!' and their concern to protect you reassures you that they do care about you. In fact, a spider in the bath can liven up an otherwise dull evening. (Some introverts are very fearful of harmless spiders. Here spiders represent the uncontrolled, dirty aspects of life.)

However, loading all your terror of annihilation on to one class of objects can mean that when one of those objects comes close to you, you can feel the full terror, and if you are among strangers you will have the additional terror that they will see how frightened you are and will despise and reject you. The lovely extravert Sarah, the Duchess of York, has been shown on our television screens dealing bravely and amusingly with aeroplanes and helicopters and all sorts of difficult social situations, but in one such situation she encountered a large snake. Until she saw this snake, some kind of python, being carried towards her, she had been cheerfully patting a whole variety of zoo animals, but once she glimpsed the snake she was overcome by terror. Her smile vanished and her face crumpled into a stifled scream. She tried to hide and stepped behind her husband who then tried to shield her while he continued greeting the animals and their trainers. The television crew kept their camera trained on her, and I, like millions of others, watched her immense distress. I hoped that she would realize that the hearts of many of those people watching her went out to her, for they knew how terrible such a phobia is when it hits in this way. Many of them would have been helped by seeing her suffer so, for they would know that they were not alone in their experience of such a fear, and many would hope that what she was showing would help unphobic people to understand how awful such a feeling is.

Sometimes the nameless dread is packaged and located, not in an object but in a situation. When I was doing a phone-in on Piccadilly Radio in Manchester a woman phoned to ask me about her special fear, which was of being murdered. This is not a totally unrealistic fear in a big city, but her fear extended to every part of her life and made her ridiculously and unnecessarily cautious. So there was more to this fear of being murdered than being murdered. I talked about how someone trying to murder her was someone who did not care about her, who was untrustworthy, who wanted to hurt her, who wanted to annihilate her, someone she would not want to be close to.

She said, 'I always pull away from people. I don't know why. I can't let anyone close to me.'

'You don't trust people.'

'I suppose I don't. I hadn't thought of that.'

If she had thought about why she did not trust people, which would lead her on to think about the hurtful, belittling things that people had done to her, she would be keenly aware of how isolated she was, and this realization would bring the terror of annihilation. Rather than face this, she constructed a fear of her body being destroyed when it was her self that was under threat.

Having a consistent object or situation to fear is a defence against being caught unawares and overwhelmed by the nameless dread. However, such defences are not always successful. Many extraverts, with or without phobias, apparently happily and successfully living their lives, find themselves suddenly, without warning, overwhelmed by terror. Typically, their response is to feel the terror in their body. Later they describe the bodily components of fear, the shaking, sweating, heart thumping, shortness of breath, weakness, pain, faintness, and when their listener (often a doctor) explains that these are the body's response to fear with preparation for flight or fight, they are unconvinced. They believe that what they felt was a forerunner of a terrible fate. They decide that the only way to avoid this fate is never to set foot in the place where they experienced these physical symptoms which doctors call 'a panic attack'. Thus they build their defence against the terror in their external reality, and earn for themselves the psychiatric diagnosis of agoraphobia.

Such extraverts, having made important parts of their territory no-go areas, find that they can no longer live ordinary lives, and then they may seek help. Since they talk about the bodily experience of fear and claim that they enjoy good relationships and had a happy childhood, doctors respond by trying to decrease their anxiety with tranquillizers, and so many such extraverts have their difficulties compounded by an addiction.

If, however, the person listening to their description of the bodily symptoms of terror and their refusal to set foot in the location of the occurrence of the terror, asks, 'If you went there again and felt this panic, what would be the very worst thing that could happen to you?' the terrible fate for which this panic is a forerunner is named.

The answer comes as one of the following,

'I would vomit, and everyone there would reject me,'

'I would faint, and everyone there would reject me,'

'I would die, and dying I would be completely alone,'

or, simply,

'I would be rejected by everyone.'

Thus, the 'very worst thing' points back to the isolation which is the source of the fear. This isolation is located within the extravert's internal reality, in a sense of being diminished nearly to the point of vanishing, resulting from a sense of essential badness and the sense of being rejected, shamed, and humiliated.

A sense of shame looms large in the internal reality of many extraverts. If your sense of existence relies on being the centre of a circle of admiring and loving eyes, then, if you behave badly in these people's eyes, they will hold you in contempt and you will feel shame. The desire never to feel shame fuels the ambition of many successful extraverts. Of course, the desire never to feel shame is always accompanied by the desire to act shamelessly, and if, as an extravert, you can, on occasions or persistently, give up your desire to be loved and admired and rely for your sense of existence on simply being noticed, you can indulge yourself in acting shamelessly. That can be great fun.

Unfortunately, for those extraverts who have to resort to the desperate defence of agoraphobia, the only shameless behaviour they allow themselves is in the demands they make on their family. Lorraine, trapped inside her home for the twenty years of her marriage, is unfailingly charming and courteous to strangers, and farewells her husband each morning as he leaves for work with abuse and the occasional hurled plate. As she told me, 'I feel really down and desperate in the morning and I can't face the day all alone. I ask him to stay for just ten minutes, and he says he has to go to work.' Her husband treats her as did her family when she was a child. 'I was the youngest of seven. An afterthought. There were lots of arguments in our family. I would be pushed aside and told to stay out of it. They made me feel like I didn't exist.'

The feeling of not existing came to Stephen as the fear of death. He was in his surgery dealing with a patient when he was suddenly overwhelmed by panic and pain. He thought it was a heart attack, and his staff rushed him to hospital. There he was examined, only to be told that it was a stress reaction and that he should consult his general practitioner. Stephen went home, puzzled and unconvinced, and found the next day that he could not go to work. Suddenly the danger of his work – he was very conscious of the dangers of AIDS – and its unpleasantnesses – complaining patients and the responsibilities of being the senior doctor in the practice – loomed larger and larger. His colleagues said, 'Take a few weeks off. You've been overdoing it,' and Stephen agreed.

A few weeks later, and Stephen found that he still could not go to work. Tranquillizers had made no difference. Someone who knew me said to him, 'Why don't you go and talk to Dorothy Rowe?' and Stephen thought he might.

He could not see any reason why talking to a psychologist should help, but, as he had nothing else to do and it was company, he phoned me. Throughout our first talk he was enormously anxious, not just about meeting me, but because he, so he told me, had always been anxious. 'I can't sit through a television programme, and I can't read a book.'

He was rapidly approaching the dreaded turning point of thirty and despaired of ever getting married. Madeline, the love of his life, had rejected him. Many of his generation have decided against marriage, so I asked him why it was important to him to be married. He said, 'To be part of a family.' I asked him what would happen to him if he was left in complete isolation. He said, 'I would go crazy or die.'

Stephen was surprised when I encouraged him to talk about his childhood. Yet what gradually emerged was the story of a boy who again and again had been threatened with annihilating isolation and who had courageously battled to hold himself together and to achieve.

His parents had never accepted him as he was. His mother wanted him to be a well-spoken, well-behaved, middle class boy, and he knew himself to be an ordinary lad who spoke with a Yorkshire accent just like his mates. He felt that he had failed her, both as a child and as an adult in not attending to her sufficiently when she was ill and dying. His father wanted him to be a cricketer as he had been, though had Stephen become a champion there would have been problems. In all contests his father made sure that Stephen never won. His father also wanted him to keep to the family tradition of medicine and to be an obedient and supportive son. Stephen, as a boy, knew that he was not a sportsman and he felt a failure. He wanted to be a vet, but he relinquished this ambition to please his father and told himself that he did not have the stamina to be a vet. He both feared and felt responsible for his father. As an adult he sorted out his father's business affairs, provided a home for him, and did his bidding without complaint, even when shamed by his father, in front of friends, saying, 'Go down to the shop, lad, and get me some cigarettes.'

His father had achieved this hold over him by threatening abandonment whenever Stephen did not behave as he wished. The circumstances of the breakup of his parents' marriage occasioned several incidents when Stephen, trying to protect his mother and himself from his father's anger was brutally threatened by his father that he would abandon them both. Being sent to boarding school he experienced as abandonment. Threats of abandonment seemed to be this family's style for bringing its members to heel. As a young man Stephen on one occasion failed to obey his grandfather, and for this his grandparents refused to speak to him, even at his mother's funeral.

Gradually, over the months that we talked, Stephen came to

see that he could not answer his two most pressing questions, 'Why can't I get back to work?' and 'Why did Madeline reject me?' until he knew both sides of the equation, what people, including himself, did *and* what he felt about what they did. For the first time in his life he confronted the question of what duty we owe our parents, and saw that, if it is correct that children should sacrifice themselves for their parents, the human species would have lasted only two generations. Free of this burden, he could seek a home separate from his father and could consider alternatives to medicine which he could choose, not as a flight from fear, but as a way of elaborating his sense of existence and become the person he always knew he could be.

Once a person regains a sense of self-worth and looks with a fresh eye at the possibilities of life, an endless number of possibilities appear.

I am frequently amazed at what my ex-clients choose to do. One, Don, I wrote about in *Beyond Fear*.

'Don described the panic attacks as a complete mystery to him. He had always been an anxious sort of person – "highly strung", he said – but he'd been a good worker, learned a trade, and had a reasonably well-paid job, with overtime, in a large factory. He earned enough to support his wife and two children, he was buying his own home, he had a car and they could afford a decent holiday each year. Then things started changing. He wasn't quite sure how, but there wasn't as much overtime and he found that they couldn't afford a holiday that year ... When he found it would be a struggle to buy the children the Christmas presents they wanted, it felt like the last straw. Then he found he was getting more and more anxious, especially in the mornings on weekdays. He'd wake up with a feeling of dread, and he'd have to force himself to get out of bed and get ready for work. He rode a bike to work, and sometimes on the way there he would be completely overwhelmed with panic. He would have to get off his bike and stand on the side of the road until the shaking stopped and his heart stopped pounding. Sometimes it was so bad he had to go back home and take the day off work. Even if he did force himself to go on, it meant he was late for work and soon he was in trouble for poor time-keeping. He couldn't explain what was happening, and so, after a lot of unpleasantness with his foreman and others at work, he was dismissed.'[3]

I wrote about Don several months after my final talk with him. One evening some weeks later I answered a ring at my front door and found a strange man smiling at me. He was tall, lean, suntanned, and dressed in the expensively casual style favoured by the rich and famous. Only the envelope with my handwriting on it in his hand told me he was Don. He was calling to say that what I had written was fine, just as he was. He was now quite well off, having seen a business opportunity, and he had given up riding his bike. He had a good car and, for a hobby, he sailed a thirty foot sloop out of the treacherous waters of the Humber and across the North Sea.

Some ex-clients undertake enterprises which are less glamorous but just as adventurous. I wrote about Helen in *Beyond Fear* because her experience of panic attacks was similar to that of many extravert wives and mothers. She seemed to have everything she needed for happiness, a good husband, wonderful children, a lovely home. The fear seemed to her to come out of nowhere. When I showed her a connection between her childhood and her panic, she was amazed. 'Are you saying that what happens to us in childhood affects us in adult life?' Yet as a teacher and mother she was constantly engaged in trying to affect children in ways which would remain with them for the rest of their lives.

A change of job for Helen's husband meant a move to another part of the country. When *Beyond Fear* was published I sent her her copy and she wrote to me, saying,

'I am enjoying life enormously at the moment. I work every morning in a local primary school and I work the occasional evening in our health centre. Then, of course, I am involved in village affairs, such as the Women's Institute, Guides, Parent-Teacher Association, etc. I don't think you would know me these days. I feel I have changed a lot over the past two years, but for the better, I am glad to say. Perhaps I have grown up at last. As for "Helen", if anyone asks you what became of her, you can truthfully say that she had finally come to terms with her fears, and is most definitely on the "right road".'

# MANIA

For some extraverts the desperate defences of anxiety, phobias and the avoidance of panic attacks are not strong enough to withstand the threat of annihilation, and so they resort to the even more desperate defence of mania.

Here the extravert is rushing around in his external reality, busily denying the fearful contents of his internal reality. When the rushing around can no longer be sustained (physically it is exhausting, and usually the consequences of such activity create increasing problems) the threat of annihilation becomes unavoidable, and the extravert has to withdraw into a depression. These alternations between manic activity and deep depressions would lead a psychiatrist to diagnose the mental illness of manic-depression.

In psychiatry it is an article of faith that manic-depression is an inherited physical illness, even though many years of research with increasingly sophisticated research tools have failed to identify a manic-depression gene. Such faith leads psychiatrists not to talk of 'curing' the manic-depressive patient, but of 'managing' the patient, with the implication that such management would be required for the patient's lifetime. Similarly, psychiatrists talk of 'managing' people diagnosed as having 'endogenous depression' and 'schizophrenia'. Belief in the genetic basis of manic-depression ensures that a psychiatrist has an increasing number of patients and that he does not have to question the effectiveness of his treatment.

The claimed 'genetic factor' in manic-depression comes not from the linking of observable genetic material with the condition of manic-depression, as has happened with the linking of observable genetic material with conditions like cystic fibrosis, hare-lip, and muscular dystrophy, but from a collusion in story-telling by the psychiatrist wanting to maintain his theory, the patient who does not want to acknowledge the contents of his internal reality, and the patient's family who wish to be absolved from all responsibility for the patient's outrageous behaviour.

Such a collusion benefits the psychiatrist most. The parents can still feel guilty about passing on a malignant gene, other family members have to worry whether they or their children have inherited the gene, and they all have to endure a so-called mad person in the family whose behaviour can continue to embarrass. One great advantage of being declared mad – either manic-depressive or schizophrenic – is that you can be as mischievous and malicious as you like, and your family cannot call you to account.

It is fortunate that there is some advantage to being told you have inherited manic-depression, for the disadvantages of being so defined are great. The treatment, usually the drug lithium carbonate, and electroconvulsive therapy when your behaviour goes beyond the bounds that your doctors, nurses and family are prepared to tolerate, has the effect of removing the excitement which made life for you, an extravert, worthwhile. Knowing that this will be the condition of your life henceforth does not inspire hope or joy, nor does it restore a sense of true self-confidence and self-worth.

The psychiatric belief that manic-depression is a genetic disease has prevented many thousands of extraverts using this desperate defence from making an inward journey to discover the source of the terror from which they were fleeing. One person who did this was David Wigoder, who has told the story of his inward journey which enabled him to give up his desperate defence. He has not given up his inward journey. That, he knows, will continue till the day he dies.

When David had completed his book, *Images of Destruction*[4] his publishers decided that the preface be written by a psychiatrist, and so the book begins with Anthony Storr, FRCP, FRCPsych, quoting David's summary of his life, 'By the time I was forty I had destroyed two successful careers, served a prison sentence, been made legally bankrupt, lost a treasured professional qualification, attempted to kill two people, and isolated myself from most of my family and friends.' Storr goes on, 'Any psychiatrist reading these words would guess that the man who wrote them was suffering from manic-depressive illness, a major form of

psychiatric disorder which afflicts at least one in a hundred
individuals in our society. The causes of this illness are not fully
understood, but are certainly multiple. A genetic factor is well-
established; and it comes as no surprise to learn that Mr Wigoder's mother was herself unstable, and committed suicide when
he was 35 years old.'

Anyone who gets past the preface and reads the actual book
will discover that it is not necessary to hypothesize a gene as the
cause of David's behaviour. No child could have grown up in the
household David was born into and become a happy and secure
adult. Time and time again David was threatened with the
annihilation of his self by the cruel and insensitive behaviour of
his parents, and he had to hold himself together as best he could.
What he could not allow himself to see was that his internal
reality contained a murderous rage. The point of change in his
life, the point where in his book he starts his story, is where he
acknowledged the existence of that rage.

When Martin came to see me I gave him a copy of David's
book. I knew it would help him understand himself, and it would
give him hope.

He needed hope. As a businessman he had, in his words,
'ruined two promising and successful careers'. Before our first
meeting he wrote to me, saying, 'I am 36 years of age and for the
past 20 years I have received intermittent periods of psychiatric
counselling. Some 15 years ago I was diagnosed as manic-
depressive. I suffer from time to time with severe depression. My
own evaluation of my depression is relationship/rejection ori-
ented. In my own mind my rejection problem is all-consuming,
causing insecurity and inferiority. I have recently lost my wife and
children after seven years of marriage. I love my wife desperately
and cannot for one moment blame my wife for leaving me. I now
realize that unless I receive some sincere help I will never be able
to overcome my problem. Each and every day I consider suicide.'

Although Martin had been in the care of psychiatrists since he
was sixteen, not one of those psychiatrists had asked him about
his childhood and his family. Until he spoke to me, he had told
no one.

His father was a successful business man. The family lived in
an elegant house in the best part of town and presented a

successful front to the outside world. What went on in that house was another matter.

From his earliest days Martin was thrashed by his father for everything his father regarded as a misdemeanour, and there were many. Until he was about ten or eleven Martin would often wake to find he had wet his bed, and he would lie there, cold and frightened, hoping that his father would leave the house without seeing him, for the bedwetting resulted in another thrashing, not in parental concern for what was actually a physical weakness. Never would his mother intervene. On one occasion when he was barely six, he had been beaten by his father and sent to his room. There, he cannot remember how, Martin broke the dressing table mirror. He heard his father's footsteps on the stairs. He flung open the window, climbed on to the ledge, many feet above the ground, and stretched out his arms, trying to grasp the drainpipe. His father's hand reached out and plucked him back, not to save him from certain death, but to thrash him once again.

As Martin talked to me over a period of six weeks I could do nothing but listen to him and acknowledge his anguish. His wife refused to speak to him, and she kept the children from him. I was not surprised when I got a long letter from him, bidding me farewell. He said, 'My mind is clear and I can tell you that my feeling of rejection was caused because I knew my wife didn't believe that I loved her. I felt the same with my father. As a little boy I loved him but I knew he did not know it because he continued to treat me so cruelly. I do so wish he had loved me, I really do . . . It is now, and only now, that I realize that my wife really is my father. For no one else could cause me so much pain and sadness . . . That I do not want to die I am aware of. But I know I must punish myself, for my father is dead, and this is my final punishment . . . Thank you for opening my eyes. I am sure that had we met sooner I might have glimpsed a life outside my "black hole" . . . I know I will not be born again. Because I dare not allow myself to consider the possibility that I would once again experience the childhood of that lonely, sad and hopeless little boy.'

A final page, written when he must have woken with a colossal hangover, said, 'Dear Dorothy Rowe, please disregard this letter.

Daylight is breaking, music is playing. Thank God for my children.'

Martin then disappeared. He phoned me from London but would not say where he was going. His solicitor phoned me, and his mother. This was a long phone call in which she complained about how difficult Martin was. 'He thinks he's got problems. He told me he had an unhappy childhood. He's got nothing to complain about. I had a much more unhappy childhood than he had, but I wouldn't complain about it. I've told him depression is in the family,' (she had been treated by a psychiatrist for depression for several years) 'and he'll just have to learn to put up with it.'

Eventually Martin arrived at his mother's house, having spent, as he told me, 'one month in the wilderness' (his solicitor thought it was Spain). He stayed there, having given all his property to his wife, and we kept in touch by letter and phone.

In one of our phone conversations he said, 'I try to talk to my mother about my childhood, but she just brushes it aside. I don't expect her to make it all right – that's not possible – but if she could say, yes, it happened and I'm sorry, I would feel so much better.'

He wrote, 'I am unable to think of anything else but my wife and children. They are with me every day of my life. I see their faces staring back with hatred and contempt . . . There is nothing wrong with life. It is the people in it that are the problem. Why do we spend so much of our precious time destroying ourselves and others? . . . All my life I had strived to be successful, believing that success would bring happiness. I now realize that happiness will bring success. It has taken me a long time to realize this. Will I be able to come to terms with it? I wonder.'

He did come to terms with it. He considered following David Wigoder's example and joining a therapeutic community, but no place was available. Instead, he embarked on a course of study, doing some A levels with a view to going to university to read philosophy and psychology. He wrote to me, 'Whilst it is true that I am experiencing an underlying sense of depression, I know that I must have purpose in my life. A sense of hope overriding a sense of fear. I cannot go on thinking in terms of what might have been – for it is!'

By now Martin understood how his intense enthusiasms and ambitious activities had been a denial of his anger and sadness. He was delighted with his new-found interest in study, but he realized, as he told me, that he should use these intellectual interests as a path to enlightenment and not as a vehicle for an emotional roller-coaster ride.

# OBSESSIONS AND COMPULSIONS

All introverts, no matter how well they have established themselves as Successful Selves, have at least one obsession. Of course, they might not call it an obsession. They would probably prefer to call it Good Organization and Maintaining Proper Standards. When they feel good about themselves, receive no criticism that they cannot discount, and life does not present them with any event of which they cannot feel in control, their obsessions are no more than regular habits. However, if their self-confidence diminishes, if criticism by others and by their own stern conscience mounts, and if life slips out of control, regular habits become obsessions, rituals which must be performed, else all will fall into chaos and they will, they fear, be annihilated.

Phobias are objects and situations in external reality which elicit from the extravert feelings of fear, anxiety and panic. Obsessions and compulsions are *ideas* which introverts may simply ruminate upon or may try to impose on to external reality. External reality is to be coerced into conforming to the introvert's ideas. The ideas always concern order, cleanliness and safety as defences against disorder, dirt and danger. So possessions must be grouped and put in designated places rather than scattered randomly, certain substances are designated as dirty or potentially dirty and washing rituals are performed to remove or segregate such dirty substances from clean, and dangerous or potentially dangerous situations are identified and defended against. Thus an introvert, before retiring to bed, will tidy the living room, wash at least one surface, usually his own, and check that the outside doors are locked and the gas taps turned off, and then, perhaps, when the perennial doubt creeps in ('Did I lock the front door?') check the locks and the taps once again.

Such ideas introverts regard as being supremely important, and so it is not until these ideas take over an introvert's life that the person sees any reason to seek to change the ideas in any way.

Thus, when June came to talk to me about how depressed she was, she did not mention any obsessions. Instead, she spoke of a nameless, overwhelming sadness, which made her weep endlessly, and a sense of being diminished, 'I feel like I'm just a pair of eyes, or a two-dimensional person.' The sense of diminishment went back at least to when she was five and her brother was born. Being herself, a girl, now seemed second best. One way of proving that she could do what a boy could do and win praise and approval was in sports where she excelled. She decided that when she grew up she would become a physical education teacher. However, the reality proved to be less than the dream. Once qualified and teaching she found herself on a plateau where no further achievement was possible, and unappreciated by her departmental head whose work, she knew, she could organize much better than he did.

Her words, 'praise', 'approval', 'achieve', 'organize', suggested an introvert, so I checked and she was. Towards the end of our conversation, when she was more relaxed, I asked if she was exceedingly organized and tidy.

June laughed. 'My mother complains that I have made my flat so neat and tidy that it's not comfortable. I think it's comfortable, but she says it's so tidy it makes her nervous. I know I'm always squaring things up, making sure everything's parallel and level. I leave out piles of laundry – but they're neat piles. I'll leave a newspaper on the table, but it'll be folded properly. I always like to be the first person to read a newspaper or a magazine. I like it to be crisp and clean, and it's not if somebody else has touched it.'

She talked of her obsessions as amusing quirks of character, not as aspects of herself about which she would complain. They were idiosyncratic aspects of her organizational skills. She longed to use these skills in business, 'be my own boss', but her low opinion of herself, part of the tragic drama she had constructed for herself as a child, held her back. She would not allow herself to pursue her ambition in the way that less self-hating people do,

'At least I can say that I tried.' Failure would be imperfection, and anything less that perfect would be unacceptable.

Like so many introverts who try to maintain their self-esteem by taking pride in high standards, June put her standards before her relationships. When her closest friend fell in love with a man of whom June disapproved, June showed her disapproval, and her friend, being forced to chose between June and her lover, chose her lover. Now June wept in loneliness. High standards and neatly arranged objects are no substitute for friends.

The problem with friends, indeed with all relationships, is that they involve other people, and people are always impossible to control and organize all the time and in every way, and emotions are always messy. In English we have words for apparently discrete emotions, 'love', 'hate', 'fear', 'anger', 'envy', 'resentment', but such emotions are rarely felt in their pure form. Usually they are fusions – anger with fear, envy with resentment, love with hate – and we find them hard to disentangle. Often we will admit to only one emotion when two or more are present. Extraverts tend to admit to fear but not to anger, introverts to anger but not to fear. People who are prepared to lie to themselves in order to believe that they are good will admit to resentment but not to envy. People who want to maintain that they had perfect parents and a happy childhood will refuse to acknowledge that love can be mixed with hate. Yet it so often is, for the people whom in childhood we loved the most are the people who inflicted on us the greatest pain and so inspired our hate.

It is this unacknowledged hate which turns the 'ordinary' obsessions of the introvert, that is, their seemingly effective way of keeping part of the changing universe under control, into repetitive ruminations and actions which seem to have the quality of being driven, something the introvert is forced to do rather than chooses to do.

The turning point in becoming able to relinquish the desperate defence of obsessions and compulsions is the realization that they are a defence.

Hence I felt greatly cheered when Russell phoned to wish me a merry Christmas and when I asked him how he was, he said, 'I've come to realize that I won't let go of these fears. It's my refusal to let go of them that's holding me back. I still have the requirement to be one hundred percent certain about something. I've got a vast fear of uncertainty.'

Four years ago, when Russell first came to see me, I had suggested to him that his obsessions and fantasies served the purpose of giving him a sense of security, even though they made him feel guilty. He totally disbelieved me. How could anyone as completely unaggressive as he choose to create murderous fantasies, and did not his efforts to avoid harming anyone show what a kind, unaggressive person he was? When I had written about Russell in my book *Living with the Bomb*,[5] I had said, 'Russell held what Alice Miller called "the absurd belief that a person can have nothing but kind, good and meek thoughts and at the same time be honest and authentic".[6] A good person, he believed, never got angry and never fought.'

However, something of what I had said over the year that we met must have seemed sensible to him, for, when his work took him to another part of the country, he found another therapist to help him on his journey of self-discovery.

When we feel hatred our immediate desire is to destroy the object of our hatred. In learning how to deal with our hatred and the wish to destroy some of us were lucky enough to have parents who did not punish us greatly for being aggressive and who accepted our 'I hate you, mummy' as a natural response to a frustrating parent. Thus we grew up untroubled by our feelings of hate and able to dissipate them in verbal expressions like 'I could have killed him' and 'Drop dead', and in fantasies where our enemies not only suffered but, if we allowed them to live, saw the error of their ways. But those of us who as children were severely punished for our expressions of our hate (a parent's response of 'How could you say that to your mummy after all she's done for you?' to 'I hate you, mummy' creates punishing guilt) find it impossible to dissipate our hatred in traditional verbal forms and in fantasy. Every possible way of expressing that hatred must be guarded against, and so the unacknowledged hatred displays itself in many disguises.

Parents who accept 'I hate you, mummy' as a natural response to the restrictions that parents put on children allow the child to discover that we frequently hate the people we love, that hatred need not last forever, and that the changing patterns of feelings in relationships do not have to be ordered into rigid categories but accepted and enjoyed in their multiple, amorphous forms.

Parents who do not accept 'I hate you, mummy' as a natural response to frustration teach the child that the intermingling of love and hate is a dark secret known only to the child and is evidence of what the child feels is his essential badness. For extravert children the dark secret must be kept hidden in the unknown and unknowable recesses of internal reality from which, when, in later life, other loved ones inspire hatred, it will spring forth as overwhelming panic. For introvert children the dark secret tells them that there can be no order in relationships with others, that chaos reigns, and there is no security.

Russell's search for one hundred percent security was doomed to failure. Nothing is certain in this world except death and taxes, and even they are filled with uncertainty. We do not know what our own death will be until we encounter it, and taxes – the demands that other people make on us – are many and varied and out of our control. The only security available to us is the security of knowing that nothing is secure and that that is a splendid truth, for in it lies our freedom. This Russell found hard to accept, for his stern conscience would accept nothing less than perfect order and perfect goodness.

Thus Russell would try to make all his written work perfect, but even as he completed a piece of work, the doubt, the introvert's distrust of external reality, would arise, and he would have to check his work again and again. However, there was for him another aspect of checking that was even more painful than this.

All of us should be able to understand why very powerful people when they travel have their pathway cleared for them. When we less powerful people try to push through a crowded supermarket or try to drive in traffic we would like to send our minions ahead to smash out of the way the people who impede us. In such situations we can momentarily feel pure hatred for those who frustrate us. However, if we cannot accept such feelings, if such hatred in the present activates the hidden hatred from the past, if we do not trust ourselves because we believe that we are essentially bad, and if we do not trust our perceptions of external reality, we find ourselves trapped in a round of fruitless searching to prove that we have not committed the crime which we had fantasied. Hence Russell, driving home from work, might find his progress momentarily impeded by a cyclist. He would drive by, and a few moments later think, 'Did I knock that cyclist over?' He would feel compelled to return to the spot to search for the supposedly injured cyclist, and when he found nobody and he was on his way home again, he would think of some 'logical' reason why he had not seen the supposedly injured or dead cyclist, and again he would return to the spot to search. Such compulsive searching might take many hours, and no amount of commonsense advice from friends would deter him. Only sheer exhaustion would force him home, and then he would awake in the night in a terror of doubt and guilt.

This kind of compulsive searching, the compulsive washing of hands to rid oneself of dirt with which one might injure others, the locking and checking of doors to ensure safety, are the easiest obsessions to describe, for the words one needs are not offensive. However, the obsessions and compulsions which trouble their owners most are those which contain images so obscene, cruel and bizarrely murderous that they are difficult to put into words.

It may seem far-fetched to claim that such fantasies which create such guilt are defences against the annihilation of the self, but indeed they are, for they are a means of trying to maintain control.

If we believe that we have committed some crime or sin and that we shall be punished, we feel very insecure and frightened if we do not know when the punishment will come and what it will be. Once we know, or, better still, we can decide what the punishment is, we can feel the benefit of such security outweighs the pain of the punishment. Russell told me how he had come to realize that the fantasies he found so vile did not come randomly but, whenever he was doing something which he enjoyed, one of these disgusting fantasies – him murdering babies or giving someone a deadly disease – would come into his mind.

Russell had grown up believing that he had to earn, and keep on earning, the right to exist, that he did not deserve any benefits or pleasures, and so when any came his way he had to pay a price. All he could do was to claim the right to determine the price, and since he so despised himself he made sure the price was high. Now Russell lives his life with greater enjoyment and humour, for he came to realize that enjoyment does not have to be paid for with suffering, and that humour can be simply pleasurable and not just a shield for pain.

The belief that in life there are no free gifts is a burden carried by a great many people and reinforced by our society. 'We weren't put on earth to enjoy ourselves,' said Malcolm Fraser, millionaire and then Prime Minister of Australia, thus echoing not just the Protestant work ethic but the old Spanish proverb, 'Take what you like, says God, and *pay for it*.' What absolute nonsense! We deserve to exist simply because we exist, and life is full of wonderful things there for us to enjoy freely, provided we do not clutter our heads with notions of rewards and punishments and keeping things under control, all the stupidities which prevent us from being ourselves and living in the here and now.

Alas, many of the obsessional introverts reading this will regard me as a dangerous person, for not only do I hold ideas which they believe are immoral, but also I threaten the structure they have created so that they will not fall apart and become what society calls mad or 'schizophrenic'. For when introverts cannot hold themselves together with their structure of control, they fall back to the most desperate defence of schizophrenia.

# SCHIZOPHRENIA

It is impossible to write sensibly about schizophrenia in relation to an individual's experience, because so many other people have a vested interest in this form of defence which requires them to insist that schizophrenia is a mental illness. There are the drug companies whose profits on the drugs used in the treatment of people so diagnosed are immense. There are the psychiatrists who have their jobs to protect. There are the Health Service administrators who like the apparent tidiness of the medical model of mental illness and whose fallacious accounting leads them to believe that it is cheaper to give people life-long, eventually incapacitating, drugs than to provide them with the sort of care and companionship which will enable them to return to ordinary life. There are the many members of society who are so frightened of change and so desirous of imposing their own ideas on others that they want anyone who shows any dissent of any kind to be locked away. There are the families, one of whose members uses this defence, who have their own secrets and who wish to be absolved of all responsibility and guilt. And there is the person, himself or herself, who wants to be safe and, in achieving this safety, both to punish and protect the people who threaten to annihilate his self.

The combined action of those people who have a vested interest in defining schizophrenia as an inherited mental illness, which is 'managed' by psychiatrists but never cured, can and does prevent introverts who would have used schizophrenia as a temporary defence from returning to ordinary life. Instead, such introverts, not having the power to challenge the people in whose care they are and wishing to be good, continue to find the defence of schizophrenia necessary. The drugs they are given, the major tranquillizers, do reduce the intensity of the fear which makes the defence necessary, but they also have the effect of slowing down thought and action, and produce other unpleasant effects, all of which prevent the person from feeling ordinary and capable of conducting his own life. Thus an intense experience of the unreality of external reality can lead an introvert to abandon his life's projects and to enter upon a much diminished way of life.

The essence of schizophrenia is not the unidentified schizophrenic gene but such a powerful threat of the annihilation of the self that external reality becomes unreal. In an attempt to regain control the introvert constructs an idiosyncratic structure of meaning in order to cope with this sense of unreality and his own feelings of badness and inadequacy.

Extraverts, in their attempt to maintain a sense of existence and to advance their own interests, often choose to be unaware of large sections of what goes on in their external reality. They can, while relating intensely to the people they see themselves as needing for their sense of existence, be oblivious of what is happening to those people. They can deny all the unpleasant, tragic aspects of their own life and the lives of others in order to maintain their sentimental, romantic view which makes them feel safe and saves them from having to think about life's unavoidable issues and what responsibilities we have for what we do. So oblivious an extravert can be of so much of external reality that phrases like 'out of touch with reality' and 'lives in a world of his own' are not inappropriate. Yet, no matter how much external reality an extravert denies, what he never denies is that external reality exists and is real.

Introverts do not *deny* that external reality exists and is real. It is their *experience* of external reality which has the quality of unreality and which leads them to doubt the existence of external reality. This feeling of the unreality of external reality comes upon an introvert whenever there is a pronounced discrepancy between what his perceptions have led him to believe is the case and what external reality apparently is. This happens when other people deny the validity of the introvert's perceptions. Brenda, in this situation, said to me, 'The world is fragile. It could become nothing.' She was engaged in a battle with officials in the Social Services and the Health Service to get them to admit that they had been negligent in their care of her granddaughter, and she was discovering that in such government institutions the shifting pattern of denials and secret reports makes the truth impossible to discover. Truth was very important to Brenda, for in her childhood she had been told many lies and received much pain from those who should have cared for her, and it was only by knowing the truth that she felt she could hold herself together. Her agony was in part for her granddaughter and in part for herself, lest she feel forced to believe that there was no one in the world who spoke the truth and who accepted her truth. For her, if there was no truth there could be no world.

Once external reality becomes quite unreal for an introvert it is no longer possible to distinguish clearly between what goes on solely in internal reality, our thoughts, feelings, images and fantasies, from our perceptions of external reality. We can then treat our perceptions as fantasies and our fantasies as perceptions, and so behave in ways which society defines as deluded and hallucinated. Such delusions and hallucinations are not random, as those who regard schizophrenia as a mental illness believe, but are part of the structure of meaning which the person has created. They, like the display of emotions which psychiatrists call 'inappropriate affect' are based, like every person's beliefs and actions are based, on the conclusions drawn from the person's experience.

If, say, you have felt your sense of self being smothered by a father who, while claiming to be caring for you, criticizes your every action and denies your truth and worth, you might well store this knowledge in an image of a powerful man holding a blanket ready to envelop you, and then, in the way that we see our fantasies in our mind's eye, see this image so clearly that it appears as a person in the room with you.

All introverts are vulnerable to this loss of the reality of external reality, but some are more vulnerable than others, for they were born into families which did not or could not provide them with the acceptance and recognition which we all need to create and to maintain our sense of existence. It is other people who tie an introvert to external reality, and it is other people who can make external reality unreal.

Babies need more than to be fed and kept warm. They need cuddles and conversations in order to feel the oneness from which the self can be created and then become separate. Noisy, querulous babies get cuddles and conversations, but so-called 'good' babies may get less than they need. Introvert babies are not being good when they are quiet. They are just maintaining their optimum level of stimulation. Mothers who define a baby as 'good' because the baby makes few demands, like the mothers who believe that a baby is 'spoilt' by having his needs met, can fail to give the baby the necessary amount of cuddles and conversation. So do mothers who are depressed, or absent, or involved in their own worries and concerns. Thus, some introvert babies fail to establish a firm basis for their sense of self. In later life, usually at the turning points in life where we have to leave a certain security behind and cope with some more demanding aspect of external reality, they find themselves overwhelmed, and the only way they can hold their fragile sense of self together is to retreat into their internal reality.

Adults can hinder a child's understanding of external reality not just by refusing to answer questions but also by lying to the child and by undermining the child's confidence in his own perceptions. This is what my mother did to me. Probably from the moment I started talking she defined me as having an unchanging characteristic which was that I told lies, I made up stories, I read things in books and tried to pass them off as true.

She did this so that whenever I said something which did not fit in with her scheme of things she could dismiss it as untrue. Sometimes she did this by mocking me, in the way that adults are wont to mock children, and sometimes she simply stated flatly that I was not telling the truth.

I was twenty-seven before I realized that I had, at last, become impervious to her ploy. When she came to see me the day my son was born she asked why I had developed toxaemia in the last week of my pregnancy. I said, 'My doctor says it was because I was working too hard. I should have stopped teaching months ago and rested.' She said, 'Oh, Dorothy, that's not true. You never work hard.' (Laziness was another unchanging characteristic she had defined as mine.) I found that I was not hurt, just amused, and I told the story to my friends and, subsequently, to many clients as an example of how sometimes we have to accept that parents do not change.

Nine years previously, I had recounted to my mother and a visitor the full story of the Japanese bombing of Darwin, something which a fellow university student (later my husband) and a soldier in Darwin at the time had told me, and which was still a wartime secret. My mother turned to her visitor and said, 'People just make these stories up,' and the visitor agreed with her. I felt shamed and diminished.

But even that feeling of shame and diminishment was not as devastating as the sense of unreality she created in me as a child when she made me doubt my own perceptions. I would say something had happened and she would say that it had not. What she always denied had to do with people, and so it was people rather than places that I doubted. I could never feel sure whether I had met a person before and whether he was who I thought he was. I was terrified that I would get it wrong and people would criticize me. Then I believed that everybody was as critical of me as were my mother, my sister and my teachers.

It is their lack of trust in their own perceptions and their attempt to avoid even more criticism which prevent introverts from acting in external reality (and not the 'lack of volition' which traditional psychiatric textbooks give as a characteristic of people with the mental illness of schizophrenia). Throughout my childhood and adolescence I often found myself paralysed, unable to act. Thus at seventeen I stood at the door of Manning House. It was another ten years before I worked out a solution to the problem of doubting my own perceptions. Instead of trying Russell's (ineffective) method of seeking total certainty, I decided to opt for the 'as if' solution. Instead of asking myself if what I was perceiving was exactly so, I decided to act as if it was the way I perceived it. It worked exceedingly well. To the problem of the fear of criticism, the cringing away from every possible situation where I might suffer another blow to my raw self, I moved, somewhat slowly, to the position where such a posture was no longer necessary. I now hold the view that anyone who criticizes me is a fool! Trying to suffer fools gladly is less of a burden than trying to avoid painful criticism.

Amused though I might be at my own solutions to these problems, I find nothing amusing about those introverts whose doubts about the reality of external reality were more powerful and pervasive than mine and who were the recipients of far more devastating criticism and humiliation than I ever was. Over the past twenty-five years I have met many introvert men and women, usually teenagers and young adults, who have had to resort to the defence of schizophrenia to save themselves from the threat of annihilation. My heart always aches for them, and I feel the shiver of fear that accompanies the memory of a near disaster. It took me some years to work out how I escaped such a fate.

I had in my early years unqualified and uncritical love from my father, my grandmother, and uncles and aunts, especially my 'Auntie Doff'. The introvert men and women whom I later knew had not received that kind of love, perhaps because their family were always unable to give it, or perhaps, just at the time they were born, their parents were struggling with some crisis. Even though I later became too self-conscious and frightened to avail myself of such love, it left me with a sufficient sense of self-worth to make me determined to survive. I would not do what those men and women did, sacrifice themselves for their family. As one young woman, whose mother was always engaged in an anxious criticism of everything her daughter did, said to me, 'If my mother did not have me to worry about she would have to worry about herself, and that would be much worse for her. I don't think she could cope with that.'

These men and women had been identified as the crazy one in the family, and by accepting this role they protected their parents and the family secrets which, when I eventually glimpsed what they were, were grave secrets indeed. It was these grave secrets, amongst other things, that led these young people to doubt their own perceptions. If your Christian father has told you that his sexual assaults on you were an act of worship, or that throughout your childhood your father was in gaol but the family pretended he was abroad, you could be led to feel very uncertain about what was happening. My family never defined me crazy, and they had no secrets (except my convict great-grandfather!) to protect, just the usual petty angers and jealousies that infest most families.

What such people need so that they can give up the defence of schizophrenia is at least one companion who is so consistently present, loyal, truthful, understanding, accepting and uncritical that external reality can take on the degree of reality which allows the creation of a structure of meaning which can be shared with other people. What such people usually get is a confusing phantasmagoria of hospital staff offering an inconsistent pattern of concern, criticism, truth and lies, a selection of drugs which, at best, make them feel dull, and, at worse, ill, and a label, 'schizophrenic' which marks them out forever as third class citizens.

Introverts create a structure of meaning to explain to themselves why external reality is as it is, and to control and predict all the changes therein. If they lose confidence in the structure they have created – as they can when external reality fails totally to conform to their expectations or when someone whose opinions they value tells them they have got it totally wrong – they feel that their structures have been destroyed, and this is a terrifying experience. However, if they can realize that the structures are simply structures and we do not have to try to preserve them at all costs, they can free themselves from the structures which inhibited them and create other structures that are more life enhancing.

In *Beyond Fear* I told the story of Jessica whose whole set of structures, what she called her judgement, fell apart when she discovered the perfidy of her companion Andy. She described how, 'I was filled with the most terrible sense of dread. It was the most horrible experience. I felt that something terrible was about to happen. It was something I was going to do, or something was going to happen to me.' Eighteen months later she was able to say it had 'not been a bad experience. Just what I needed really. You have fixed pictures in your unconscious and you don't have access to them, although they exert a strong influence. In that experience of madness everything gets well and truly mixed up. That was good for me.'

Out of such an experience a greater creativity can come.

Alexander Thynn, eleventh Viscount Weymouth, artist and writer, is an introvert who first had to battle to maintain his identity and then, through that battle, was able to discover and to use the skills and talents of an extravert. Many people regard him as an extravert, for his way of living is most unconventional and flamboyant, but he is well aware that he is not. He knows that if we see that the rules and conventions of our society are man-made fictions, not Absolute Truths, we can realize that we no longer need to follow them blindly but that we can create our own rules. This is what Alexander has done.

Alexander lives at Longleat in one wing where he is creating his murals. He described to me how he had been born into a family which was organized in a strict hierarchy with his father, the Marquess of Bath, at its head. His father expected complete obedience from his children and for the early years of his life Alexander was an obedient child who tried to please his father, and, like so many obedient children, he became, as he described himself, 'a shy, sensitive little boy'. He did quite well at school and so decided to go to university.

This did not suit his father at all. The Thynn family, his father declared, were not intellectuals, and no son of his was going to university. But Alexander insisted, and off he went to Oxford. He had hoped to get a good Second Class degree and prove his father to be totally wrong. But he got a Third, and his father said, 'I told you so.' Some very bitter quarrels followed.

Alexander said, 'It was an identity crisis. Mine was a bullying upbringing and there came a point when I was not going to be told what my identity was going to be. University gave me the tools to destroy the attitudes which had previously been imposed on me.'

The battle with his father was for Alexander more than a simple disagreement between two people with different points of view. His father attacked Alexander's basic judgements about himself and what he could achieve, and Alexander began to doubt his own judgements. 'I felt a great deal of doubt. Could he be right? Could it be I'm not fitted to be what I thought, ambitiously, that I could go on to be? In the uncertainty of my own assessment of myself, the uncertainty of the feeling I gave to others when I was in their company, I was withdrawing and cutting off from previous contact. I became a recluse. But later as my confidence was gradually found, and, as the battle was won against my father, or at least he'd stopped trying to enforce his attitudes on me, and then, gradually, I emerged in what could be regarded as a more natural self.'

Alexander found his confidence through painting. His murals fill some sixteen rooms, vast, colourful, and highly individual. He divides them into 'cocoons, therapies and fantasies' but altogether they form Alexander's attempt at a total explanation and a philosophy of life is perhaps summed up in a banner which runs the length of one long room, 'Heaven and Hell are what we experience here on Earth, in the relationships between our fellow human beings.'

The theme of the therapy mural which Alexander calls 'Paranoia' concerns his relationships with his family. He said, 'I always imagined that if you're allowed to paint you get better, and I'm always getting better. This is where I've painted paranoia which at times in my life, in my post-university years, was quite bad. I was convinced that people were listening through walls, and I think they were too. A paranoiac can see the world much more clearly than all you sane people. Doctors are innocents. They just don't see the reality. Anyway, this is where I tried to paint out my worry, my anxiety phase, my paranoia, so that I can treat it lightly and take it humorously. It begins inside the womb, we have a father figure, mother figure,' he gestured to the many figures on the walls, 'The all-seeing eye ... the war machine ... elder sister figure ... here I'm sending it up all round, filling it with goolies and goosties and the things that go bump in the night, and at the centre of all one's paranoia is one's parents.'

At the end of the long room were two portraits, painted by some conventional portrait painter. They were of Alexander's parents, painted in the 1930s. The Marquess looked very urbane and sophisticated. To my eye he had the expression of that kind of man who thinks that the best way to relate to small boys is to challenge and tease them. Perhaps he did not realize that it is necessary also to be kind.

The reason that Alexander had found his father's criticism of him so devastating was that from his earliest days he saw his father as setting the standards which he had to attain because he wanted his father's love and approval. The introvert gives to the standard setter the power to attack the basic premises on which the introvert has built his whole edifice. Thus the standard setter can become the persecutor, and, when the standard setter is the parent, the standard setter becomes a persecutor twice over. The actual parent becomes a persecutor, and the internal parent, that representation of our parents that we carry around inside us, becomes a persecutor too. Alexander found himself under attack in both his external reality and his internal reality, by his father and his father's image, his persecutory conscience. In such a situation introverts who have lost confidence in themselves find it hard to maintain a clear distinction between the two persecutors. Then they need friends who can help them distinguish between the events when they are under attack from real people and when they are under attack from their internal objects. Unfortunately, they most frequently meet doctors who say, 'But of course your parents aren't persecuting you. They love you and want the best for you,' and who give the diagnosis of the mental illness of paranoia or paranoid schizophrenia.

Alexander found his therapy not in doctors but in art. He wrote and he painted. He abandoned his father as the measure of his achievement and established contact with a group of people against whom he could measure his success. In doing this he found what he called 'a sense of release from isolation'.

It is a kind of isolation which is the essence of the experience of the defence of depression.

# DEPRESSION

Suppose you come to suspect that most of the important things in your life are not what you thought they were. You worry that perhaps all your relationships are changing for the worse or disappearing. You are doubtful whether your future will turn out as you planned and you can see no definite, acceptable way forward. You doubt whether you interpreted past events correctly and you are not sure what the correct interpretation should be. You question your judgement and your ability. You are suspicious of other people's feelings towards you. Do they really mean what they say? Life seems to be slipping out of your control. You wonder if there is anyone you can turn to, if there is any end to this uncertainty.

The uncertainty is unbearable. The fear is overwhelming.

So you create certainty for yourself.

You cannot say everything is absolutely perfect, for obviously it is not.

So you say to yourself, 'I am an absolutely bad person. This is why bad things have happened to me in the past and why only bad things will happen to me in the future. Because I am bad everyone is certain to reject me. If they say they will not they are lying. Because I am bad everything I do will fail. I am responsible for everything that happens to my family and friends, and I have failed totally to meet my responsibilities. Everything is my fault.'

Now the dangerous uncertainty has vanished. You are absolutely certain. You are safe.

Safe inside the prison of depression.

The essence of the experience of depression is that you are alone in some kind of a prison. You can describe your prison. You might see your prison as being at the bottom of a deep pit, or locked inside a cage, or wrapped in a shroud. You might feel that you are stumbling across a stony desert, or through a thick fog, or that a large black bird is crouched on your shoulders, making it impossible for you to move. Whatever your image, you are alone, and in this prison you are both the miserable prisoner and the cruel gaoler. When we are simply unhappy, no matter what terrible fate has befallen us, we still feel a connection to the rest of the world and to ourselves. We let others comfort us, and feel warmed and supported, and we comfort ourselves. But when we are depressed, no warmth or support comes through our prison wall, and we punish ourselves most cruelly.[7]

Without the defence of depression the human race would not have survived. By shutting ourselves in this prison we keep out all the dangers and uncertainties that otherwise would overwhelm us. By making every day in the prison the same as the next, we deal only with the bare minimum of issues that we can manage to deal with, and we make sure that nothing new gets in to frighten and stress us. By concentrating on just ourselves we do not have to face what is happening to others. Locked in our prison we can avoid acknowledging the inescapable disasters that the human race is prone to – death and loss and the tragedies that nature or our own cruelties and stupidities bring upon us. In depression we can give ourselves a breathing space before we confront all this again, or we can keep ourselves safely locked away forever.

Depression is the most popular of all the desperate defences. It is equally available to extraverts and introverts, and we always have the foundation ready laid.

**The foundation of our prison of depression is our belief that, No matter how good I appear to be, I am bad, evil, unacceptable to myself and to other people.**

We can go through life being very good at being good, and so keep our sense of being bad, or not good enough, well hidden from ourselves. But being good at being good means working very hard, and as we get older we lose the resilience and strength of youth. We get tired. We do not get as much done. Our list of mistakes and wrong decisions gets longer. When something happens to shake our self-confidence we can no longer trust our ability to be good at being good. We can no longer ignore our sense of being essentially bad and unacceptable.

The reason that we as children so readily accepted our parents' teaching that we were bad and had to work hard to be good was that, harsh though this teaching was, it contained a promise. *If you are good, nothing bad will happen to you.* We believed it. When bad things did happen to us, we blamed ourselves. We had not been good enough. So we worked harder, tried to achieve more, to do things better, to put other people's needs before our own. Secretly this belief gave us a sense of power. Through our own efforts we could control the system of rewards and punishments that governed the universe. Instead of feeling helpless, we felt guilty. Instead of saying, 'There was nothing else I could have done in that situation, given the information and experience I had,' we said, 'I ought to have done better,' and persuaded ourselves that we were wiser and stronger and better informed than we actually were. By feeling guilty we could feel that we were both virtuous and not helpless.

So we lived in a world of illusion of our own making. Then one day a terrible disaster befell us, and we cried, 'I have been good all my life. Why has this happened to me?'

We found ourselves contemplating, or trying to run away from, a truth which our parents had hidden from us.

### No amount of goodness will prevent disaster

Perhaps the disaster was something that other people could see and share – our child dying of leukaemia, our partner's faithlessness. Perhaps the disaster was our secret disappointment – that the goals our parents had set us and we had dutifully fulfilled led not to a life of glory and achievement but to a life of quiet desperation, that no matter how hard we tried to be good, our parents would never give us their unstinted, uncritical love. Whichever kind of disaster befalls us, and some of us have both, we cannot avoid the question, 'Why did this happen?'

Of any disaster, there are only three ways of answering the question, 'Why did this happen?'

(1) I caused it.
(2) They caused it.
(3) It happened by chance.

If we choose 'I caused it', we feel guilty.

If we choose 'They caused it', we feel angry and resentful (and if 'they' are people we are not allowed to criticize, we then feel guilty for feeling angry and resentful).

If we choose 'It happened by chance', we feel frightened, for it is out of our control and could happen again.

We can put off the recognition that no amount of goodness prevents disasters, that is, disasters happen by chance, by events outside our control, by moving into the prison of depression where we live in a turmoil of guilt, anger and resentment.

For some people the stay in the prison of depression is relatively short. The pain of it makes them review their beliefs and attitudes. Perhaps they had already had some understanding that if you build your life on the belief that you are bad and have to work hard to be good you then have to live with some very unpleasant implications of that belief.

If you believe that you are bad and unacceptable, then it follows that you are always frightened of other people. They might find you out how bad you are and reject and criticize you, or they might be like you, bad and pretending to be good, and so are untrustworthy. If you fear other people for long enough you come to hate those people, and when you fear people you never get close to them to see the troubles they are bearing, and so you envy them. You can never have close relationships with people if you fear, hate and envy them.

If you believe that you are bad and unacceptable and have to work hard to be good you believe in some system of rewards and punishments contained in your beliefs about the purpose of life and the nature of death. Whatever these beliefs are, you draw from them the conclusion that as you are bad you will get more punishments than rewards and so for you life is terrible and death is worse.

If you believe that you are bad and unacceptable you are unable to look back at your past with pleasure and towards your future with hope. Only bad things have happened to you in the past and only bad things will happen to you in the future.

If you believe that you are bad and unacceptable you see your anger as evidence of your badness. Thus you cannot cope with your anger or anyone else's anger.

If you believe that you are bad and unacceptable you always feel weak and vulnerable, and so you resort to the defence that weak people use – never forgive an injury (and, of course, you never forgive yourself).

For some people their stay in the prison of depression is long, for they have invested a great deal in the beliefs which build the prison of depression and they are loath to relinquish them. The physical treatments for depression, anti-depressant drugs and electroconvulsive therapy, can make such people more cheerful temporarily, but until they have confronted truthfully their belief about their inherent badness and its attendant beliefs the shadow of the prison will always be upon them, a cruel place of safety when annihilation threatens.

Over the years I have seen many people not only find their way out of the prison of depression but thoroughly dismantle it. Here I shall tell of just one of those people.

Elizabeth's life, as she told me on her first visit, was, to outside observers, a simple, happy story. She had been born to parents who loved her greatly. She did well at school, worked as a civil servant during the Second World War, married a longtime boyfriend who became a successful doctor, had three children who grew up to be fine, successful people, and now she and her husband could look forward to a comfortable retirement.

Yet, what lay behind this story which tinged it all with sadness and at times locked her in the black prison of depression?

Disloyalty.

Her husband Roger had betrayed her again and again, not with other women but with one woman, his mother. She was a difficult woman who punished those who offended her with implacable silence. When differences arose between her and Elizabeth and Roger, and they often did, Roger always sided with his mother and left Elizabeth alone and unsupported.

Roger, like his mother, sulked, and this Elizabeth despised. In other respects Roger was a good husband and father, and so even though the glory and trust had vanished from her marriage, Elizabeth felt that she should take her own mother's advice and stay with Roger.

Throughout her story Elizabeth had made many references to her mother – what a wonderful woman she was, how close Elizabeth was to her, how distressed Elizabeth was at her mother's death. There was just the faintest hint of criticism in that perhaps her mother had given her the wrong advice about her marriage. This was quickly negated by Elizabeth pointing out that in those days a woman with three small children could not have separated from her husband. Her mother had just been stating the obvious.

The next time Elizabeth came to see me she talked about her mother and, in doing so, revealed how even the most truthful of us can not only censor our story but also forget that we did so. However, Elizabeth valued truth, and when her memory of her censorship returned she did not hide from it but confronted it with all its pain.

She told me how one day, when her mother was very old, her mother told her that there was one thing she had done to Elizabeth which she regretted. Elizabeth hastened to reassure her mother. 'No, mum, everything you did was fine. You've nothing to regret.'

Her mother insisted. She said that she regretted preventing Elizabeth from joining the Women's Air Force during the war.

Elizabeth said, 'No, mum, you didn't prevent me. I decided that it wasn't a good thing for me.'

Elizabeth described to me how in that conversation with her mother she had a distinct memory of herself weighing up the pros and cons and coming to the conclusion that leaving her position as a civil servant to join up was most unwise. It was not till much later that she remembered what had really happened. At eighteen she was bored and frustrated in her work. She applied to join the WAF and was accepted. Then she told her parents, and her mother was amazed and hurt. The subject was brought up again and again, with her mother saying, 'I've sacrificed myself to give you an education so you could get a good job, and now you're going to throw it away just to please yourself,' and all the while looking distressed, miserable and lonely.

Elizabeth could not carry this burden of guilt. She withdrew her application, remained in her job and with her mother, and dealt with the pain of her mother's selfishness and her own guilt by forgetting this part of her story and putting a fiction in its place.

However, even if we rewrite our stories, we still act in response to what really happened. Elizabeth knew that her mother would not want her to leave home to get married, and when, three years later, Roger finished his training and asked her to marry him, Elizabeth firmly told her mother that this was what she was going to do, and her mother acquiesced. At least as a married woman Elizabeth would still be open to her mother's guidance, and her mother had definite views about a wife's role as the servant and helpmate of her husband. 'His dinner should be on the table as he comes in the front door.'

Elizabeth had been brought up with the adage 'If a job's worth doing, it's worth doing well', which she interpreted as 'worth doing perfectly'. She did not allow herself to realize that she had embraced so many duties that she had lost her freedom. As she said to me recently, 'I remember early in the Sixties listening to a radio programme about Women's Liberation and thinking that it didn't apply to me. I was free. I didn't realize I was so loaded down with chains I could barely breathe.'

What she could not hide from herself was the frustration and fear that her husband created in her. Throughout their marriage she wanted to get things sorted out, to understand what went wrong between them, and to draw some conclusions so that in the future they would act more wisely. The things she wanted to get sorted out related to her feelings, her husband's understanding of her feelings, and his support of her. She found it hard to get him to engage in such a conversation, but occasionally he would agree to talk. Then he appeared to listen and to discuss, and at the end of the conversation he would agree that in future he would behave differently. So he did, for a short while, and then he slipped back to the old ways of ignoring her feelings and not supporting her. She was left frustrated, feeling that for all her efforts nothing had changed. She described one of these occasions where he refused to acknowledge what was happening to her as an experience of the near annihilation of her self. 'I felt that I was floating between heaven and hell.'

Elizabeth can now look back on the time when she was depressed and contrast it with now. She said, 'When you're depressed all you're interested in is survival. How can I get through the day? Now I feel that I've found myself again.'

She was able to make this change because she was prepared to examine aspects of her life that she had previously regarded as unquestionable. She allowed herself to see that by allowing her mother to influence her decision about what she should do with her life she had done much less than she might, but, rather than spend time regretting this, she resolved to make the most of her future. She came to accept that her husband was what he was and that she should give up trying to change him, and he, as we are all wont to do when people stop pushing us to change, changed, and became much more aware of and concerned for her. She recognized the power ploy in feeling guilty, and gave up berating herself for past failures. 'I did what I thought best at the time. There was nothing else I could have done.'

She saw, too, that, as parents, whatever we do for our children, we are likely to get it wrong, even if it is the best we can do. As any psychologist can tell you, the best way to teach anyone anything is to reward the right responses and ignore the wrong ones. Elizabeth's parents knew this without needing a psychologist to tell them, and they brought Elizabeth up with a constant supply of rewards and praise, just the sustenance an introvert needs for her sense of existence to be secure. Elizabeth said to me, 'I just expected that when I did something well I would be rewarded. I didn't realize that when you're a wife and mother you don't get rewards. I didn't expect praise for my housework, and my husband and children appreciated the meals I cooked, but that wasn't it. I was looking for proof of regard and caring, and it didn't come. I'd work and work, in a way testing him again and again, with the idea, "If I create this situation, then you'll show me that you understand." But he never did. I couldn't work out what was happening. I thought there was something wrong with me.'

Because she had been so intent on winning rewards by pleasing others she had never developed adequate skills in pleasing and rewarding herself. The lack of outside rewards made her feel diminished, just as her husband's lack of affirmation of her made her feel diminished. Once she saw this, she did not need to cling to the belief, 'If I am good I shall be rewarded', for she knew that this belief is the demand for that kind of security which makes impossible spontaneity, joy and hope.

# WINNING NEW BATTLES INSTEAD OF LOSING OLD ONES

What keeps us excluded from the spontaneity, joy and hope that allow us to live life to the full is that we keep on fighting old battles, instead of recognizing that we are engaged in new ones, and using the inadequate weapons of our childhood, instead of our adult wisdom and guile. The arguments that bedevil every workplace are rarely about the here and now. They are usually action replays of a child's unresolved battles with his parents.

John told me that he and the head of another department had to work out a programme together and that he dreaded this, for his colleague was an overbearing man who wanted his own way, regardless of other people's interests. John described their first discussion in which John felt frightened and overwhelmed, in fact, just as he did as a small boy when his bullying father overwhelmed and defeated him. I said to John that perhaps his colleague behaved in this irrational and unhelpful way because he was interpreting this new situation in the way he interpreted similar situations in his childhood. 'Oh, yes,' said John, and went on to tell me that his colleague was the son of a woman famous for her ardent political campaigning. Her son had never forgiven her for not giving him enough attention. Now he demanded that everyone give him the attention and acquiescence that his mother had denied him. So here were two grown men with a current and very serious business issue to resolve between them and each engaged, not in talking to one another, but in battling with a long dead parent.

Of course, all we can use in interpreting a new situation is our past experience, but if we continue to draw on only one part of our experience in the same way every time, instead of using the resources of our past experience creatively, we continue to make the same mistakes.

Even the best of therapists do this! My friend and colleague Jo Pearce was telling me about some of her current problems with her extremely difficult father, problems which distressed her greatly and played no small part in the headaches which plagued her. Such headaches had an additional worry. Her mother had died quite young of a brain haemorrhage. Not only did her headaches make Jo worry that such a fate lay in store for her, but they reminded her how, as a child, she had blamed herself for her mother's death.

Jo told me how, all through her mother's illness, she had been constantly warned, 'Don't upset your mother.' Her mother's death left her feeling that she had upset her mother by wanting her attention and concern, and that her mother had found this all too much and so had abandoned her. Now, when she tells her friends of her problems she is afraid that if she loads too much on them they will reject her.

Jo, being an extravert, has an image and an expectation of people rejecting and abandoning her. I, being an introvert, have an image and an expectation of people crumbling if I load my worries and needs upon them. I grew up with the admonition 'Don't upset your mother' ringing in my ears, for mother would get an asthma attack whenever she was upset, and as she disapproved of almost all of the universe there were plenty of things that upset her. My father would look very worried when mother was ill, and it seemed to me that he, too, was in danger of crumbling. So I kept my problems to myself and, very foolishly, strictly limited my expectations that people would listen to me and help me with my burdens.

Of course, another reason I refrained from telling others of my problems was because I would not run the risk of criticism. I always think my clients are very brave, putting themselves in a situation where I can criticize them. And, of course, I do, for criticism is implied whenever I try to make obvious the implicit meaning in their story.

In our first talk Stephen told me in a very hurried fashion about how Madeline had ended their relationship after he had told her about a previous relationship where the girl concerned had had an abortion. Madeline had not simply refused to see him again but had gone to some trouble to make him feel thoroughly shamed and rejected.

In listening to this I assumed that this had happened shortly before his first panic attack which left him thinking that he was dying, but I was wrong. The events had happened over two years previously, but the pain of that memory had not ameliorated one tiny jot.

At our second meeting Stephen talked about his need to be truthful and honest. He wanted people to accept him and to like him as he was, and being honest and truthful was an essential part of this. He could not lie. He could manage fibs – 'That's a nice dress' or 'I enjoyed the meal' – but he could not lie in important matters.

In theory speaking the truth is the best way to behave, but in practice speaking the truth causes problems. If you want people to like you it is often best to keep your thoughts to yourself.

Stephen and I talked about this in terms of how hard he found reprimanding his staff. He mentioned again how much he wanted people to accept him as he was, and went on to speak of the conflict in his childhood, when his father and teachers expected him to be tough, manly and good at sport, and his mother wanted him to speak and act like a well brought up boy from a middle class family. His mother did not approve of his mates. Stephen told me how one day she told him that he was not to play with them. They were common working class boys, socially beneath him. For some months he did not see his mates. Then one day they met, and they asked him why he was staying away from them. Unable to lie, he told them that his mother had ordered him to and why. In the telling he did not condemn and reject his mother, and so his mates condemned and rejected him.

I pointed out the similarity between this story and the story of how his girlfriend had rejected him. He agreed in some surprise, for he had not seen the pattern himself. But at a deeper level he had, for later in our conversation he told me of a recurring dream where he is out shooting and the bird he shoots turns into a plane and crashes, injuring people. Then he goes to a house and confesses what he had done.

In each of these incidents, with his mother and his mates, with Madeline, and in his recurring dream, Stephen is trying to deal with the dilemma, 'If I tell the truth I get rejected, but if I don't tell the truth I can't be myself.'

Stephen solved this dilemma by realizing that life was livable only if he was himself, and that if other people did not accept him that was their problem, not his. Once he allowed himself to be himself he could also let himself know that he really is a very likeable person, and that he was in no danger of being universally rejected.

Of course, once we allow ourselves to be ourselves we can have problems with those family members who have a vested interest in us remaining as we were, irrespective of our sufferings. Once Stephen became himself he could make decisions, and some of these decisions did not suit his sister. She fought back with the one weapon which had always brought him to heel in the past, shame. 'If you do this you'll never be able to live with yourself again,' she flung at him, and Stephen felt himself falling back into the old, anxious ways. But his father came to his rescue. After a lifetime of ordering Stephen about, he now said, 'You do what you want to do. It's your life.'

If Stephen had not risked being himself he would never have discovered that his father had changed and was no longer a totally overbearing ogre. Similarly, if Margaret had not risked doing what she feared most, she would still be trapped.

I wrote of Margaret in *Beyond Fear*.

'Margaret cannot bear to be touched. She cannot bear to be alone, but when she is with people she cannot bear them to come too close. When she first came to see me she told me that she knew she was a bad person. She had known this ever since she was a small child. She knew that she was bad through and through. She spoke of herself as a child without any sympathy or concern because, as she told me when I asked, she did not deserve any. She said that as a child she had done something terrible but she would not tell me what it was. If she told me what it was I would see how bad she was and then I wouldn't want to have anything to do with her. This was the theme of our meetings, every fortnight for more than two years.'

Eventually, she told me how, as a child, she and her friends were involved in some sexual games, and how, when the adults found out, she bore all the blame. Her friends 'never played with me, not ever again. And they told other people about me. When I went to secondary school, some of the boys from the boys' high school knew, and they'd say things. That's why, when I left, I went right away. But I'm always frightened they'll find out where I am and they'll tell people and I'll lose my job and nobody will talk to me.'

She had left home as soon as she was old enough and never went back. Nor did she keep in touch with her mother. However, after she told me her story she was able to take up more social activities and enjoy them. She also became a devotee of Quentin Crisp, whose recommendations that we should be ourselves made more impression on her than mine did. Then one evening she phoned to ask whether I thought she should phone her mother and wish her a happy Christmas. Knowing that she had already decided to do so, I gave the therapist's usual non-directive answer. Some weeks later she went to visit her mother, and found that one of her friends, Betty, a partner in the shameful misdemeanours, lived next door. Betty welcomed her with open arms, and, summoning all the other old friends and their families, organized a welcome home party for Margaret. Now Margaret can let herself be the warm, wise and witty person she has always been.

I have a friend, Gregory, whom I visit when I am in the USA and with whom I have a regular correspondence about our families and our work. Gregory is interested in the history of scientific and religious phenomena, with a special interest in concepts of the supernatural. I had sent him a copy of *Beyond Fear*, and shortly after received the following letter,

'I am working through a great and liberating psychological crisis of my own. It was reading your books on depression that made me first wonder if I was a depressive. Recently experiencing mounting anxiety, hopelessness, and fear (for no objective reason) I went to a psychiatrist and was promptly diagnosed as a typical lifelong depressive. I'm quite sure he's right as I fit almost every criterion.

'You won't be surprised that the psychiatrist put me on anti-depressant drugs right away, but his approach was sensible in that it was combined with therapy with a clinical psychologist. I must have been unconsciously ready for it, because almost immediately a whole new level of my psyche came to light. It was very poisonous and had to be coughed out.

'How right you were when you said that my work on demons was "really" about my father. I have finally been able to admit, to my enormous relief, that my father hated me like poison from the time I was a small child. The image I have of myself as a small boy is lying there in bed at night with a hideous, dark, mothlike thing fluttering above me sucking my life out. Have you ever seen a fly that a spider has finished with: it's a dry husk with an empty space inside where the fly's whole being has been drained away. That's what I felt like – only not quite, because there remained (fortunately) a part of me that was still alive. But in order to survive that terror that self had to surround itself with armor and isolate itself.

'With incredible and wonderful rapidity, within a few days of these terrifying revelations I began a marvellous process of healing. I was able in fantasy and with deep emotion to make contact with that small boy, to reassure him that he was a good, strong, loving person, and, above all, a lovable person and I loved him very much. I was able to go into his room where he lay terrified at night and pick him up and hug him and *take him out of there*. For some reason I wanted to take him to a sidewalk cafe, and we sat there in the sunshine watching the people go by and talking. And I told him I would never leave him.

'It was one of the most powerful experiences I have ever had.

'Then I went to make contact with the miserable adolescent me. This was much harder, for he had so much time to build up his defenses. Here was this homely, pimply child with greasy hair and a fragile, husklike persona surrounding vast emptiness, and inside this emptiness a huge amount of plate armor surrounding himself. Whereas I could get quickly into a state of deep love for the small boy Greggy, I found it difficult to convince the adolescent Greg that I loved him because in fact it was really difficult to feel the love, and he knew it.

'I finally got through to him by using an experience that he had that I can still emotionally resonate to. I have always called it my God experience. It may well have been God.

Whatever it was, it was an enormously affirming experience to a miserable, depressed, isolated child. I was alone in my room in my grandmother's house (I was visiting her), and without warning I suddenly felt what I can only call an absolute presence, which seemed to say, simply *I am here*. Somehow that steelplated shell of the adolescent opened in that love, and I was able to enter through that opening and finally love that boy. I convinced both him and myself that he was not the husk or the emptiness or even the armor but that loving self deep down in there.

'I then went to him at his most miserable: all those grey mornings when he got up and made ready for school with a feeling of dull dread in his stomach, a sense of total greyness and isolation. I went into his room on one of those mornings and said, "We're getting out of here."

'At first I had the fantasy that I would take him to the same cafe and the three of us – the small Greggy, the adolescent Greg, and the adult, could get together, but somehow that didn't work. So I asked the boy Greg what he would like and he said to go on a long car trip through the west. Then we were driving together through the Nevada basin and range area, and I told him, "I love you, and you are *never* going to see that school again, or that house again, or your father again, *ever*." What about my mother, he seemed to ask, and I said, "OK, your mother really loves you, and we'll see her again. But the rest of it, *never again*." The boy seemed to expand and became animated.

'These contacts were followed by the most powerful physical sensations, which continued for many days. It was as if I could feel those steel bolts holding the steel protective plates around me popping loose one by one, and each popping gave me a surge of pleasure. There have been hundreds of poppings, and more to come (I hope and trust) because the plates are still there, but they are certainly coming apart. I feel myself filling out; my body is more alive than I have ever felt in it.

'I still have a way to go, but I have found "the way out of my depression", and I actually have the wild hope that I won't be depressed any more. For the first time I am accepting positive feelings about myself. I can't tell you how much I love and admire those children, especially their strength and courage against those terrifying, incomprehensible attacks. They might have been annihilated; they might have turned into something bitter and vicious; but somehow they kept their love and creativity. Loving them for the first time, I'm finally ready to love myself (of course they are myself!).

'Your earlier books on depression helped me prepare myself for this, but your recent book, which I read just as I started psychotherapy, was perhaps of really crucial help. It helped me identify the underlying feeling of my childhood as sheer terror. Until a month ago I would have described my childhood as a happy one, with some problems, and I already understood my father's ambivalence. Ambivalence, hell, he hated my guts. I know he did have some positive feelings as well, but the underlying feeling was an annihilating hatred.'

People like Gregory who have made such discoveries and changes in themselves do not put these experiences behind them but rather find in such experiences an endless source of wisdom. As time goes by they are able to see these experiences with greater and greater clarity, and are able to give an account of the wisdom derived from them. Sheldon Kopp[8] has written a great deal about his experiences when he developed a brain tumour which threatened his life and his sanity. He now describes the wisdom he gained from such experiences in the following way,

'At the time I fell ill, I still believed that life had inherent meaning, and that I had an important part in what was to happen to me and to those around me. My tumor seemed an undeserved and tragic fate. How the hell did that fit into the grand scheme? Not only had I started out as the innocent victim of my parents' mistreatment, but nobly transcending that unfair disadvantage, I had gone on to transform my suffering into a continuing fight against injustice. Why should a good guy like me end up with a brain tumor?

'It took me two more years of therapy to resolve this pseudoinnocent question. Knowing that my mother hated me was not enough. I remained excessively vulnerable to life's random mishaps. I could not keep myself safe from making too much of my occasional bad luck until I realized that though it is probably true that my own mother hated me, it was nothing personal.

'Any kid living in that house at that time would have served as a suitable target. It was my misfortune to have been the one who wandered in. There was no special meaning to it all, no compensations for that less-than-perfect beginning. As an adult I was free to choose to do what I could to alleviate the suffering of others. I need only to understand that this compassionate activity would neither avenge my past nor assure my future.

'The first time I entered into therapy my question had been, "Why am I such an awful person?" The answer turned out to be, "You are not an awful person. You only feel that way now because as a child you were treated as though you were bad." This time my question was, "Why me?" The answer turned out to be, "Why not?".'

Only when we can accept that 'Why not?' are we ready to be our Successful Self.

# The Successful Self

# 7

# Creating Your Successful Self

It is our ability to accept 'Why not?' that gives us our freedom. There is no special reason why we have been singled out for bad fortune, any more than there is a special reason why we have been singled out for good fortune. 'Why not?' enables us to enjoy good fortune without guilt or the expectancy of an inevitable bad fortune to follow, and to cope with our bad fortune as best we can, unhampered by the feeling that somehow we must have deserved it.

By freedom I do not mean from work and responsibility to others, for bodily survival requires work — even on a tropical island the coconuts have to be collected — and from giving and receiving, for we live with other people. Nor do I mean freedom from the consequences of our acts. All our acts have consequences, usually different from what we expected and far wider than we can ever know.

By freedom I mean freedom within ourselves. We are not constrained, boxed in: we are not driven to act. The world is available to us, and full of wonderful possibilities. Even at our busiest, we can take time to listen, to look and to wonder. As we take our ease, we speculate upon possibilities for action and create a multitude of plans.

Such freedom comes with the realization that you are not a puppet moved by the decree of some Grand Plan of Universal Justice, where your striving to be good is properly rewarded, and when it is not you are left confused, frightened and resentful. You realize that our suffering is not a punishment for our wickedness. Our suffering comes from three sources: the planet, which is not particularly adapted to our needs and shows an impartiality to the survival of each of the species on it; our body, which is of limited life span and prone to malfunction; and from ourselves, for, in our refusal to understand ourselves, we injure ourselves and others. It is our refusal to understand ourselves that is the cause of most of our suffering.

Realizing that there is no Grand Design of rewards and punishments does not mean viewing the world as a causal connection of atoms and particles and we as merely the result of chemical changes. Such a view is just as constrained and demeaning as the view that God is a touchy and irascible old man with strong views on sexual activities but not on war and famine, and who has a peculiar sense of justice, or is frequently blind, deaf and forgetful. Realizing that there is no Grand Design of rewards and punishments means that we have to apply ourselves to trying to understand life, while knowing that our understanding can never be complete, and to understand why we act, and what the consequences of our actions might be.

Realizing that there is no Grand Design of rewards and punishments frees us from the battle to protect our self from annihilation. This is one of the stages in the creation of the Successful Self.

**The Successful Self is not engaged in a constant battle to avoid the threat of annihilation of the self.**

Those desperate defences which earn us the label of being mentally ill are not the only defences used by people still engaged in the constant battle to avoid the annihilation of the self. There are a great many people who are apparently leading normal, successful lives, but whose every action is motivated not so much by positive plans and desires as by the anxiety to avoid a danger which is not understood, rarely brought consciously to mind, but is known to the person as a shameful, secret weakness.

Against this fear these peope have developed a whole range of defences which they regard as habits. The nameless fear can be turned into named *worries*, and the world is full of expert worriers, capable of turning every aspect of life, however joyful, into a worry. The nameless fear motivates and is temporarily assuaged by *work*, and the world is full of workaholics, who dread empty weekends, holidays and growing old.

If there was an Olympics of worrying and working, both introverts and extraverts would be equally talented competitors, but in keeping the universe apparently organized and under control the introverts would win, and in getting people to need you and depend on you the extraverts would win. In the omnipresent and continual Olympics created and maintained by the belief that being good is always rewarded and being bad punished, the contestants, wanting to claim that they are successful through their own efforts, have to blame themselves when they fail. So much of what nowadays is called stress is the only partially successful and always debilitating attempts by people to ward off through worry, work and trying to be good the threat of the annihilation of the self.

Why do people persist in behaving in this way, causing themselves and their loved ones so much unhappiness? Why don't they change?

Medieval theologians once drew up a list of the Seven Deadly Sins and, of these, they said, the Deadliest was Pride, because *pride stops you from changing.*

It is pride that stops us from confronting our fear of annihilation, naming it for what it is, and seeing that it is something we created in childhood and that it has no claim on us once we cease to be children. It is our pride which makes us call our defences against an illusory fear virtues, and we take pride in our virtues.

Thus, introverts try to protect themselves from what they believe is the greatest danger by setting themselves high standards of organization, achievement, clarity and control, and not only do they take great pride in their high standards, but they take great pride in setting standards for other people (particularly their unfortunate children) to emulate. Extraverts try to protect themselves from what they believe is the greatest danger by charming, controlling and manipulating people into doing what the extraverts want them to do, that is, to form and maintain groups to which the extravert belongs. (Their unfortunate children are never allowed, emotionally, to leave home.) Extraverts take great pride in being lovable.

When, at your very core, you know yourself to be weak and frightened, how can you give up the few rags of glory that cover your nakedness? If you are not a standard setter or a much loved person you have no claim to fame or distinction.

Hence many people are stuck in these roles, unable to journey onwards. Those who do make the journey onwards have usually been pushed by events to confront their fear. Such introverts have had the experience of being overwhelmed by their emotions and losing all control, and extraverts the sense of emptiness which creates the fear that they cannot go on, for there is nothing to go on with.

While it is pride's inevitable fall that can force us to confront our fear of annihilation, such a confrontation does not necessarily have to result from the extremes of distress. It needs simply to be *the decision to change*. How can we begin?

Our emotional experiences, as well as being felt in our body and mind, and described in words, are felt in an *image*. When we talk about what we are feeling we draw on this image. By making the image clear and explicit to ourselves we can see its meaning more clearly and thus decide whether that meaning should still apply in our life.

Stephanie Alexander did this when she wrote to me shortly after reading *Beyond Fear*. She wrote,

'I want to describe, before it gets away from me, what fear looks like to me. It is a vision I have half-seen many times in a kind of horror but as I've read your book it has appeared in three dimensions, very vivid. The scene is a small white room with tall walls, and I am attached to the figure trapped in it, but also above her and looking down. I cannot see her face: it is held down and out of sight. She is naked, the skin dark red as if flayed, and she hugs herself and seems even smaller then she really is (I am quite a large person, but this Self is tiny). She-I experience how soft her flesh is and how brittle her bones. There is nothing to prevent her from being eliminated, annihilated – she's as vulnerable as the most vulnerable of the molluscs – the soft, soft, soft, vapidly pretty sea slugs most of whose beauty relies on the buoying effect of the water. The threat is not of attack by people. It is of an attack by nothingness. The tiny room is in a great complex of empty white walls which open imperceptibly on to a land of complete barrenness – flat, chewed-looking, khaki-coloured grass and not even the empty beauty of a sandy desert. I suspect the tiny room is actually in an airport, where one is merely a small and transient piece of flesh and bone which could be easily lost – just swept away by a puff of air.'

She went on,

'As I drifted off to sleep, I got a stern message that this picture of fear is incomplete, and that those white concourses open from time to time to admit swarms and swarms of people. A thousand counters with incomprehensible ever-changing neon signs; hundreds of inaudible announcements; and those people knowing exactly what they're doing and where they're going. Only I do not know and dare not ask. And even if I cling to a pillar I cannot stop those millions of people walking through me on their purposeful way.'

When Stephanie first wrote to me in 1983 after reading my book *Depression: the Way Out of Your Prison*, she lived a life where people did walk all over her, and she believed that as she was such a bad, useless person she should not object. When she decided that she would take charge of her life, she found that the image ceased to have such a hold on her. Her letter went on,

'I set all this down smiling, because it has the quality of a memory and not a present reality. It has elements that are a bit anxious-making, but certainly not paralysing and that means many steps forward have been taken ... The joy is in saying, I too can lay out my terrors; I too can understand that I have them, and even why I have some of them. To me they are real and terrible terrors and it is marvellous to be given permission (or to give myself permission) to look at them and describe them and say hello to them and put out a hand and stroke them – and so great shapeless monsters rearing out of the dark become manageable creatures. With love perhaps they can become purring cuddlies – a grotesque hope at the moment, but why not indulge in something way out for once.'

The way to turn these 'real and terrible terrors' into 'manageable creatures', if not into 'purring cuddlies' is to recognize that the threat of annihilation of the self is an illusion. When we feel that our self is shattering or disappearing, what is happening is that it is not our *self* but the *structure of meaning* we have created which is shattering and disappearing.

The structure of meaning is a set of interrelated sentences or propositions which describe what we believe is our self and our relationship with the world. Usually we take this structure of meaning to be real, solid and true, and when we find that it is not, that, whatever reality is, it is different from what we thought it was, we feel frightened. It is as if you are in your car driving along a road and, suddenly, the car, the road and the very earth have disappeared and you are falling through space. Thus an extravert woman's structure of meaning may revolve around the proposition, 'I am married to a good, kind, truthful man whom I love and who loves me, and we shall spend the rest of our lives together.' When she discovers that he has embezzled his firm's money and fled to South America with his longtime mistress, a large part of her structure of meaning has disappeared, but she feels this as if she is in danger of disappearing. An introvert man's structure of meaning may revolve around the proposition 'I am an extremely competent businessman and in ten years' time I shall be managing director of this firm.' On the day he is fired most of his structure of meaning is shattered, but he feels this as if *he* is shattering.

Many people spend their lives trying to insist that their structure of meaning is the Real and Absolute Truth, and that the world *must* conform to it. Thus the woman whose husband has deserted her can insist that he has done what he has because he loves her, that the story about his mistress is not true, and that one day they will be together again. The business man who has been fired can insist that he is the victim of a vendetta and that he will punish those people and force the firm to reinstate him with apologies and promotions, no matter how much this costs him and how long it takes.

Alternatively, this woman and man can say to themselves, 'I got it wrong', and with this statement *distinguish between the self that endures and the structure of meaning which, though it can shatter and disappear, can always be rebuilt.* Then they can acknowledge and endure their disappointment and anger, restore their self-confidence with statements like, 'I'm well rid of that man', and 'I was too good for that firm', and so build another structure of meaning which becomes their life.

When we are able, in our own lived experience and not just in intellectual thought, to distinguish our sense of self from the structure of meaning which our sense of self has constructed, we know that even if we get the structure of meaning wrong, our sense of self remains. Left completely alone, we may be unhappy, but we do not disappear. Seeing our structure of meaning as structure enables us to recognize that everything that is is in a state of flux, and what we see as our rigid and permanent categories of organization and control are fictions, illusions of permanency in a changing world. Recognizing this, we no longer feel compelled to control and organize, and do so only to amuse and to take care of ourselves.

Life *is* change, and that is what makes it interesting. We can waste our lives demanding that we should not be expected to change our structure of meaning, or we can spend our lives in the delight of always discovering something new.

Part of our structure of meaning is the set of propositions we apply to our self. If we apply propositions like, 'I value and accept myself, and that includes my weaknesses as well as my strengths' we have no difficulty in seeing our structure of meaning as simply a structure, and feeling strong enough and confident enough to change it as the need arises. However, if we apply propositions like, 'I am weak, bad and unacceptable and must strive to overcome my weakness, badness and unacceptability by being very good' the merest suspicion that our structure of meaning is no more than our ideas and that our ideas might be wrong comes to us as 'real and terrible terrors'.

Our propositions about our self are not always presented in sentences. They can exist most powerfully in images.

'Stephanie's image is of a self too weak to object to what other people, who seemed to care nothing for her, did. The origins of this were in her childhood. An only child, she was taken by her parents to live in South Africa, and encouraged, especially by her mother, to feel that they formed an exclusive and self-sufficient family unit – far away from English relatives her mother hated, superior to South Africans. Although her parents determinedly resisted "spoiling" her (discouraging demonstrativeness, "conceit" and "self-pity", and favouring stoic self-discipline) they were kind and generous. For Stephanie home was special and a happy place.'

'Stephanie was grateful to her parents for giving her everything that they had lacked in their own youth. She knew that they had the right to expect – and the power to demand – perfection from her in return. Besides, she secretly feared that as the least significant member of the charmed family circle she might lose her position – be banished in some way, perhaps – if she did not work hard to retain it.'

'The circle was beginning to relax naturally while Stephanie was away at university, but when she was twenty-one it shattered unexpectedly. Her parents were killed in a motor accident while she, though injured, survived. Alone and suddenly aware of physical fragility, she sought to protect herself by re-forming the circle, and so became the weak and vulnerable victim of parents grown more powerful in death – for she owed them everything – and whose imagined demands she could never meet. Worse, she began to give the same power to others, working to be good, to please and appease. Every failure etched more deeply the picture of herself as a nonentity without any rights and of others as solid, powerful and in control. They did not care for her because there was nothing in her to care for.'

'The more deeply etched the picture, the more it became an immutable part of the landscape – and the less possible it was to understand that she had drawn it herself and so could erase or paint over it herself.'[1]

Until we realize this, we are trapped forever in childhood. We look at our relatives, our friends and acquaintances, our colleagues, our bosses, and everybody in some position of authority, doctors, police, politicians, shop assistants and prime ministers, bus conductors and presidents, and we see them as powerful giants. We expect them to use their power to look after us, and when they fail to do so, we feel greatly wronged. At the same time we are frightened that they will use their power against us and punish us for our misdemeanours. So we try hard to be good.

However, if we acknowledge that we are adults in a world of adults, we see that the so-called 'authority figures' are nothing more than ordinary men and women, some of them fallible, hypocritical and ignorant, and others, fallible too, but honest and caring, capable of inspiring our respect but never our awe. As adults, we have outgrown hero worship. True, as adults we have to give up the hope that other people will look after us the way good parents look after their children, but how can you be free so long as you are always expecting to be looked after? When people look after us they expect us to do as we are told.

As children we are in the business of constructing our sense of self. Introvert children, knowing that they must achieve but needing to find standard setters who will guide and suggest possible goals, hope that their standard setters will give them approval and admiration, but they always find that criticism comes as well, and that criticism can be devastating. Extravert children, knowing that they need to gain membership of groups, hope that other people will accept them and like them, but they always find that rejection and dislike come as well, and that rejection and dislike can be devastating. It seems to children that the only way to avoid criticism, rejection and dislike is to be good.

**As children we do not realize that other people can criticize, reject and dislike us only if we let them. So long as we do not recognize this, we remain children.**

As adults we know that other people can say all the words and do all the actions that to them mean criticism, rejection and dislike, but if we do not want to accept these we do not have to do so. We can hold firmly to the belief that, 'Anyone who criticizes, rejects or dislikes me is a fool, and I don't take any notice of fools.'

So as not to be too pig-headed and vain, we can modify this belief to accepting thoughtful criticism from those whose opinions we respect and who respect us, and to allowing that other people may have attitudes and predicaments which lead them to reject or dislike us, but we do not take such rejection and dislike personally. Their dislike and rejection does not diminish us in any way.

However, we can reach this position of the Successful Self only when we have abandoned our belief in our essential badness and unacceptability.

# VALUING AND ACCEPTING YOURSELF

**The Successful Self feels valuable, self-accepting and self-confident.**

Discovering 'Why not?' means that you no longer have to take yourself seriously, and *not taking yourself seriously is an integral part of being self-accepting and self-confident, just as it is an integral part of being free.*

When we are under threat and have to battle to survive we take ourselves very seriously indeed. Like soldiers in a war, we have to be constantly aware of where there might be danger in our surroundings, and we have to keep ourselves alert and ready for battle, but, unlike soldiers who get periods of rest and relaxation, we must be constantly on guard. ('Life is a battle' is an interpretation of life which is held by many people.) Thus we have to be constantly aware of every word and gesture, even, or especially, those made in jokes and teasing, that other people make, in case a seemingly innocent word and gesture is really a dagger aimed at our heart. We have to be aware of our own every word and gesture as a defence to ward off injury or a provocation inviting more attacks. We see ourselves as being in danger because we know ourselves to be weak. Knowing ourselves to be weak, we suspect that we are insignificant and have no part in the scheme of things. The fact that people attack us and hate us means that we are of significance to them. So we make no attempt to step out of what we see as our fight for survival, for to do so, we believe, would mean that we would become a nothingness, or a minute figure in an empty desert. Survival, then, is no laughing matter.

The trap of seeing yourself in danger because you are weak, and needing to be in danger in order to invest yourself with some significance is further complicated by the need to strive for the rewards of goodness and the avoidance of the punishments for badness, and with that the belief in a just world where the good are rewarded and the bad punished.

Many people say that we must have a system of rewards and

punishments because if we did not everybody would choose to be bad. Such people are not aware that they are generalizing their sense of their own badness to everyone. They see babies as being born inherently bad, and fail to observe how children *enjoy* cooperating with and pleasing their parents, provided what their parents expect of them is within their capacity to achieve. There is no greater pleasure in life than sharing and caring and being with and enjoying one another's company, but this is possible only when we accept and trust one another. Parents, instead of loving their children as they are, see in them wickedness or potential wickedness, and, instead of letting the children grow naturally, as a flower unfolds, control and punish their children, and, as a flower bound and cut will not blossom with its natural beauty intact, neither will the children. Thus the parents rob their children of their potentiality, and deprive themselves of the joy of being with their children, sharing, caring and accepting one another. Fortunately for us, unlike flowers, we are capable of reflecting upon ourselves, and, from such reflections, change.

**We can discover that we see people as bad because we are frightened of them, and not that we are frightened of people because they are bad.**

However, as small children we cannot understand that our parents see us as bad because they are frightened of us. (They are frightened of us because they fear their own weakness and inadequacy, and are frightened that they will lose their children or let them get out of control.) Instead, we grow up believing that somehow, no matter how good we try to be, we are bad and unacceptable (and so grow up to be frightened of our children as our parents were of us).

How can we rid ourselves of this belief? *How can we find again the capacity to be ourselves that we were born with?*

The sense of badness and unacceptability is like a huge, heavy box strapped to our shoulders and weighing us down. What we need to do is to take the box off our shoulders, open it, and sort through its contents. There will be one or two pieces which, when we examine them, prove to be not vast, unmanageable, weighty horrors, but valuable tiny trinkets we can slip into our pockets.

Thus we can empty the box, discard it, and travel lightly and freely.

Among the rubbish we can throw away are the negative ideas we have about what we look like and what we are capable of doing.

So much of the criticism that is thrown at us as children concerns what we look like, and this worries us terribly. We are always too tall or too short, too fat or too thin, our hair is too straight or too curly, our skin is too pale or too brown, our legs are too long or too short, our nose is too big or too small, and our awareness of those parts of ourselves that other people approve of is totally outweighed by our awareness of those parts that other people disapprove of. As we grow up we cannot get rid of these worries because the message that comes to us from magazines, newspapers, films and television is that if you are not young, thin and beautiful you are of no importance at all.

(If we spent as much time and effort in appraising how well we get along with one another as we do in appraising one another's appearance our lives would be transformed.)

Conscious of this all-pervasive criticism, we can remain unaware that our impression of what we look like (what psychologists call our *body image*) is wrong. We look in the mirror and see something that is not there.

Like many children, I grew quite quickly when I was ten and eleven, and this was a never-ending source of comment and complaint by my mother, especially when I became taller than she was. Not that this was any great height. Mother was five foot three inches, and I grew to my full height of five foot five inches. However, my image of myself was that I was unnaturally tall, towering over people who were the right and proper height. My image was reinforced at school where the teachers would order the children to stand in line from the tallest to the shortest. Three of us would be singled out to head each line.

This sense of being immensely tall, along with the sense of being immensely overweight (my sister would refer to me and my friend Joyce, who was similar to me in build, as 'the elephants') combined with my perception of other people being likely to crumble if I was too forceful. I withdrew more into myself and, at the same time, became very protective of the people I cared for.

If I had drawn a picture of how I experienced these relationships it would have been of a large me, bending over, arms curved protectively over small, vulnerable, but perfectly formed, people. (What I am trying to convey here is that our body image is not just a mental picture of 'what I look like' but is an integral part of how we see ourselves relating to the world and to other people.)

At thirty-nine I was still using this image and not recognizing it as false. I had by then two good friends, Jake and Janet Empson. We were doctorate students with lots of worries in common. I felt protective to them both, but to little Janet in particular. I had no doubt as to what our respective heights were. If one of my erstwhile teachers had ordered us to stand in line, thin, gangly Jake would have gone first (I had no difficulty in seeing that a man could be taller than me, for I never grew taller than my father), then me, and then little Janet.

One evening when the three of us were together in my flat I said something which included a reference to the fact that I was taller than Janet.

'No, you're not,' said Janet. 'I'm taller than you. I always think of you as little Dorothy.'

I was astounded. How could an intelligent young woman, a psychologist, be so mistaken. I protested that she was wrong. I was taller than she was.

Jake, ever the experimental psychologist, said, 'Stand back to back. Over there, where you can see in the mirror.'

We did as he said, and there, to our mutual astonishment, Janet and I saw that we were exactly the same height.

This discovery did more than enable me to see myself and Janet as women of average height. It also enabled me to relinquish a protective posture towards my clients. The wise, kindly, caring therapist, leaning protectively over the client prevents the client from becoming a fully grown adult and preserves the therapist in a false and essentially empty role. My image of therapy became that of two people in a vast and bottomless deep well of water. My client is thrashing around and, in so doing, is in danger of drowning. My sole advantage is that I know that if you remain still and *trust the water*, it will bear you up and support you. I do not let my client cling to me, for then we would both drown, but

I stretch out my arm and with my finger tips support him until he discovers for himself what I already know.

For some people reassessing their body image requires a great deal of effort, for their childhood experiences left them feeling that they did not own their own body.

One of our tasks in early childhood is to construct a sense of self which is co-terminous with our body. We do this by developing control over our body, discovering what I-and-my-body can do and can choose to do. However, children lose this control over their own body and the unified sense of I-and-my-body when adults treat the child's body as an object. This happens when the adult vents his or her passions on the child's body in rage or sex. It also happens when parents, with their desire to be good parents and believing that this includes taking a keen and intrusive interest in their child's bowel movements, handles the child's body like an object in examining the child's rectum and genitalia. Similarly, doctors, who as a profession find it easier to treat people as bodies rather than people, can refuse to recognize the necessity of respecting a child's right to bodily privacy. Many children find the way they are treated by their parents and doctors in the name of vigilance and good health indistinguishable from sexual assault. These experiences can leave the child experiencing his body as an object separate from himself instead of being a unified I-and-my-body. The separation of body and self means that the person does not care for 'this object my body' in both senses of not caring for, that is, not liking and not looking after. The images such a person has of 'this object my body' contain a sense of separation of body and self and memories of what it felt like being treated as an object.

Just as we need to sort out and change as necessary our image of what we look like and how we relate to others, we need to sort out our beliefs about what we can do. The kind of criticism and contempt flung at us as children by parents and teachers led us to believe that our abilities were limited even in those areas where our parents and teachers expected us to achieve. Many things that we would have enjoyed doing were forbidden to us, for they were 'sissy', or 'girls don't do those things', or 'vulgar and cheap', or 'not our style', or 'not for the likes of you', or 'no use to you in earning a living', or 'a waste of time since you'll be getting married'. We entered adulthood not just with a very limited range of skills and interests, but with an unawareness of the possibilities that life offers. Our perception of ourselves as having limited skills, interests and abilities prevents us from elaborating our sense of existence and from taking the step which enables us to accept and value ourselves.

As I write about the need to give up the belief that we are bad and unacceptable it can seem that this is easy to do. But it is not. You can change your belief 'Brand X soap powder is no good' to 'Brand X soap powder is good' without having to alter anything much of your structure of meaning and your actions. But changing 'I am bad and unacceptable' to 'I like every bit of me, even my weaknesses' means that every part of your structure of meaning will change in some way and with that your every action and thought will be different in some way. It seems that with things like soap powder we can change our mind, but with more profound meanings we need to do more.

Over the years I have seen many people change from 'I am bad and unacceptable' to 'I like every bit of me, even my weaknesses' and they have all done the same sort of thing. They begin by deciding that their life is just too miserable to endure any longer and that they are going to do something about it. They find a therapist, or join a group, or take themselves off for an encounter weekend or a drama therapy course. They read Eric Berne and Fritz Perls, Alan Watts and Sheldon Kopp, and Dorothy Rowe of course. They work their way through *Passages* and *The Cinderella Complex*, *The Women's Room* and *The Female Eunuch*. They may venture into Freud and Jung, or if religiously inclined into more inspirational texts. They may become the best read client in the history of therapy, and at the end of it all they know that they need to accept and value themselves. They know, in terms of almost every psychological and philosophical theory why this is so, but such knowledge is only intellectual knowledge. It is in their heads, not in their hearts. Until it is in every fibre of their being nothing much has changed.

A little has changed. Instead of the absolutely rigid structure of meaning, there is a little bit of flexibility, what Gregory experienced as 'those steel bolts holding the steel protective plates around me popping loose one by one'. Some forgotten events have been seen again, and some remembered events have been reinterpreted. Whatever, out of this flexibility an idea emerges, 'I shall do something.' This something may be something very revolutionary – get a job, when every argument as to why this was impossible was well known to all who would listen – leave the marriage, when previously any suggestion that the marriage was not perfect had been vigorously rejected – study for a degree, when previously age and imbecility obviously precluded such a course. Or this something may be simply finding again something that was lost – returning to the sport that had been relinquished for family responsibilities, painting a picture just for oneself and not for others, sending a card to a friend with whom one had quarrelled. Whatever the 'something' it forms an action in which the internal and external realities are united. It is not the extravert's usual rushing around, avoiding the difficult parts of external and internal reality, or the introvert's obsessional organization of external reality. It is *an action which unites internal and external reality in a thoughtful and yet spontaneous way, a creative, new act*. It is not in response to a direction by someone else, but a personal decision. It is risky, for it may fail. It is difficult, for the necessary skills and experience are lacking to some degree, but an act without personal responsibility, risk and difficulty would not have the effect this act has, which is to change the core of the structure of meaning. Out of such an act 'I am bad and unacceptable' gradually becomes 'I like every bit of me, even my weaknesses'.

The creative act which restores a sense of self-worth enables the person to unpack the most feared contents of the box, the hidden memories of childhood and the hidden sense of badness.

*The hidden memories of childhood concern those events which led us to believe that we were bad and unacceptable*. Retrieving them and looking at them from the perspective of an older person, we see a small child suffering through the actions of an adult. If we still dislike ourselves, we look at the child we were without pity, but if we care for ourselves we feel pity for the child, and pity is a painful emotion.

Looking at the adult is even more difficult.

From earliest childhood we have been taught that only wicked and ungrateful children criticize their parents. Some of us never dare to do so, and hence remain, no matter how old we may become, obedient and grateful children. Some of us went through the teenage rebellion stage where we criticized our parents endlessly, but always feeling guilty for doing so. This made our rebellion very painful and confused, and, unless we had parents who tolerated our bad behaviour and did not use our guilt to manipulate and punish us, we emerged from this stage even more estranged from our parents but still unable to see them as people struggling with their own concerns in which we were more an object for their feelings rather than a person in our own right. Criticizing our parents still made us feel guilty.

Feeling guilty and trying to deal with our guilt by propitiation and expiation (for instance, phoning home, regular visits there, present to parents, having parents to stay, before every decision asking, 'What would mother think of this?' even though mother has been dead some twenty years) is a defence against acknowledging the mutual hate that exists in a parent-child relationship.

Feeling guilty and trying to deal with the guilt by propitiation and expiation also serves the purpose of stopping ourselves feeling pity for our parents. As children, if we loved our parents, as most of us did, we sometimes pitied them, and so we discovered how painful feeling pity is. I always remember how when I was seven I asked my mother to buy me a pencil case to take to school. I explained to her that it was very important that the pencil case contained a pencil sharpener. When she returned from town she gave me the pencil case she had bought. It was a nice blue one, opening out to show the pencils strapped inside. However, there was no sharpener, just a pointed metal cover to go over the tip of a sharpened pencil. I showed this to my mother, and she said, pointing to the pencil cover, 'Isn't that a sharpener?' I remember standing suffused in pity for my mother who did not know the difference between a pencil sharpener and a pencil cover. I hastened to assure her that the pencil case was fine, even though secretly I was bitterly disappointed. Looking back now, I am sure that my mother did know the difference between a pencil cover and a pencil sharpener. She was sorry she had not taken the time to look at what she was buying, but, typically, she defended herself by pleading ignorance rather than admit she had made a mistake. When I got older I saw this way of her behaving, but at seven all I saw was her vulnerability. Now when my clients become angry and fearful as our discussion verges on some criticism of my client's parents, I know that it is not just the possibility of guilt but of pity as well which creates this fear and anger. Pity is often far harder to bear than guilt.

Guilt is a horrible feeling, but it has some saving graces. We show that we are good by feeling guilty when we lapse from our standards of goodness. We can assuage our guilt with acts of expiation and propitiation. We can predict and prevent guilt by acts of omission and commission. Whereas pity can catch us unawares. Our heart contracts with a sudden pain which then showers sharply through our body, and tears spring to our eyes. We do not know what the tears are for. Have they come from the pain, or are they for the object of our pity, or for ourselves? Perhaps all three, for in our pity we perceive not just another person, but the ultimate sadness of life and our own intimate relation to that sadness.

Painful though pity may be, it is through our capacity for pity that we can return to those scenes of childhood which taught us to believe that we were bad and unacceptable, re-experience the fear, hate and helplessness, but without the sense of being trapped as we were as a child, and with the understanding that human beings, through their ignorance and aggression, injure one another. We may not yet be able to forgive our parents, for forgiveness is a very slow process, but we can pity them, just as we can pity the child we once were, and so remember our past with sadness and mourning. Those of us who suffered in child-hood, and most of us did, can never again live in total bliss, but it is better to live freely with sadness than to trap ourselves in denial and depression. Acknowledging our own sadness allows us to acknowledge the sadness of others, and through that draw closer to them.

Acknowledging and accepting our own sadness helps us in acknowledging and accepting those parts of us which we see as evidence of our essential badness.

Out of this feared darkness arise those forces which, in order for us to survive and to press on with our lives, make us want to push aside all those people and objects which frustrate and threaten us. When those forces are felt as rage and hate and the desire to kill they seem evil, and if we let ourselves express them as cruelty, violence and murder we do evil, harming others and the world we live in. When these forces are felt as the determination to go on living, to protect other people, and to create, they are felt as courage and vitality which we value.

> **Our problem as human beings living together is always how to control our evil destructive forces while not crippling or eradicating our creative forces, for both spring from the same source, a living being.**

The function of all living beings is to live. All of us, from single cells to people, strive to go on living. I cannot say what an amoeba feels like when its striving to live is frustrated, but I can say what happens to people. The moment we are frustrated prevented from proceeding on with our living, be it in taking the next breath or in building a multinational company, we feel anger, and just as swiftly the anger turns to aggression, the drive and feeling which insist that we shall go on living and proceeding along the path we have mapped out for ourselves. As complex living creatures we have developed a multitude of ways of expressing our aggression, from the rage of a newborn baby trying to avoid suffocation, through the violence of a warrior or murderer, to the intricacies of the legal mind, but whatever, our responses as living creatures every day and in every way follow the same pattern.

frustration → anger → aggression

There is just one way in which all societies in all races and cultures and in history have dealt with the problem that we need aggression to survive, yet aggression within a group is very destructive to that group. Each group says of itself, 'We are not aggressive. It is our enemies who are aggressive. We have to defend ourselves against our enemies.' Thus aggression within the group is projected outwards, the members of the group can then think of themselves as virtuous, and young men, whose vitality is a threat to the group's peace and stability, can be sent off to fight and die as heroes. Enemies are a necessary part of how we organize our society.[2]

While we kept our wars small and local by fighting on a

battlefield and not in towns and villages, while the group's leaders actually took part in the fighting, and each man made his own weapons, this was a way of dealing with aggression and envy which caused hardship and suffering to a great many people, but it did not threaten our existence as a species. However, when the ritual of war was abandoned and civilians were caught up in the fighting, when the leaders retreated to the safety of their bunkers, and the armament manufacturers began amassing wealth and power, the dangerous aspect of aggression, its blind destructiveness, became uncontrolled within that one group to which we all belong, the human race, and when blind destructiveness is loose in a group that group will be destroyed. So now, even if we do not destroy ourselves through a nuclear war, we shall soon make this planet uninhabitable by our species, for we are busily and aggressively engaged in the destruction of the resources of the planet.

What stands in our way of finding another way of living together is not just greedy and power hungry leaders, but our own inability to understand how aggression is an essential part of our being. We, and not just our enemies, are aggressive.

I am often asked by organizations involved in world issues to give a lecture on the function of enemies, and always, at the end of my lecture, I am advanced upon by Peace People, declaring most aggressively that they never have and never will feel the slightest twinge of aggression. I am always tempted to say, 'Who are you kidding?', knowing that the only person they are fooling is themselves, but I feel myself under a physical threat and, not wanting to be beaten up, I become charming. If the charm reduces their aggression I might then point out that, even as they declare that aggression is totally and absolutely absent from their being, if I closed my hands across their nose and mouth, blocking off their breath, they would suddenly discover their aggression. Not for a moment would they sink passively into death. They would fight back, because no matter how good we want to show ourselves to be, a larger part of us wants to go on living. Similarly, the man who advanced upon me, telling me that *never* had he felt aggressive and that he brought his children up with *love* (I could see him punishing his children while declaring, 'This hurts me more than it hurts you, because I *love* you') as much as he hammered his children with his *love*, had those children been threatened by someone else he would have placed himself between his children and their aggressor and turned on the aggressor aggression aimed at saving his children.

We are in the business of surviving. We would like to do this gracefully, intact, serene and superior, but if we cannot we will do it as best we can and with every means, however low and cunning and destructive. We would like to believe that we are not in the business of surviving but in being good, and we do not like to admit to ourselves that we are good in order to survive. So we are loath to admit to ourselves that all our bad behaviour when we become difficult – crabby, irrational, impatient, dissatisfied, aggrieved, discontented, inconsiderate, acrimonious, resentful, censorious, argumentative, weepy, distracted, demanding, abusive, blackmailing, manipulative, violent – all forms of aggression – we are unscrupulously and necessarily trying to survive. We may believe that we are caring, considerate, unselfish and self-effacing, and we may believe that a beneficent God will save us, but when the chips are down and our backs are to the wall we know that the only person who will save us is ourself. We want to survive both physically and as our self. If we cannot have both we will choose our self. This is why some of us choose suicide.

Aggression is both a feeling and an action, and both encompass our attempt to impose our structure of meaning on a world which may be reluctant to conform to it. Our structure of meaning may include the plan, 'I'll open this door', and when the door refuses to budge we feel frustration, anger and aggression in swift succession as we push or kick the door. Our structure of meaning may include, 'My children must obey me', and when they fail to do so we hit them (a form of aggression called violence), or say, 'How can you do this after all I've done for you' (a form of aggression called making people feel guilty), or 'If you do that I won't love you any more' (a form of aggression called the threat of abandonment).

The reason that some people refuse to admit that they are aggressive is because as children it had been impressed on them both that being aggressive is wicked and that they have no natural right to exist. Hence, when they are under attack they have no right to protect themselves, and if they protect themselves in the slightest degree they are wicked. Since responding to attack with aggression is as natural as breathing, they need to protect themselves and fight back while at the same time pretending not to do so. When someone like myself comes along and blows their cover it is no wonder that they are annoyed, aggressive even.

Yet, so long as we deny our aggression we are unable to develop effective ways of dealing with it. Over the past few years psychologists have developed some excellent courses called *assertiveness training* which I would recommend to anyone who has difficulty in being aggressive and in dealing with other people's aggression. Using various techniques such psychologists assist their students to discover in themselves both their own aggression and their right to exist. If you value yourself you can develop many flexible, skilful and effective ways of expressing your own aggression without being destructive and of dealing with other people's aggression without being injured and taking such aggression personally, that is, letting it diminish you.

Part of the reason why many people are reluctant to admit that they are aggressive is because their aggression is mixed with envy.

Simple envy, 'Gosh, I wish I had that!', can be pleasant when it is mixed with admiration and, if accompanied with a sense of self-confidence, can be a spur to action to obtain what is envied. However, when we envy what we see as beyond our capacity to achieve because we are weak, incompetent, unjustly treated and undeserving, our envy becomes mixed with hatred, resentment and destructive aggression.

In childhood most of us are taught, usually in circumstances involving punishment, guilt arousal, ridicule and contempt, that to be envious is to be wicked. Many adults have great difficulty in sharing their possessions with others because as children they were forced in the name of learning, to be good, to share their toys and other treasures long before they had the mental capacity to understand the concept of sharing. In adult life they may manage to share some of their possessions with their children – extensions of themselves – but they bitterly resent their taxes being spent on the welfare of strangers. If all parents would let their children discover, as they developed, the satisfactions and benefits of sharing instead of forcing such 'good' behaviour on to the child the structure and function of politics in our society would change out of all recognition. What would politics be without greed and envy? Unfortunately such a change in child care will not occur until all of us can confront the murderous envy lurking in the blackness which we experience as our essential badness.

Until we confront this envy we cannot recognize that it is inappropriate. Most of the objects of this envy are no longer enviable. Sure, you envied your ten-year-old brother when he was tall and brave and dashing and could do all sorts of exciting things, while you were small and weak and had to stay at home with mother, but how can you envy him now he is an insurance broker with a beer gut, a receding hairline and a string of broken marriages? Surely anger and pity that he made so little of his chances are more appropriate emotions? Meanwhile, some of the things we envied are within our grasp, if we still want them and if we have the self-confidence to try.

Often our murderous envy is not just hidden in our inner darkness but parades about disguised as virtue, a very strict virtue. As obedient children we envied other children who could run about and enjoy themselves, and as adults we deplore the 'children of today' and support measures to force children to be controlled and obedient. 'Educational standards are falling,' we say, and extol the merits of public examinations and an inflexible curriculum that turn learning from a joy to a penance. We deplore 'the youth of today' who do things that we secretly wanted to do but dared not, and we support compulsory military service and prison regimes of punishment rather than rehabilitation. Murderous envy wants to destroy what it cannot have.

Denying our own envy means that we cannot be ourselves. It has another bad effect. We do not always realize that we are the object of other people's envy. We find people doing strange or terrible things to us, we do not understand why, and so we cannot defend ourselves properly.

If you have been taught that envy is wicked and so have repressed and denied your own envy you become unaware of the immense prevalence of envy in our society. If you have learned to think of yourself as incompetent and of little value, you do not realize that another person can see you as competent and valuable and so envy you. Not seeing this envy directed towards you, you do not experience the pleasure and uplift of being the recipient of admiration and envy, nor do you protect yourself against murderous envy.

Freud and the Freudians made much of the way that women envy men and called it 'penis envy'. Feminists responded by pointing out that it was not men's penises that women envied but their power. In these arguments the fact that men envy women was overlooked, and indeed many women find it inconceivable that men should envy them. I remember my shock when my friend Nan said of my errant husband, 'He envies you.' I have seen that same shock on the faces of my women clients when I have pointed out that their husband who is so busy being sane and competent envies his depressed and anxious wife. Yet the pattern of the relationship is that the man has steadily, unscrupulously and often in the guise of being a caring, supportive husband, undermined his wife's self-confidence. He does this, if he is an introvert, to keep her under control and fitting in with his organization, or, if he is an extravert, so she will not leave him. Envy is always present in a relationship between an extravert and an introvert, for while each may admire the other's competence in the less real reality, each envies such competence.

It is only by perceiving and accepting our own aggression and envy that we can perceive clearly and dispassionately the aggression and envy directed at us by others and so be able to defend ourselves adequately against the destructive elements in such aggression and envy. Becoming depressed is not an adequate defence.

We can protect ourselves against other people's destructive aggression and envy by not allowing ourselves to be manipulated into situations where this aggression and envy can be expressed. When it is impossible to avoid such situations, most commonly when the people expressing such destructive aggression and envy are our loved ones (the envy parents have of their children is often the source of the bitter criticism parents make of their children), then the appropriate defence is not to take the attack personally. We can adopt the attitude that the envious aggression is their problem, not ours. If that is how they feel, then, that is how they feel, and we are under no obligation to respond or even feel bad about it. We do not have to apologize for having qualities and advantages which other people envy, we do not have to deny our qualities and abandon our advantages. We do not have to apologize for existing, nor do we have to accept that our nearest and dearest have the right to criticize us cruelly and unjustly and to abuse us physically or verbally.

When we are able to see the destructive aggression and envy directed at us as the other person's problem, not ours, we are then able to see the other person as perhaps needing our understanding and support. By letting the person say all kinds of outrageous things to us we can allow the person to get rid of the feelings of rage, hate and envy. Part of coming to accept our own feelings is realizing that *no emotion lasts forever*. Just as we cannot go on laughing indefinitely, nor expressing sexual feelings indefinitely, so we cannot express anger indefinitely. We hurl a few words or objects, or even fling ourselves on the floor and scream and kick, and then the anger subsides. It is enormously comforting to have someone let us be angry, and not criticize our excesses and exaggerations, nor make us feel guilty, nor humiliate us for losing control, nor take our performance personally. Families who accept one another as the individual that each is treat one another with respect and allow one another to behave badly or excessively from time to time without guilt arousing post-mortems or recriminations.

By looking into the hidden recesses of our self and discovering there our aggression, envy, rage and hatred we lose our sense of superior virtue, but we discover a sense of unity with all other human beings. This helps us understand why some people do such terrible things.

By 'understand' I do not mean 'excuse'. Psychologists and social workers who talk of understanding criminals, or adolescents, or drug addicts, or homosexuals, are often accused of being 'do-gooders' who are dangerously permissive and actually promote wickedness. The accusers are always law-abiding citizens who were very obedient children. To become an obedient child you need parents who do not understand you. Being understood is a desire we all have, and an unmet need creates an ache, an emptiness, and envy. Much of the competition between men which is expressed as an envy of power and possessions is really an envy of and a longing for the tenderness and understanding which a boy loses when he enters upon the traditional education of becoming a man. Not wanting others to be understood means that you have not been understood.

By 'understanding' I mean *seeing connections*. If we understand how aggression is a response to frustration, and if we understand how a certain young man has created a structure of meaning in which he sees himself as lacking all recognition except in his knowledge about guns, if he feels that he is frustrated in everything that he wishes to do, then we can see the series of connections which culminated one day in this young man shooting his mother and his neighbours. We do not approve of his act, but neither do we see it as a sudden, inexplicable action.

This is the kind of understanding we need to develop if, from time to time, we are to find ourselves enjoying the serenity of forgiveness. Bad things happened to us, or we did bad things ourselves, and the memory of these events with their pain, anger, resentment and desire for revenge becomes a heavy weight we have to drag along with us. Only forgiveness can sever our connection with this weight.

Much nonsense is talked about forgiveness. People are always saying it is something we can choose to do. This is nonsense. Of course we can say, 'I forgive him for the terrible wrong he has done me,' and present ourselves as being virtuous, or other people see us as virtuous when really we are trying to avoid further trouble. When Gordon Wilson was pulled from the rubble of the Enniskillen bomb which killed his daughter he said that he bore the men who had placed the bomb no ill-will. This was his very wise attempt to forestall any acts of revenge. He was not saying that he would never feel angry that his beautiful daughter with her life still before her had died in this way, nor that he would not mourn her, nor occasionally wonder why his God moves in such mysterious ways. He loved his daughter, and so her death is something which he has to carry with him for the rest of his life.

People who say, 'I forgive but I don't forget,' are wanting to appear both virtuous and tough. Sometimes 'not forgetting' is bitterness and the desire for revenge, and sometimes it is simply remembering where the danger lies. If you have lost one leg to a crocodile it is foolish to put your other leg within the range of his jaws. Whichever the 'not forgetting' is, it means that you are still burdened with the memory of an injury. It is something you cannot afford to forget, and so you have not yet entered the state of forgiveness.

Forgiveness is not something we do but, like happiness, is something which arises spontaneously from what we do. It is not a virtue but a blessing. We cannot make ourselves forgive any more than we can make ourselves be happy. We can create the conditions where we can be happy, and we can do the things that make us happy, but happiness remains a by-product of what we do. Similarly, we can do the things for which forgiveness is a by-product. We can seek to enlarge our understanding of why these hurtful events occurred. We can do the things which restore a sense of continuity to our life and a sense of value to ourself. It is much easier to discover forgiveness for a faithless partner if you go on from your marriage to a life of fame and fortune than to a life of obscure penury. It is much easier to discover forgiveness for yourself if you actually seek to understand yourself and to undertake new and creative enterprises. By concentrating on the understanding and the actions we can one day discover that we have lost a burden, and that state of lightness is forgiveness.

Gregory's account of his journey into his inner reality did not end with his recognition that his father hated him. He had to deal with his own hatred and he did that using his aggression through imagery.

In his next letter Gregory reminded me that

'These visions and conversations are/were not hallucinations but imagery. I found that I could deal with that which is within me through imaging and personifications.'

He went on,

'My psychologist suggested several months ago that after I had really succeeded in "killing" my father I might one day want to resurrect him in transfigured form. At the time I said, "NO! He's dead and I want him to stay that way!" Recently, however, the reconciliation has occurred. I do not discount my father's hatred of me or my hatred of him in return, but I am now able to see the positive, good side of him and myself and the whole relationship. It was an ambivalent one: that is to say, he both hated and loved me. I had to accept the reality of the hatred and then later I could accept the reality of the love. I am also now able to understand *why* he hated me and to some extent empathize with his feelings. Visiting my mother at Christmas, I went to his grave and for the first time (he has been dead fifteen years) embraced his gravestone and wept tears not of anger or regret but of love. I also began (occasionally, not obsessively) wearing a sweater and jacket of his that I had inherited and had not wanted to put on.

Even after the episode which I have described with the adolescent Greg I felt that Greg was standoffish – when I pictured us, he would let me hug him but would not hug me back. All the reassurances I gave him that in spite of his introverted, pimply unattractiveness he was a good, bright, loving person, and that the horrors of our family life were not his fault – all these seemed to rebound on him: he wasn't having it. He still felt resentful – and of *me:* somehow he felt I was betraying him by not being honest with him.

I kept offering him this and that and failing to get through till finally I sensibly asked him what *he* really wanted.

What he *needed* was for me to accept the destructive hatred in him. What he wanted was to go back to the town where he lived and for me to go with him. In fantasy we acquired an armored tank. We lined up the kids at school who had snubbed and mocked him and shot them, then buried them in a trench out in the lifeless desert. We drove the tank back to town, parked it across the street from his school, and shelled it (I'm glad to say that it was empty of people at the time) into rubble. Most painfully, we drove it to the house where he lived and aimed our guns at it.

"Do we really want to do this?" we asked each other, for the house had many good associations as well as the evil ones. After some soul searching we decided we did, and shelled it. We then went down to look at the damage. Everything was destroyed. Everything *except* my father's couch, the throne from which he issued his awful commands and reprimands. The couch would not burn; it smouldered evilly, sending off an oily smoke that choked us. "It'll kill us," Greg screamed. I ran and got a flamethrower, and together we reduced it to ashes.

Later, having destroyed my father's throne, I could reconcile with his memory.

Greg was now much happier and would hug me, but
without enthusiasm. "What do you want *now*?" I asked him
with some irritation and impatience.

What he needed now was for me to accept his *self*-hatred.
This was one of the most painful episodes in my whole
therapy. The image of his self-hatred was a long, fiery
tapeworm lodged in his intestines and pulsing red with
hatred. It was too much for my ego to handle on my own,
and I became immobilized with terror. The thing would not
leave my vitals. I called on Jesus for help. Jesus appeared in
my driveway, driving an old VW bug (!) "Get this out of
me," I called to him. His reply: "Stop panicking. Calm down.
Just ask it to leave and it will leave." "Are you *kidding*?" I
demanded of Jesus. "Just ask it to leave," Jesus replied. So I
did, and immediately it obeyed. Slowly it uncoiled, left my
body, exited the house, and crept into the back seat of Jesus'
car. Jesus drove off with it.

To my horror, a few moments later Jesus returned in his
VW and asked me: "Do you want to see It again?" "NO!" I
shouted. "Are you *crazy*? I told you to destroy It!" Jesus
smiled quietly and opened the door of the VW. Out It came
– no longer a red, hideous work, but an angel of such awful
whiteness, beauty, majesty, and loving power that I scarcely
dared look at it.

The result was (a) Greg gave me a huge hug and the
reconciliation was complete, (b) my long-term digestive
problems have improved enormously. Do you wonder?

I am finding that I have reservoirs of new energy and that
I am increasingly able to pass this positive energy on to other
people now. It is a wonderful feeling.'

Feeling that we are in essence bad and unacceptable and so
have to work hard to be good uses up an enormous amount of
energy. It is no wonder that when we relinquish our sense of
badness with its compulsion to be good and thus find that we can
simply *be* we discover enormous resources of energy and enthusiasm. Now we are free to elaborate our sense of existence.

# ELABORATING THE SENSE OF SELF

**The Successful Self has developed flexible and creative ways of elaborating the sense of existence.**

Before we can elaborate our sense of existence we have to feel at home in our sense of existence, and to feel at home in our sense of existence we have to feel that our way of experiencing our sense of existence is right and proper for us.

Some years ago when I was running a workshop for psychology students I showed them how to ladder and then asked them to form small groups and ladder one another. One of the students was Rachel, a very beautiful, vivacious young woman from, as she told me later, a well-off Jewish family. After she had done the laddering with her partner she came to me in a state of great excitement and asked me to ladder her. She wanted to check what she had found. So she chose some other objects to describe, and we went through the process. At the top of her ladder was, yet again, the sense of existence as individual development and achievement. Her pleasure in making this discovery was enormous.

Later she explained why. All her life her family had assumed that she would follow the traditional pattern for a woman. While her parents had been pleased that she had done well at school, they did not place the emphasis on her education that they did on her brother's. They saw her going to university as a suitable way of filling in her time between school and marriage. They emphasized the importance of her looking attractive and dressing well, and Rachel could please them in this, for she enjoyed nice clothes and compliments. Yet all the time she felt a sense of unease. She thought that she should have been looking forward to marriage and a family, and when this prospect filled her with foreboding rather than joy she felt that there was something wrong with her.

Now all was clear. She was not a people person after all. It was all right for her to want to achieve as a psychologist. In herself, she had come home.

Rachel had sufficient self-confidence and sense of self-worth to feel that she could persuade her parents to accept that, while she might become a wife and mother, these were not going to be the only roles that she would play. She would not ignore her sense of existence in order to fit in with what her family wanted. Many people do. There are many introvert women who blame themselves for not enjoying a life made up of family relationships, and many extravert men who live in constant anxiety, trying to please their families by achieving. When such introvert women and extravert men are praised for fulfilling so well the roles their families have selected for them, they feel that they are imposters.

By contrast, when we feel at home in our sense of existence we find that fulfilling the requirements of our sense of existence – achieving or relating – comes naturally. Of course, we encounter obstacles, but there is a sense of ease and rightness that illuminates and motivates everything we do. Events in our outside world may demand that we make some hard decisions, but we always know which decision is right for us. Decision-making becomes less of a weighing up of the arguments for and against, and more of listening to the answer which arises from within us. We know that if we ignore our inner voice then, even if our decision is made to please other people or to avoid unpleasant consequences, no good will come of it. We shall be left feeling false, having betrayed ourselves.

When we look to other people to tell us what to do and what to think, to tell us how well we are achieving and to relate to us so that we know that we exist, when we feel that other people have to give us the right to exist, we lose touch with our inner voice. We have no way of knowing what is right for us, but not knowing what is right for us does not prevent us from feeling at odds with our self when we act against our nature. We may want to spend all our lives being good, obedient children because we believe that what we give up in the effort to be good and obedient is worth the protection and security we gain, but inevitably we find that we have traded our self for an illusion. Being good does not protect us from disaster.

Over the months that I have been writing this book many people in Britain and the United States have been reeling in pain, shock and horror from the discovery that the people whom they thought were looking after them have not done so. In Britain the

National Health Service has existed for so long that many people have taken it to be an order of nature. Illness and infirmity need not be feared, for the NHS is there to care for us. Now when the government says, 'There is not enough money to meet the demand,' and proceeds to close hospitals, the protests against this are fuelled by the passionate feeling, 'I've been good. I've paid my taxes. You've got to look after me.' Similarly, in the United States many people have taken the strength of the American economic system and the mighty dollar to be an order of nature. They maintained their belief that as loyal, obedient American citizens they were safe, even when the United States joined the Third World as a debtor nation, but when the dollar slid downwards and the prices of stocks and shares crashed, they saw with horror that they were not safe and that their government did not act swiftly and effectively in protecting them.

In our desire to find good parents who will look after us we transfer our hopes from our own parents, mere fallible people, to our government and believe the politicians when they say they will protect us and care for our interests. Of course, politicians always say that (they are ever ready to play the good parents to our good child), but, of course, they cannot do so. No government can control the economic forces which envelop the entire world and affect every person. Similarly, no government can control the climate which envelops the entire world and influences every person. Economic and climatic forces interact. For instance, both big business and peasant farmers benefit in the short term from the cutting down of the rainforest, but the depletion of the trees is part of the 'greenhouse effect', the warming of the planet, which is having far-ranging and eventually, for us, devastating effects on the climate worldwide. At present most governments, wishing to be seen as protecting their people, are doing so by denying that there is a problem.

Even if all our politicians were completely altruistic, totally without greed, the desire for power, and without commitments to other wealthy and powerful people, they could not govern the country in such a way that they never betrayed or hurt or failed to protect one of their citizens. If in addition to all these virtues they added the virtue, rare in politicians, truth telling in all circumstances, they would have to say that not only do economic and climatic forces exist outside the control of the most powerful dictator, but even in matters within their control there are issues where no matter what decision is made someone will suffer some disadvantage. It is a basic condition of life that once we act on a decision we have excluded all other possibilities of choice. You can't have your cake and eat it too. If the government decides to build a factory on natural woodland, some people will gain by being given work, and others who value the woods will lose. There is no event from which all that follows is totally good or totally bad. The life of Jesus has inspired many people to act with love and concern for others, and it has also inspired many people to violence and murder. While English children died during the Second World War, for the first time in the history of Britain the government attempted to ensure that all British children were adequately fed.

When we realize that as adults we cannot blindly entrust our welfare to others we have then to take a much keener and wider interest in what is going on around us. We can never make ourselves totally safe, but the better informed we are, the better able we are at identifying possible dangers and ways of avoiding them. Many people believe that if they do not read about nuclear war, or if they refrain from watching a television programme about earthquakes these disasters will never occur. This belief saves them from the hard work of acquiring the knowledge and carrying out the actions which could prevent the first disaster and mitigate the effects of the second. Their laziness is understandable for they have had the kind of education which taught them to dislike learning. As children they were punished for being curious, and much of their energy is absorbed in the battle to be good and to ward off the threat of annihilation of the self.

Freeing ourselves of the burden of being good in the hope of a reward, and allowing ourselves to be ourselves experiencing our own sense of existence, we discover that we have immense energy and enthusiasm which will enable us to elaborate our sense of existence. We need to be aware of how limited our education has been. We may have our degrees and diplomas, but few of us have explored the artistic potential we were born with. We might have travelled, but, in the way that we have been taught to see everything in terms of 'my country' (good) as against 'not my country' (bad) our travels have not enlightened us. Now, in the cause of elaborating our sense of existence we can go where we have not dared to go, see what we have not dared to see, and do what we have not dared to do.

Sometimes daring to go, to see and to do involves all kinds of hazardous quests and adventures. Sometimes it involves dangers not so much like climbing an active volcano as the even more risky business of daring to say, 'No' to those people who believe that they know what is best for us. Two people who dared to do this are Baroness Masham of Ilton and Dr Su Brinkworth.

Lady Masham has always been passionately fond of horses and riding. When a young woman she entered a point-to-point, something went wrong, and she was severely injured. A week later she had to face the fact that she would spend the rest of her life in a wheelchair.

Lady Masham could have chosen to become an invalid with people to look after her for the rest of her life. Instead she married, adopted two children, maintained her interest in horses and riding, and entered a life of public service. As a member of the House of Lords she became passionately involved in all matters to do with health and especially the needs of the physically handicapped.

I had often seen Lady Masham on television, usually with her talking energetically to reporters as they gathered around her on the footpath outside the House of Lords. As I found when I talked to her, she much prefers to talk about the issues which concern her than about herself. However, in a more formal television interview the interviewer did ask her how she had come to terms with her disability and she said, 'When one door closes another opens.'

I was delighted to hear her say this. I am so used to talking to people who hold firmly to the belief that, 'When one door closes, God slams every other one in your face.'

Lady Masham, I found, had met many people who held firmly to such pessimistic views. She was scathing about 'the experts' in the field of spinal injury who always advised about the patients, 'Don't raise their hopes.' She said, 'In the disabled field you come against this. I started the Spinal Injuries Association because some of our people were having real difficulties and they really needed someone to fight for them, on their behalf. If someone had said to me, as they did, you won't be able to ride a horse, I said I will ride a horse. A lot of my fellow paraplegics have that sort of attitude. A doctor told one young man, a pilot, who had broken his neck, that he wouldn't be able to drive. That is a ridiculously stupid thing to say to someone, because you never know. You must have hope. In all these things you must have hope. Anyway, he did drive, and he took great pleasure in driving up to the hospital and showing the doctor who told him he couldn't drive.'

Her work brought her into contact with many people who were depressed and suffering. She realized that bad experiences as well as good can be used to elaborate our sense of existence. She said, 'I got depressed once. I'm not a depressive by nature, but I know what it can feel like, and it's a good thing because now I've been able to understand other people better.'

Lady Masham summed up her life and work with, 'In parliamentary life we work in groups because that's how we get things done. I also work in isolation, but I do look for advice from other people. I like to have the support of others. I prefer to work with other people. I believe that if a thing can be made better it should be made better. I always think it's very important that I can feel, that I can respond to other people.'

Lady Masham, an extravert, elaborated her sense of existence by building a set of relationships with many different people in many different ways, all of which required her to acquire knowledge, skills, awareness and understanding. Su Brinkworth, an English psychologist working in New York and crippled with rheumatoid arthritis used the disaster which had overtaken her as a way of elaborating her sense of existence.

Su, an introvert, told me how important it was to her to regulate her emotions 'so that I have predictability and a stability which gives me a potential for growth. I think that the loss of the self is not only chaos and falling apart, but it's also being stuck. It's being in limbo. It's not developing, not growing, not participating in the world as a whole. It is tremendously important to let go of resentments and hurts and fears, and be able to progress on. I have a great need to understand and shape, if not control, at least to do something to make things – me, my life, the lives of others – better. I think that life consists of getting knocked down, picking yourself up, getting knocked down, picking yourself up, but if you learn that you're going to be knocked down, you see the punch coming and you can duck, so that actually you don't get knocked down anywhere near as often as you might do if you didn't prepare and didn't learn and didn't envision the possibilities. Each time you pick yourself up, you grow a little. You become stronger, deeper, and more versatile.'

Su had had plenty of experience of picking herself up. She, healthy and happy, had gone with her husband to New York, but after she became ill she and her husband separated, leaving her without the qualifications necessary to work as a psychologist in New York and without money or a family to support her.

She described to me how the arthritis began some ten years ago. 'I was sitting watching television and I felt I'd been struck by a bolt of white-hot lightning in my left shoulder, and it zipped from joint to joint, usually waking me around three o'clock in the morning. I had difficulty in getting out of bed in the morning, but by the time I got to the doctor's surgery I had loosened up. The doctors insisted that there was nothing wrong with me. So it was misdiagnosed for the first eighteen months, by which time it had done a lot of damage. Then there was a different kind of damage when the internist diagnosed it in a burst of glee at how clever he was. He brought in several medical students who stood around my bed in little white coats looking like a soap commercial. He informed me it was the worst case – or possibly the best case – that he'd ever seen, and that it had done a lot of damage in the period of not being diagnosed. I would "lose the use of my hands in two years, and be in a wheelchair in three years", and even though I would go into periods of remission "it would still be eating away at the joints". I was what the physicians would describe as a good patient, because I just lay there while he picked up one limb or another and demonstrated the difficulties I had. I was actually in shock. After this guy left I looked in the mirror to see if I was still in one piece, because I felt quite fragmented at that point. I wasn't able to speak. Then after about three days of being numb, I got angry, which was one of the best things I could have done. I thought, "Right – I'm damned if I'm going to lose the use of my hands, or be in a wheelchair, but if that happens I shall put a motorbike engine on the back and paint it red and run this guy down, and fly up and down Fifth Avenue with a flag on the back." '

Su endured vast pain and discomfort and multiple operations, and in that time finished her doctorate and qualified to work as a clinical psychologist. (Qualifying as a clinical psychologist in the United States is not about learning how to be a competent psychologist and a wise human being. That is something candidates have to do for themselves. It is about learning and regurgitating vast amounts of information, and about being knocked down and picking yourself up over and over again. Before the Big Daddies will let you into the Club, you have to demonstrate that you are a good and obedient child, able to take much chastisement.) Su told me how now she is employed she can function so much better. 'In the beginning I was terrified because I couldn't afford to eat every day. I was always terrified that I would get thrown out of my apartment because I couldn't pay the rent and I'd be on the street with the bag-ladies. Once I could feel secure about eating and having somewhere to live I could buy clothes and feel better about my body that way. I learned a lot, and now I'm able to put that knowledge together and give it back to the medically ill patients that I'm working with. That makes me feel it's all been meaningful and worthwhile, so that does a tremendous amount to integrate me. I feel I've coped in different kinds of ways at different times.'

One of the things Su had learned and which she used with her patients was the power of imagery. She said, 'I can envision different, alternative ways to deal with a situation. Like difficulty with the boss, or planning the next step. If you can image them in a whole multi-faceted fashion, you can pre-live them, and you do make something happen there. You make yourself grow faster, you don't just wait for experiences to happen through which you learn, you make experiences happen mentally. That was one of the things I found when I was very ill. You're stuck in hospital, you can't go on vacation, you can't play golf. But you can in your head, and you get the same feelings that you would do if you went and did it. I can envisage how it used to be that I could run. Then I can feel the wind in my hair and on my skin, and I can feel the blood racing and my legs pounding. I haven't been able to run like that for ten years. But I can get a lot of the mental energy and the emotional feelings from imagining doing that.'

I asked Su if she had not considered the alternative of becoming an invalid. She said, 'Early on when I was floundering I went to a clinic where there was a woman who used to sit in her wheelchair looking totally pathetic with her hands like wilted plants and crying all the time. I thought, "Well, I could do that." There was another woman who was so furious that she just sliced people up all the time. I thought, "Well, I could do that too." But I saw what it did to other people. If I did that I would cut myself off from other people. I used my intelligence to look at my choices, and I had also had a lot of experiences when I was growing up when I felt really beaten down and I hadn't succumbed. No matter how overwhelming my circumstances were, there were still things I could do. There are always things that one can do, even if they are only tiny. So long as I've got a bit of energy, I can come up with alternative creative possibilities to be able to go on to the next step. I have actually come across doctors who tell me that I am not doing what I am doing. They told me I would not work full time, and not only do I work full time, but I also teach and have a private practice and have a social life. It still scares me. It could be a bleak future, but, funnily enough, I'm happier now than I ever was. I have the potential for more happiness than previously.'

Su referred often to her friends and the warmth and loving that flows between them. She explained, 'At first I coped by being very sad and very angry and concentrating on my studies so I could use my brain even if my body rotted. Then I realized that I was trying to be hyper-independent because I felt so abandoned by my family and my husband and I couldn't trust anybody else. There were a lot of people who could help and would help if somehow I could accept that and let them in and help them help me. The more I could accept and love other people, the more I could accept and love me. The more I've been able to accept my limitations and to accept me as a whole person again, the better my functioning has become.'

Su had discovered that she could not be a whole person if she retreated to the reality she trusted, her internal reality. To be whole she had to venture into her less real reality.

# MAKING THE LESS REAL REALITY REAL

**The Successful Self has made the less real reality real by developing the skills necessary to live within that reality.**

One day when I was twenty-two I boarded a train at Central Station to go to Bankstown, a suburb of Sydney thirty miles to the west. This was to be my first day as a teacher. When the train reached Sydenham a group of young women got on and sat a few seats down from me. One of them caught my attention. She was beautiful, tall, slim and sparkling. She talked and laughed with great warmth and vivacity.

All the group left the train at Bankstown, and as I followed them down the street I realized that we were all going to the same place, Bankstown Home Science School. Later that morning I met the group in the staff room of the school, and thus began a life-long friendship with Nan Olive, Nan Purnell as she became on her marriage a few years later. In England, when people ask me, as they often do, 'Don't you miss Australia?' My truthful answer would always be, 'I miss Nan Purnell.'

Nan's generosity is limitless, and I could write a book about all that she gave me, but here I want to describe three important things I learned from her.

As a teacher I was hopeless. I had no idea how to interest a class and get them to cooperate with me. I wasn't interested in becoming a better teacher. But I was interested in finding better ways of getting along with people. At university I had managed to learn how to get into Manning House, but I was still very frightened of entering many other social situations. I enjoyed conversations about topics which interested me, but I had no idea how to converse with everybody who came my way.

Nan did. She had ways of greeting people that made them feel warm and wanted. She remembered something about every person she met, so that when she met that person again she could mention what she remembered, and thus make the person feel important. She observed people carefully, picking up signs of things about which they might not have spoken. She had endless means of getting people to talk about themselves. She asked questions, never in any critical way, but out of genuine interest, and as the person answered, she looked at that person, and listened, absorbed and intent. When she talked of her own experiences, it was in the context of what her listener found interesting and important, and not in the context, as many extraverts do, of making herself the centre of attention. When she said farewell, it was with messages of concern and optimism.

I watched all this and noted it carefully. Then I started to copy her, initially not very successfully, but, as I absorbed her skills and made them my own, the whole business of meeting people and talking to them became less and less difficult. Now, thirty-four years later, I never answer the phone, or chat to my neighbour across the fence, or respond to my client, without drawing on what I learned from Nan.

Nowadays psychologists talk of social skills and run groups to teach shy people these skills. Many people benefit from learning such skills, but unless the skills are absorbed into the person's own structure of the self, they remain no more than party tricks, likely to desert the person in times of stress.

Learning the subtle and complex art of conversing with other people can mean for a shy extravert the blossoming of a natural talent, and for the shy introvert a means of making external reality more real, solid and unchanging.

I found that all the introverts I interviewed who led successful lives and appeared to have all the necessary social skills could recall the events which led them to decide to acquire these social skills and the people from whom they learned these skills. Susyn Reeve, a management consultant whom Ron Janoff described to me as 'the most successful person I know', told me how the earliest memory she has of her older sister is of her being 'very social'. She said, 'What I learned from her is now part of me. In the past I used to watch myself in action and I would imagine that I was her.'

However, Susyn still had 'some degree of shyness that I hold on to because it's a kind of protection.'

Shyness is a necessary protection for introverts against the criticism which can come from any person whose approval they desire. Susyn said, 'I'm real chatty, but there's another part of me that's the opposite. I can scare myself and make a test of a situation. I can make the people I'm with my judges. Then I just don't know even how to talk about the weather. Yet what I do in my work is to create situations for other people to talk to one another. To stop myself making people my judges I remind myself consciously that I'm going to make this experience with this person be of value, no matter whatever decisions could follow from it. This point in time is going to count, and that gives me freedom. I'm not so future focused, thinking about my work and my contract. I'm in the room with the person, paying attention to what is going on.'

What Susyn is describing here is the process of paying attention to external reality, and through that process of attention achieving a coordination of internal and external reality. This is the *here and now experience* where we feel at our most alive. All thought of past and future have no place in such an experience, including the anxiety that this present experience will not prove to be in the future as self-annihilating as similar experiences in the past.

The ability to live in the present, enjoying what is when it is, is something that the Successful Self values and often uses.

Another ability valued and frequently used by the Successful Self is to be happily and securely alone.

Being alone comes naturally to the introvert, for internal reality, the essence of aloneness, is always real. Not only can introverts be alone with their thoughts, many can also be alone without their thoughts. What such people describe is the experience of entering upon an internal space, 'a soft brownness', as one woman described her space to me, and just being there without thinking. (There is a famous *Punch* cartoon of a gracious lady visiting an old farmworker who is sitting alone at his fireside. She asks him how he fills in his time, and he replies, 'Sometimes I sits and thinks, and sometimes I just sit.') In that space even the stimulation of thinking is stilled, and the jangled, painful feeling that comes from too much happening at once fades away.

Not all introverts have retained this ability. I suspect that it is an ability introverts are born with, but most abandon its use as the need to achieve and not to waste time presses upon them. Those who retain this ability can find it disturbing. A psychologist colleague described to me how when she returned home at the end of a difficult day at work she would just sit without thinking for some minutes. She was uncertain whether to regard this as a sensible recovery technique or something sinister. But then all our abilities can become handicaps when we feel under great threat. The woman who enjoyed the peace of her 'soft brownness' found that it turned to icy blackness when she was depressed, while introverts who have lost confidence in themselves and are no longer able to distinguish internal reality from external reality find their ability to stop thinking both a relief from the confusion and a handicap, the 'thought stopping' which psychiatrists regard as a symptom of mental illness.

The ability to be alone requires *the ability to distinguish between being alone and loneliness.*

The ability to be alone means realizing that our sense of existence is not dependent upon the presence of other people. Left completely alone, we all, extraverts and introverts, go on existing. Such an existence may be painful, for we are lonely, and long for other people.

Terry, who some years previously had spent hours haranguing and complaining to me about the iniquitous way his family, friends and colleagues had failed to meet his need that they always be there supporting his sense of existence and doing what he told them to do, called one day at my office just, so he said, to let me know how he was getting on. Very well, as it had turned out. He had resolved his confused relationships with several women and he had relinquished a job where he had been in public view, something which appalled and delighted him, and had taken up farming. The cows, he said, were all the appreciative audience he needed. How, I asked, did he achieve this?

Terry said, 'I discovered that when I was alone I didn't die.'

He went on to describe how this discovery had been forced on him. At the same time as his firm had insisted that he take some months' sick leave all his women, his family and most of his friends decided that they had had enough of his impossible behaviour and they refused to be with him. All his life Terry had been rushing around, trying to avoid such a situation, believing aloneness meant annihilation. Now he had discovered that it was not. He had been preparing himself for this discovery. He had been studying Lao Tsu's *Tao te Ching* and some works on Zen, and had learned to meditate, and had found how to be in his internal reality without needing to keep his thoughts constantly occupied with events in his external reality.

Many extraverts when they are lonely and frightened that their sense of existence will disappear avoid being alone by creating fantasies of activities and relationships in the outside world. These fantasies can also serve the purpose of denying that their world is as boring and unpleasant as it is. The format of these fantasies is that the extravert, playing some dramatic and exciting role, is engaged in relating to a host of characters. Sometimes one or two of these characters become real figures in the extravert's external reality, and accompany him at all times. Usually these 'imaginary playmates' are left behind as the child moves into adolescence, but sometimes they remain as a secret companion to the adult extravert.

Lonely, misunderstood extravert children very sensibly use fantasy to comfort themselves, to hold on to themselves, and to give themselves the courage to survive and look forward to the future with hope. But, when the child spends most of his time in his fantasies and treats his external reality as a stage on which he acts out his fantasies, such a survival technique is at the cost of the child's relationship to the real world and the actual consequences of his actions. Absorbed in fantasy and wanting to avoid the unpleasant aspects of reality, the child fails to notice and remember much of what goes on around him. In adult life his memory of his childhood is patchy and limited. Moreover, it is only by observing closely in childhood what goes on around us that we can develop our understanding of why people behave as they do and why one event follows another. The extravert child, absorbed with fantasy figures does not develop an empathetic understanding of real human beings and fails to realize that there are connections between what we do and what others do. Thus the extravert child can fail to see a connection between his arriving home late from school and his mother punishing him for doing so, and even more can fail to see that his mother's anger arises from her distress. In adult life he is amazed and annoyed when his wife is angry and upset simply because he stayed drinking with his mates in the golf club instead of being home early to take her out for a birthday celebration.

Another deficit that the child's absorption in fantasy produces is a lack of the development of skills in dealing with issues within internal reality. Instead of finding ways of dealing with 'I am frightened, weak and helpless,' the child resorts to compensatory fantasies of being brave, strong and powerful. Imagining yourself as Superman is great fun, but, unlike Clark Kent, you cannot become Superman when you are being terrorized by your parents, your teachers and your mates. Whereas, if you recognize and name these feelings and see the connection between them and what people are doing, you can work out effective ways of talking to yourself to increase your courage and bolster up your self-confidence. Reciting to yourself, 'Sticks and stones will break my bones but names will never hurt me,' will stand you in greater stead than Superman.

The imaginary playmate which seems so real is always some part of the child's internal reality projected into external reality, and, while the imaginary playmate does provide a kind of company to which the child can relate to maintain his sense of existence, the conflict it represents cannot be resolved in external reality. For instance, the imaginary playmate may be a child in need of care and comfort. In trying to look after his imaginary playmate the extravert child is denying his own need for care and comfort, and since he will not acknowledge his need he cannot develop ways of meeting it. He can be so busy being a good friend to his imaginary playmate he does not realize that the one person he should be a good friend to is himself.

So it is that many extravert adults say of themselves, 'I was born an anxious person. I had a happy childhood. I don't remember much of it. But people don't, do they?'

However, many other extraverts have grown up without the need of an all-absorbing fantasy life, or have realized the dangers of such a life, and so have been able to acknowledge, explore and accept their internal reality, and with that acquire the ability to be alone.

To some extent we all, extraverts and introverts, find ourselves pulled back into our preferred realities. As introverts we can give up acting upon our external reality and withdraw into our thoughts, or the space where our thoughts can be. As extraverts we can do what an extravert friend of mine said he did. 'I can think and think and think, and then I get tired of thinking and want to act.'

When we, as Successful Selves, withdraw into our preferred reality, it is to use it not as a retreat but as a resource.

# CREATIVITY

**The Successful Self uses the preferred reality not so much as a refuge as a resource for creativity.**

Susyn Reeve distinguished very carefully between using her internal reality as a resource and as a refuge. She said, 'I've always been seen as a good worker. I deliver. I grew up around a lot of good workers, and as a child I got a lot of praise for doing a good job. But the other side of it is, I actually want to do nothing. I want to do nothing as an activity. I'm not so driven in that I work all the time and every day. One of the reasons I left a full-time job was for the quality of life. I wanted time to go to the park during the day. I wanted to be able to wake up in the morning and not have to rush to start my day. I like to hang out and day-dream. I do that a lot.'

Day-dreaming for her was crossing over into a peaceful, creative space, which could come from listening to music, or a relaxation tape, or going for a walk and 'listening to the birds and seeing the leaves. That will get me connected with myself. I then discover what my next step is.' That is, in the quietness of her internal reality she listened to her inner voice.

There had been a time in her life when, jobless and divorced, she was depressed and had retreated into her internal reality. She emerged from that retreat to start a new job and a new life but, some years later, as she said, 'One of my fears when I left a full time job and started my own practice was that I would go back to the time in my life when I was so scared when I woke up in the morning I wouldn't want to get out of bed. So the rule I made was that I make my bed immediately I get up. Nowadays I follow that rule ninety-seven per cent of the time, and there are those other three per cent of the time when I want to rebel against it, so I'll get back into bed. My fear used to be that I'd just curl up into myself.' Now Susyn would not do that. If she stayed in bed it was to meditate, to dream, and to plan.

As a child and young woman Susyn had seen her competence and hard work rewarded, and so she simply regarded this as a rule of life. Good work brings rewards. When she reached a point in her life where hard work, competence, and trustworthiness were not being rewarded, indeed she was suffering no matter how hard she tried to be good, she felt herself and her world shattering, and she retreated into the safety of depression and her internal reality and her bed. In this retreat she eventually realized that she could not rely on an Absolute Rule of the Universe that goodness, or even the best of hard work, is rewarded. She had to rely on herself. Instead of waiting for rewards to come as spring follows winter, she had to make her own decisions, act for herself, be the sole judge of performance, and to reward and encourage herself.

Retreating into our preferred reality is our way of avoiding taking responsibility for ourselves and of avoiding the risks of acting creatively.

**Taking responsibility for yourself means making your own decisions and accepting responsibility for your mistakes. Acting creatively means doing things which are new and therefore risky.**

Jennifer described to me how her need to be good got in the way of her creativity. She could see very clearly how for most of her married life she had collected needy people, in fact, she said, she was an expert in need. She came to consult me because she wanted me to help her give up her need to be needed and free her to get on with her artistic work. It was the risk that held her back. There was the financial risk. Leaving her husband meant leaving a comfortable home and money for comparative poverty until she established herself and her work. She acknowledged this, just as she acknowledged the even greater risk that once on her own she might not prove to be the great artist she thought she was. The belief, 'I could have been a great artist (writer, musician, sportsman, etcetera) if only my family had not prevented me' is a useful comfort blanket when it is our own lack of self-confidence and refusal to take responsibility for ourselves that prevents us from using the resources of our preferred reality to be creative. The world is full of introverts sacrificing themselves for their ideals and extraverts rushing around in service to all the needy and demanding people they can find, and all of them believing that it is wicked and selfish to take responsibility for yourself and to make your own decisions in accordance with what your inner voice tells you, if only you can hear it.

Listening to our inner voice, we can open the door to the creative process.

*Trusting yourself is an essential part of creativity.* You must still your criticizing conscience and let the process flow. The flow is spontaneous but not uninhibited. There is channelling, but channelling by wisdom and experience, not by inhibition and negativity. There is a sense of the rightness of things, and the creative process comes, burgeons, and closes with the sense of roundness and completion, yet, until the whole enterprise is complete, there is a link, an opening to the next stage in the creative process.

All of us are born to function in this way, and we each have a multitude of talents that we can apply the creative process to, but our education and our belief in our limitations and inadequacy inhibits us.

We can use the process of creativity not just in producing works of art, but in developing our relationships with other people, in enlarging our competence in our less real reality, in knitting together our two realities, and in mastering our experience.

The ways in which we usually relate to one another are very conventional and restricted. For instance, we all know how important touch is to us, yet it is only in recent years that men have been allowed to hug one another, and even now such hugging is restricted to the sportsfield or is done by men who pride themselves on their awareness and sensitivity. When Mathias Rust was sentenced to four years in a Russian labour camp, his father, farewelling him, shook his hand. If ever Mathias needed to be held, it was then, but if Mathias had had a father who hugged him he probably would not have felt the need to uphold his ideals and prove himself by landing his plane in Red Square. So many of my clients have told me how their parents would never say to them, 'I love you,' and any touch was a slap, not a cuddle.

We can be creative in taking something from our internal reality and putting it out in our external reality (a thought, a feeling, an image translated into an action) and be creative in taking something from our external reality and putting it in our internal reality (an action or an observation translated into an image). In this two-way process we co-ordinate our two realities and make them equally real.

It is through this two-way action that we *master our experiences.*

When something happens to us which surprises, shakes or frightens us we begin a process whereby we have to deal with the emotions aroused in us. Denying our feelings, or saying, 'I'm upset,' without knowing whether 'upset' means feeling angry or feeling frightened, prevents the first step in mastery, which is the acknowledgement and naming of the feelings. Only then can the feelings be dealt with in an appropriate way, first, perhaps, by crying, shouting, and then, as the pressure of the feelings subsides, by thinking over what has occurred, establishing its meaning, looking for its implications. Then it becomes clear what is the appropriate action to take.

Throughout it is very helpful to have someone there who can tolerate the sight of our pain, listen as we tell our story (perhaps over and over to help the emotion aroused subside), act as a sounding board for our ponderings without criticizing and advising us, remind us of our worth if the event has reduced our self-confidence, and, if the experience to be mastered is a loss, accept our sorrow and understand that our grief may be with us for a very long time. Never does a companion tell us to pull ourselves together or that we 'should be over it by now'. (I should not advocate this kind of companionship for, if we could all do this for one another, all therapists would be without clients, all psychiatrists would be without patients, all psychiatric hospitals would be empty, and there would be no market for books telling us how to live.)

Mastering our experience is the process whereby we alter our structure of meaning so that we take in something new and assimilate it into our structure by giving it a meaning which allows us to go on with our lives without feeling inhibited and restrained by this experience. Not mastering an experience means hedging it about with denials which prevent us from learning anything from experience, and, as Santayana said, 'Those who do not remember the past are condemned to relive it.' Thus some of us go through the pain and disappointment of ending a marriage, and, by mastering the experience, go on to a fuller, different life, and others of us, not mastering the experience, continue to marry the same kind of person and suffer the same pain and disappointment over and over again.

When we fail to master our experiences the story we construct of our lives contains gaps and inconsistencies, unlike the stories constructed by Successful Selves.

# A FULL LIFE STORY

**The Successful Self has created a life story without the gaps and inconsistencies which inhibit and cripple, and which goes forward in courage and hope.**

Memory is always a reconstruction. It is not a filing cabinet where something can be put away and later taken out completely unchanged. Everything that happens to us we absorb by linking it to what we already know, and in that linking and absorption, change it. Even learning something 'off by heart' is a reconstruction. We memorize the material by seeing similarities in it to other things. We remember a phone number because it is similar to our own, or it can be put in a familiar rhythm, and so on.

All the events which make up our life story are reconstructions. There are events which might be called 'facts' and which several people can agree did occur, but each person interprets the event differently. A man might die, and his mother be so overwhelmed with grief that she dies not long after, his wife, presenting herself as the grieving widow, secretly rejoices at her escape from an unhappy marriage, and his son, twenty years later, might say, 'I was fourteen when my father died and I was completely shattered, but now I've a son of my own who reminds me of my father I feel that I am part of a cycle of life and that makes me feel secure.'

Just as the story of our past is a construction, so is the story of our future. We tell ourselves the story of what our future will be.

We might try out several stories as a way of looking at alternatives and planning what we might do, or we might feel that our future is already determined and unchangeable. If we are wise, we know that it is not.

It is our story which gives our life significance. Without our stories we would be born, live and die, like a flower or an insect. We listen to one another's stories in order to confer a greater significance on each story. A story which is not told is significant only to the owner of that story. Lives, mean and despicable, can become full and glorious in the telling of their story. The insignificance of human beings in the vastness of the planet is never more apparent than in the open spaces of the American West, and the lives of the people there in the nineteenth century were made up of grinding hard work, loneliness, suffering, and petty, murderous squabbles, yet the telling of their stories, many times reconstructed, has conferred on them a significance not enjoyed by the stories of most of the crowned heads of Europe.

The power struggles among people are very much concerned with whose story gets told. In families it is the most powerful person, the father or the matriarch, whose story has the greatest significance, and from which other people in the family must learn and to which they must pay deference. In my family my father's story of him as a soldier in the Somme was the compelling story. My mother's story of the First World War years, when she worked in a little country town at a job far inferior to what her intelligence would have allowed her to achieve, was rarely mentioned.

History is the story told by the people in power. Until recently all our history was written by white, capitalist men. Only relatively recently has history been written by Marxists, or women, or blacks. When people's stories are reconstructed as literature or film, these stories are about the people in power. I spent my novel-reading years reading about the middle class English and my film-going childhood and adolescence watching stories about men. These novels and films showed me that my story, that of a working class girl, had no significance. In the 1950s being working class became fashionable for a while, so perhaps one day a black woman in Brixton, or an Asian woman in Bradford, or a Mexican woman in San Diego might see her life upon the screen, full of significance.

Giving significance to our stories need not be part of the power struggle. We can cooperate in this. I listen to your story, and you listen to mine. By giving one another's story significance we support one another's self-confidence and self-worth.

The problem about listening to another person's story is that there are usually parts of it which are painful to listen to. Helplessness and pity are painful emotions, and if the person we are listening to is a relative, we can feel in some way implicated in his distress. To avoid this many people adopt the practice of always getting very upset whenever a family member attempts to tell them something which is not a thousand per cent pleasant and perfect. This way you can train your family to say, out of your hearing, 'Don't tell Mother. She'll get upset,' or, 'Don't tell Dad. He'll just get angry,' and you save yourself much bother and hassle.

Of course, the disadvantage of this practice is that your family have secrets and your children grow up strangers to you. Perhaps a better procedure is to learn how to listen.

One of the attributes of a good listener is to be *there*.

I had not appreciated clearly and consciously how important structure and control are to an introvert until, twelve years after Nan Purnell and I had met, my husband left me, which meant that my son and I were homeless and, apart from what I could earn, penniless. I felt the terror of things falling apart. But Nan and her husband John remained for me as real and solid as rocks and always welcoming me and my son. Years later, working in psychiatric hospitals with lost and frightened people, I remembered the Purnells' friendly solidity, and realized that this was the most important function of a therapist. Initially, when the client is in the grip of the fear of annihilation, the therapist's friendly solidity can counter the extravert's sense of disappearing into nothingness and the introvert's sense of things falling apart. Later, when this terrible fear has receded, the friendly solidity of the therapist can allow the client to risk entering that vast uncertainty of changing her structure of meaning.

When Nan and I were young mothers, she with two daughters and I with my son, we spent a lot of time together. Across dirty nappies and cans of baby food, ice cream and wet swimming costumes, we talked endlessly about everything and everybody, but often about our mothers. Nowadays, in psychotherapy it is fashionable to talk about being 'given permission' to reveal our secrets. Nan with her uncritical sympathy and interest gave me permission to talk about mine.

This was the first time I had talked in any depth to anyone about my mother. My sister, six years older than me, regarded criticizing our mother as worse than criticizing God. I had never shaken off my mother's injunction, 'Don't talk about family business to strangers.' But Nan was not a stranger.

Nan came from a large family and had many friends, so she knew a lot about mothers and daughters. I realized that I was not alone in my experience or wicked to feel such anger and hate. Nan, listening to me, let me get rid of most of that anger and hate. In later years, endless conversations with my clients about their mothers helped me dissipate the last of that anger and hate, and to return to a sense of closeness with my mother. Talking and listening to Nan, I sorted out the story of my life.

If we share in listening to one another's stories we come to realize how differently we each interpret matters, and how these interpretations change over time. Once we see that our story is something that we have constructed, we realize that our story does not have to be our fate. We may have constructed our story on the premise that we live in a just world where the good are rewarded and the bad punished, and so our past history is all about us working hard to be good and our future is about receiving the rewards of that goodness. When these rewards fail to materialize we are faced with the choice of constructing a story of our future where disappointment, betrayal, misunderstanding, and resentments abound (for the introvert, a tragedy, and for the extravert, a romance with an unhappy ending) or revising the premise.

Revising the premise frees us from the story. Realizing that the world contains no special order of justice, that bad things can happen to good people, and good things happen to bad people, and that we can all be lucky, and we can all be unlucky, allows us to reconstruct our story. We have to reinterpret our past (this can involve retrieving memories repressed and emotions denied) and rewrite our futures.

Once we realize that we are free of the constraints of some universal system of justice we then have to decide upon the rules which will set the boundaries of our story. If we neglect to remember that all our acts have consequences, we may make our rule that there are no rules, and live to regret this. If we remember always that our acts have consequences we will create rules which we hope will guide us in our actions so that we do not cause too much pain to ourselves and others. Thus do we take responsibility for ourselves.

One of our rules needs to concern courage in the face of uncertainty and loss. We can try to reduce uncertainty by making everything secure, but then we lose our freedom and our hope, for hope is possible only where there is uncertainty. We all suffer loss — loss of loved ones, of youth, of hopes, of things that we enjoyed doing, and things that we would have enjoyed doing had we had the chance to do them. Loss leaves a legacy of sadness, and if we are wise we acknowledge this sadness and live with it rather than run from it, for by accepting our own sadness we, as Su Brinkworth said, increase our potential for happiness.

Our story, then, needs to take full account of our losses and our sadness. In the accounts that depressed people give of their lives they will begin by saying, 'There is no reason why I should be depressed,' and then go on to tell a story of loss — a self-confidence boosting pastime given up through injury or marriage, a burglary in which nothing was taken but a sense of security lost, taking a conventional job and losing a dream, having a child and losing freedom. The depressed person will tell of such losses, but deny their significance, claiming that it is foolish to have such needs and selfish to feel the loss in their non-fulfilment. By being depressed the person tries to deny the sadness and thus refuses to mourn. However, mourning is a natural process which once gone through comes to an end. Refusing to acknowledge sadness and to mourn means that the sadness has to be carried and defended against, a gross and ugly burden.

We can acknowledge and mourn our loss, and eventually relinquish it by constructing for ourselves a story which knits together our internal and external realities. It is not enough to give, as an introvert, an account of thoughts, feelings, images and theories without relating these to external reality, nor is it enough to give, as an extravert, an account of activities without meditations upon these activities.

When Laura Geller, a rabbi, reviewed the autobiography of Dr Ruth Westheimer, the Dr Ruth of sex therapy fame, she said,

> 'Ruth Westheimer's lifetime has been extraordinarily full – she has lived in five countries, experienced more tragedy than most people will ever deal with, lived as an active participant in two of the most important events of modern Jewish history – the Holocaust and the birth of the state of Israel – celebrated personal joy and triumph and achieved more success than she ever dreamed possible. The book is filled with minute details of that life, who she knew, what she did, how her life evolved. What is missing from the book is a thoughtful analysis of how the events of her life have shaped her as a person. We learn a great deal about what happened to Karola Siegel as she became Dr Ruth, but we never learn much about the human being behind the events. It is an interesting story, but a story without a soul. Perhaps all those years of being like that German doll that bounces back when it is down makes real introspection impossible, or maybe confronting her soul is just too painful.'[3]

In contrast to Ruth Westheimer is Nora Ephron who, when her husband, Carl Bernstein, the journalist of Watergate fame, left her for another woman, confronted her pain and dealt with it by writing a very perceptive and funny book, the definitive account of the break-up of a marriage from the woman's point of view. At the end of the book she recalled how

> 'Vera said: "Why do you feel you have to turn everything into a story?"
> So I told her why:
> Because if I tell the story, I control the version.
> Because if I tell the story, I can make you laugh, and I would rather have you laugh at me than feel sorry for me.
> Because if I tell the story it doesn't hurt so much.
> Because if I tell the story I can get on with it.'[4]

Getting on with it means leaving the past behind and continuing the journey.

# 8

# The Journey Continues

The Successful Self is not a state but a journey. An unsuccessful self might claim from the depths of ignorance and arrogance that he knows it all, but the Successful Self is, like Socrates, the wisest person, for, as Socrates said, while all men know nothing, he knew that he knew nothing. Socrates was of the opinion, however, that 'The unexamined life is not worth living.'

Examining life, while it is endlessly interesting, is a dangerous occupation. It may not provide many answers, but it provides endless questions, and questions are not what people in positions of power want. Good, obedient children are seen and not heard, that is, they do not ask questions. Some parents might tolerate questions, and some teachers, wanting learning to remain a joy, encourage their students to explore, but the forces of reaction are powerful in society and government, and education is concerned not with letting children develop naturally as themselves and becoming themselves, but in turning natural children into good, obedient children who will become good, obedient adults. It is not in the interests of people in power that children grow up to be independent, questioning adults who are responsible for themselves, or that good, obedient adults change into independent, questioning adults who take responsibility for themselves. Neither the education system nor the psychiatric system aim to produce Successful Selves.

The reason that the forces of reaction are so strong, that people in power wish to prevent people from becoming Successful Selves, is that they themselves are still locked into the belief that goodness is rewarded. Of course, since the circumstances which happened to befall them have resulted in them having the power and wealth to reward themselves, so they might not have the same difficulty that poorer, less powerful people have in maintaining this belief. Whatever, the system whereby children learn to be obedient is a hierarchical one, and in many hierarchies, while it is not pleasant being at the bottom, there is the hope that we can move up the hierarchy. Born children, we can become parents, and so good, obedient children become good, obedient parents, and do to children what was done to them.

Thus, it is in Britain as I write we have a Prime Minister who is known as 'nanny', and politicians of all political persuasions who lecture us in the tones of 'we know best' reasonableness, talking to us as if we were children who could be quite adult if we tried, the tones teachers and parents use when they want children to be 'responsible', that is, obedient even when they are not being supervised.

We can assume the parental role in more ways than just being parents and politicians. We can become psychiatrists, psychologists, and therapists of all persuasions.

The psychiatric system puts the patient at the bottom of the hierarchy, a permanent child with no chance of advancing upwards, and only a slight chance of escaping from the system altogether. The psychiatric system is not interested in creating Successful Selves and neither are most therapists.

Being a therapist is a position of great power, for the client coming as a child-like supplicant, invests the therapist with power, wisdom and magic. If the client then grows up, takes responsibility for himself, and so sees the therapist as an ordinary, fallible human being, the therapist loses his power. Hence, many therapists do not want their clients to grow up, and they use their power to undermine and belittle their client.[1]

If on your journey to and through Successful Selfhood you think it might be interesting or useful to consult a therapist, you should look for one who is on the same journey as you, and not one who is involved in compensating himself for what he lost as an obedient child by becoming a powerful parent.

This is not something that therapists list with their qualifications. You will have to judge from what you can find out about the therapist. Here are some of the things you can look for.

# THE THERAPIST AS A SUCCESSFUL SELF

(1) S/he is not engaged in disputes with other therapists about theory and practice.

(2) S/he, while using one or other psychological theory as a structure for understanding what goes on in therapy, does not regard this theory as the Complete and Absolute Truth, and the practice of therapy developed from this theory as the Only Right and True Way To Do Therapy.

(3) S/he does not regard her/his beliefs, attitudes and opinions as correct and the client's beliefs, attitudes and opinions as incorrect, but s/he regards the client's beliefs, attitudes and opinions as the conclusions drawn by him from his experience and, while they may cause him pain, they are *not* invalid or illogical. It is for the client, not the therapist, to decide whether and how these beliefs, attitudes and opinions should be changed.

(4) S/he does not know what is best for the client and s/he knows and admits that s/he does not know.

(5) S/he reveals her/his beliefs, attitudes and opinions to the client so the client can be aware of and deal with the therapist's biases and prejudices.

(6) S/he does not manipulate her/his clients into becoming a credit to her/him as a therapist, but accepts and supports the decisions the client makes about his life.

(7) S/he does not hide behind a barrier of receptionists, waiting rooms, rigid appointment systems, or acting the role of being a warm, wonderful human being, but can simply be her/himself.

(8) S/he enjoys loving and accepting relationships with spouse, children, relatives and friends. Her/his children are neither a credit nor a disappointment to her/him, but simply a joy.

There are such therapists around. I call them good friends.

Good friends let us be ourselves. Good friends are our equals, and when they help and comfort us we do not feel belittled.

As children we were belittled quite enough.

# OURSELVES AS SUCCESSFUL SELVES

The most profound and far-reaching experiences we have as children are those where we find ourselves totally helpless and afraid. Before those experiences occur we live our lives just by being ourselves, innocently relating our sense of good and bad to what is pleasant and what is not. Those childhood experiences of helpless terror introduce us to an implacable morality in which good feels safe and bad means not safe. We extricate ourselves from the danger of total helplessness by defining ourselves as bad and our persecutors as good, only to discover that being bad is equally dangerous, for bad things happen to bad people.

As bad children we were slapped, beaten, shouted at, criticized, put in isolation, deprived of what we needed, humiliated and made to feel shame and guilt. We were told that bad adults had even worse things happen to them. We resolved that we would try to be as good as we possibly could be. That way we would be safe.

Being good, so the adults around us told us, meant being clean, tidy, obedient, unaggressive, never envious or jealous, but always kind, generous, unselfish and responsible, where responsible meant not making your own decisions but being obedient without being told to be obedient. Often we failed to reach these standards, and often we were told that we were bad and we felt that we were bad. Whenever we felt an impulse to be dirty, untidy, disobedient, selfish, greedy, envious, mean, jealous, aggressive or irresponsible we had either to reject it, or express it and afterwards feel guilty. We became secretive, not wanting to let other people know that we were not always totally good. These secrets cut us off from other people, and we discovered that *being good means being lonely*.

Still, what's a bit of loneliness so long as you know you're safe? Maintain the right amount of goodness and nothing bad can happen to you.

The problem was what was the right level of goodness? Once we were old enough to read newspapers and watch the news on television we realized that people are having bad things happen to them all the time. Quickly we learned how to defend our belief that goodness is rewarded and that in the end people get what they deserve by using the method of *blaming the victim*. 'People can get a job if they try. Unemployed people squander their dole money on drink, drugs and colour televisions.' 'The starving of the Third World just wait for handouts. They don't try to help themselves.' If we had learned, as many boys do, to equate good with strong, we are contemptuous of the weak and feel that they deserve their suffering.

Blaming the victim works very well, so long as you are not the victim.

One woman, rescued from the capsized car ferry in Zeebrugge, told on television how she had pulled herself out of the water and on to a ledge where also sat an eight year old girl. In the watery darkness they waited a long time to be rescued. The little girl kept saying over and over, 'But I've been so good. I haven't told any lies.' Perhaps out of all the possible misdemeanours she might have chosen to mention, telling lies came to the fore because in that perilous place she was being forced to consider the possibility that the people she loved and relied on had lied to her. No amount of goodness will ensure that car ferry doors are closed when they should be, and that other people will always look after you as you expect.

All of us discover as we go through childhood and enter adulthood that goodness does not create safety as the night follows the day. Indeed, in the course of an ordinary life, we find that we can be kind, generous and caring, and still people reject us. We can work hard, and do everything we are told to do, and still we do not win the prize. These discoveries make us feel that the system of justice which we believe is functioning in the world is not working properly, and that we are being treated unfairly. We feel angry, bitter and resentful. We see other people apparently being rewarded for their goodness (not half as good as ours) and we feel envious. Our anger, bitterness, resentment and envy cut us off from others and this adds to our loneliness.

So locked into the struggle to be good and do good that we do not realize how our best efforts to be kind, caring and generous to other people actually alienates us from them. Because we believe that we are intrinsically bad, and being good is the effort we must make to keep this badness in check, our kindness, generosity, concern, and love rarely flow easily and spontaneously. We divide up the possible recipients of our goodness into the deserving and the undeserving, and we would no more waste our goodness on the undeserving than we would throw our money down a drain.

In my middle-class shopping centre, Broomhill, carol singers collecting money for a Christian charity for the famine victims in Africa had their collecting boxes filled. After Christmas, two young women offering to sell cheap trinkets 'because our kids need food' were spurned. In psychiatric hospitals doctors and nurses commonly divide patients into the deserving and the undeserving. If you are considered to be undeserving then you will be given drugs and electroconvulsive therapy and perhaps put in seclusion (locked in a small room on your own) rather than being given conversation, and certainly not referred to psychologists for therapy.

Those patients who are sent for therapy come with the belief that goodness must be rewarded. They often reveal this when, having ventured to become happier and less anxious, they then encounter some crisis and retreat back into depression and anxiety. Then they say to me, 'I didn't want to tell you because I don't want to disappoint you. You've been so good to me.' I try to point out to them that my disappointment or satisfaction is not part of the therapy. I am paid to give my client my undivided attention for an hour or two. Presumably I would be disappointed if I did not get paid, but whatever my clients choose to do, whether they become the most Successful Self of all time, or whether they become the most Profoundly Depressed of all time, is their business. They do not have to please me. If I sit through a therapy session apparently exuding goodness it is because I want to do whatever it is I am doing and not because I expect a reward.

Such statements initially cause great puzzlement, because my clients are still locked into, 'If I am good bad things will not happen to me: bad things have happened to me: that means that I am much worse than I thought and/or I have been treated unfairly.' As my clients come to see that this dilemma is one of their own making all talk of disappointing me disappears. They might feel disappointed in or annoyed with themselves when they resort to the old defences of depression and anxiety, but that is another matter.

This expectation that goodness must be rewarded is very common amongst therapists and counsellors of all persuasions. There is the feeling that 'I gave Mrs Smith an hour of my time and so she should show an hour's worth of improvement.' Patients who fail to reward their health care professionals and volunteers (including the vicar) with improvement commensurate with the time and effort given get labelled 'ungrateful' and 'undeserving', receive less attention, and, if they complain about this, are labelled 'attention seeking'. Patients who realize that in our society it is more important to reward goodness than to tell the truth, will insist that, no matter how ghastly they privately feel, whatever time they are spared by these good, kind, generous, busy people they have benefited greatly. (It is this response which greatly inflates a doctor's impression that the drugs he prescribes actually work.)

Goodness, and its rewards, turns relationships into transactions where everyone feels exploited and cheated. To give without expecting something in return is seen as weakness. To receive without giving back is seen as greed. So the immense pleasure of giving without needing gratitude or love or appreciation or the sense of feeling good about being good can never be felt to the full, nor the pleasure of giving to someone the right and opportunity to feel that pleasure. Had we retained the capacity to feel such pleasure we would not have reduced Christmas to a sentimental charade and a commercial transaction.

Expecting that our goodness will be rewarded robs us of more than the immense pleasure of giving and receiving freely. We also lose our sense of wonder. As babies and toddlers we were constantly amazed at the wonder of the world, but once we were made conscious of our badness and our need to be good we could no longer look at the world with this sense of wonder. We could see the world only in relation to ourself. The sun no longer simply shone. Its shining was either good for us or bad for us. The world became nothing but a resource which we could plunder, a peg on which to hang our fantasies, and a backdrop for our life drama. Yet it is this sense of wonder which makes us feel alive in the here and now, part of everything and at the same time an individual perceiving the wonder.

We never actually lose the sense of wonder. We just let it fall into disuse. It resurfaces now and then to be put to use as we try to decide what meaning we shall give to life. Gazing at the moon we might ask, 'What's it all about?' and eventually come up with an answer which seems right for us. The particular religious or metaphysical answer we arrive at seems right for us because it contains in it an attempt to maintain our sense of existence and to ward off the threat of annihilation. Thus an extravert who has experienced the threat of abandonment all too often develops a system of beliefs which involve the presence of loving spirits or a heaven containing a loving Father, angels and departed loved ones now much kinder and loving than they were on earth. Never again will the extravert be alone, either here or in the hereafter. The introvert who has been threatened all too often with chaos develops a system of beliefs about a supernatural order concerned with individual achievement, acclamation, glory and perfection. Never again will the introvert be overwhelmed by chaos, for the supernatural order shines through the natural order and only perfection lies ahead. Provided, of course, we are all very good.

Thus we can create a system of beliefs which we hope that, when people fail us, will give us a defence against the threat of annihilation. Doing this we hope that we shall not feel the pain of loss and the weakness of helplessness. But it is a vain hope, for losing the people we love is always painful, and there are many events, including our own sickness, old age and infirmity, where we, helpless, are made aware of our weakness. Moreover, if in such situations we insist that we are not actually feeling the pain and the weakness, that such unpleasant feelings are excluded by our belief in some power outside ourselves, we cut ourselves off from other people who might wish to help us and who might be experiencing their own pain and weakness. We deny what they are experiencing, and fail both to support them and to experience the closeness and unity that people sharing their suffering can create. Even worse, if the situations which create our pain and weakness diminish our self-confidence (as they are prone to do) and make us aware of our own sense of badness, we find that the protection which our belief was supposed to give us is not available to us, for its protection depended on us being good. Thus we can suffer a double loss, the disaster which has befallen us and the belief we hoped would protect us from disaster.

Worst of all, a belief in some supernatural or religious system which, we hope, will protect us from the pain and weakness which threaten the annihilation of the self prevents us from knowing that our defences against the threat of annihilation are unnecessary, and that we are ourselves both unique in our individuality and part of the continuous web of life. We are born knowing this, so, if we can still those inner voices that are forever crying, 'I must be good. I must be safe', we can let ourselves know what we know.

Sometimes this knowledge comes to us in experiences like that which Gregory called his God experience. Such an experience is very common.[2] Sometimes this knowledge comes to us as we meditate, or in the sense of wonder as we gaze upon the natural beauty of the world. In all of such experiences our true self is speaking. As much as we feel weak and helpless and about to be annihilated, there is always a part of us that takes the right to existence for granted. If that part did not exist we would not feel frightened by the threat of annihilation. We would, without protest, disappear like smoke in the wind. In that part of ourselves, the part that we, in our efforts to be good, have denied and ignored, is the knowledge that we are a unique individual and that we belong. If we have one such experience of this knowledge and then insist that it was solely and utterly of some power external to us we are still denying that essential part of ourselves. However, if we acknowledge our truth, the knowledge stays with us as a quiet certainty. We are no longer on the treadmill of feeling bad, trying to be good, and being frightened. We can simply be. We are no longer locked into relationships of dominating the other or being dominated by the other. We can simply be with others, our fellows and our equals.

Such certainty does not save us from pain and weakness, and we would not wish it to, for we are our unique self and part of the continuous web of life as much in pain and weakness as we are in joy, strength and love. However, such certainty allows us to see that we do not have to fear our weakness, for we no longer experience weakness as the threat of the annihilation of our self.

Our self is secure, and we do not give to others the power to threaten to annihilate us, even though in our weakness we sometimes have to tolerate as best we can the foolishness of the people in whose care we find ourselves. We do not have to fear our pain, for as we do not fear our weakness we can allow other people to care for us and witness our pain and weakness and support us. When the pain is the pain of loss we can let ourselves feel the pain, for the pain would not have been there if we had not loved. It is the condition of human beings to love and to mourn, and so long as we have loved there will be others to mourn us just as we have mourned. Recognizing this, we are not depressed, for depression is the refusal to mourn, but we are sad, and in our sadness, as well as in our love and joy, joined to other people.

In such certainty we achieve our own individual synthesis of being an introvert and an extravert. Of course, as a born extravert we keep looking around for some extra stimulation, and as a born introvert we keep organizing, but, tolerating our long established idiosyncrasies, we achieve not merely the idealized notion of being both an individual and a close-knit member of a group, but the real, lived experience of being one's unique self and an integral part of the continuous and continual life of the planet, as much a part of life as a wave is part of the ocean.

# Notes

## CHAPTER 1

(1)  D. Rowe (1987), *Beyond Fear*, Fontana, London.

(2)  D. Adams (1979), *The Hitch-hiker's Guide to the Galaxy*, Pan, London.

(3)  D. Rowe (1978), *The Experience of Depression*, Wiley, Chichester, re-issued 1988, as *Choosing Not Losing*, Fontana, London.

(4)  *Beyond Fear*, op. cit.

(5)  D. Rowe (1985), *Living with the Bomb: Can We Live without Enemies?*, Routledge, London.

## CHAPTER 2

(1)  C. Jung (1981), *Psychological Types*, Hogarth, London.

(2)  I. Myers-Briggs (1986), *Introduction to Type*, Consulting Psychologists Press, Inc, Palo Alto, California.

(3)  H. J. Eysenck (1947), *Dimensions of Personality*, Praeger, New York.

(4)  H. J. Eysenck (1973), *The Inequality of Man*, Temple Smith, London, pp.192–194.

## CHAPTER 3

(1)  *Beyond Fear*, op. cit., pp.150–159.

# CHAPTER 4

(1) H. Eysenck (1964), *Crime and Personality*, Routledge, London.

(2) J. Horne (1987), 'A morning slickless', *The Guardian*, October 17.

(3) W. P. Colquhoun (1984), Effects of personality on body temperature and mental efficiency following transmeridian flight, *Aviation, Space, and Environment Medicine*, June.
  T. H. Monk and S. Folkard (1985), Individual differences in shiftwork adjustment, in *Hours of Work*, edited by S. Folkard and T. H. Monk, Wiley, Chichester.

(4) J. Marks and P. Greenfield (1987), How the CIA assesses weaknesses: the Gittinger Personality Assessment, in *The Power of Psychology*, edited by D. Cohen, Croom Helm, Beckenham.

(5) S. B. Kopp (1971), *Guru*, Science and Behavior Books, Palo Alto, California.

(6) G. Brown and T. Harris (1982), *The Social Origins of Depression*, Tavistock, London.

(7) R. Totman *et al.* (1980), Predicting experimental colds in volunteers from different measures of recent life stress, *Journal of Psychosomatic Research*, 24.
  D. E. Broadbent *et al.* (1984), Some further studies on the prediction of experimental colds in volunteers by psychological factors, *Journal of Psychosomatic Research*, 28, 6.

(8) R. Ruark (1978), quoted in *Contemporary Authors*, Permanent Series, Vol 2, Gale Research Company, Detroit.

(9) R. Ruark (1958), *The Old Man and the Boy*, Hamish Hamilton, London, pp.112, 114.

(10) Q. Crisp (1986), *The Naked Civil Servant*, Fontana, London.

(11) Q. Crisp (1981), *How to Become a Virgin*, Fontana, London.

(12)   L. Braudy (1986), *The Frenzy of Renown*, Oxford University Press, Oxford.

(13)   *ibid.*, p.10.

(14)   See Chapter 6 and *Beyond Fear*, op. cit., pp.280–318.

(15)   D. Rowe (1983), *Depression: the Way Out of Your Prison*, Routledge, London, pp.65–66.

(16)   A. Miller (1983), *The Drama of the Gifted Child*, Trans. R. Ward, Faber, London.

(17)   *Beyond Fear*, op. cit., p.139.

(18)   *The Mind Box* (1985), Everyman Series, BBC TV.

(19)   *Depression: the Way Out of Your Prison* and *Beyond Fear*, op. cit.

(20)   Chuang Tsu (1974), *Inter Chapters*, Trans Gia-Fu Feng and Jane English, Wildwood, London.

(21)   N. Ephron (1984), *Heartburn*, Pavanne, London, p.54.


## CHAPTER 5

(1)   C. Garvey (1984), *Children's Talk*, Fontana, London, pp.165–166.


## CHAPTER 6

(1)   *Beyond Fear*, op. cit.

(2)   R. D. Scott and P. L. Ashworth (1969), The shadow of the ancestor: a historical factor in the transmission of schizophrenia, *British Journal of Medical Psychology*, 42, no.1, pp.13–32.

(3)   *Beyond Fear*, op. cit., p.231.

(4)   D. Wigoder (1987), *Images of Destruction*, Routledge, London.

(5)   *Living with the Bomb*, op. cit. p.184.

(6)   A. Miller (1983), *For Your Own Good*, Faber, London, p.265.

(7)  *Depression: the Way Out of Your Prison, op. cit.*
    *Choosing Not Losing*, Fontana, London.

(8)  S. Kopp (1987), *Who Am I – Really?*, Jeremy P. Tarcher
Inc., Los Angeles, p.163.


## CHAPTER 7

(1)  S. Alexander (1988), unpublished notes for an
autobiography.

(2)  *Living with the Bomb*, op. cit.

(3)  L. Geller (1988), The Long Life of a Short Woman, *Los
Angeles Times*, January 10, review of *All in a Lifetime* by R.
Westheimer, Warner Books, 1988.

(4)  N. Ephron, op. cit., p.154.


## CHAPTER 8

(1)  D. Smail (1987), *Taking Care*, Dent, London.
    J. M. Masson (1988), *Against Therapy*, Atheneum, New York
and (1989), Fontana, London.

(2)  A. Hardy (1979), *The Spiritual Nature of Man*, Oxford
University Press, Oxford.
    D. Hay (1981), *Exploring Inner Space. Scientists and Religious
Experience*, Penguin, Harmondsworth.

# Index